FORGED

ALSO BY BART D. EHRMAN

Jesus, Interrupted: Revealing the Hidden Contradictions in the Bible (and Why We Don't Know About Them)

God's Problem: How the Bible Fails to Answer Our Most Important Question—Why We Suffer

Misquoting Jesus: The Story Behind Who Changed the Bible and Why

The Lost Gospel of Judas Iscariot: Betrayer and Betrayed Reconsidered

Studies in the Textual Criticism of the New Testament

Peter, Paul, and Mary Magdalene: The Followers of Jesus in History and Legend

Truth and Fiction in the Da Vinci Code: A Historian Reveals What We Can Really Know About Jesus, Mary, and Constantine

A Brief Introduction to the New Testament

Lost Christianities: The Battle for Scripture and the Faiths We Never Knew

Lost Scriptures: Books That Did Not Become the New Testament

The Apostolic Fathers

Jesus: Apocalyptic Prophet of the New Millennium

After the New Testament: A Reader in Early Christianity

The New Testament and Other Early Christian Writings: A Reader

The New Testament: A Historical Introduction to the Early Christian Writings

The Orthodox Corruption of Scripture: The Effect of Early Christological Controversies on the Text of the New Testament

Didymus the Blind and the Text of the Gospels

FORGED

Writing in the Name of God—

Why the Bible's Authors Are Not

Who We Think They Are

BART D. EHRMAN

HarperOne
An Imprint of HarperCollinsPublishers

HarperOne

HarperCollins books may be purchased for educational, business, or sales promotional use. For information, please write: Special Markets Department, HarperCollins Publishers, 10 East 53rd Street, New York, NY 10022

HarperCollins website: http://www.harpercollins.com

HarperCollins®, ■®, and HarperOne™ are trademarks of HarperCollins Publishers

FIRST HARPERCOLLINS PAPERBACK EDITION PUBLISHED IN 2012

Designed by Kevin Estrada

Library of Congress Cataloging-in-Publication Data

Ehrman, Bart D.
    Forged : writing in the name of God : why the Bible's authors are not who we think they are / Bart D. Ehrman.
        p. cm.
    ISBN 978–0–06–201262–3
    1. Bible. N.T.—Authorship. 2. Bible. N.T.—Controversial litera-ture. 3. Bible. N.T.—Evidences, authority, etc. 4. Bible. N.T.—Criticism, interpretation, etc. I. Title.
    BS2330.3.E375   2011
    225.1—dc22   2010034177

12 13 14 15 16   RRD(H)   10 9 8 7 6 5 4 3 2 1

To Sierra, granddaughter extraordinaire

Contents

Acknowledgments ix

Introduction: Facing the Truth 1

1. A World of Deceptions and Forgeries 13

2. Forgeries in the Name of Peter 43

3. Forgeries in the Name of Paul 79

4. Alternatives to Lies and Deceptions 115

5. Forgeries in Conflicts with Jews and Pagans 143

6. Forgeries in Conflicts with False Teachers 179

7. False Attributions, Fabrications, and Falsifications: Phenomena Related to Forgery 219

8. Forgeries, Lies, Deceptions, and the Writings of the New Testament 251

Notes 267

Index 293

ACKNOWLEDGMENTS

I WOULD LIKE TO THANK everyone who helped me in writing this book. Thanks first of all to the National Humanities Center, which provided me a fellowship in 2009–10 that allowed me to do the research. The staff, from the top down, were absolutely marvelous. Special thanks to the amazing library staff, Josiah Drewery, Jean Houston, and Eliza Robertson, who have gone far beyond what anyone could hope for in providing research assistance. May their tribe increase.

Several smart and insightful people graciously read the manuscript in its final stages, and I owe them a huge debt of gratitude: Dale Martin, of the Department of Religion at Yale, who is never afraid to tell me when I'm wrong; Jeff Siker, of the Department of Theology at Loyola Marymount, who occasionally lets me know when I'm right; Joel Marcus, of the Divinity School at Duke, who after all these years continues to wield a mighty red pen; an anonymous reader for the press who provided numerous challenging insights; my daughter, Kelly Ehrman, who is unusually gifted in recognizing literary inelegance; and above all my beloved wife, Sarah Beckwith, professor of medieval and renaissance English at Duke, who is uncannily smart and insightful and is, on top of it all, a walking bibliography.

Thanks as well to my insightful and encouraging editor at Harper-One, Roger Freet, and all the other Harper folk who have always provided extraordinary help and support: Mark Tauber, Claudia Boutote, Mickey Maudlin, and Julie Burton.

Unless otherwise indicated, translations of ancient texts are mine.

I have dedicated the book to granddaughter number two, Sierra, who has seen the light of day for just a year, but is already shining, herself, with an extraordinary brilliance.

Introduction:
Facing the Truth

On a bright sunny day in June, when I was fourteen years old, my mom told me that she and my dad were going out to play a round of golf. I did a quick calculation in my head. It would take them twenty minutes to get to the country club and about four hours to play eighteen holes. After a bit of downtime, they would drive home. I had five hours.

I called up my friend Ron down the street to tell him my parents would be gone all afternoon, and that I had snuck a couple of cigars out of my dad's consistently full stash. Ron liked what I was thinking and said that he had cobbed a few cans of malt liquor and hidden them out in his bushes. The joys of paradise opened before us.

When Ron came over, we headed upstairs to my bedroom, where we threw open the windows, lit up the cigars, popped the cans of brew, and settled in for an afternoon of something less than intellectual discourse. But after about ten minutes, to my horror, we heard a car pull into the driveway, the back door open, and my mom yell up the stairs that they were home. The golf course was crowded, and they had decided not to wait forty minutes to tee off.

Ron and I immediately switched into emergency gear. We flushed the cigars and the beer down the toilet and hid the cans in the trash, then pulled out two cans of deodorant and started spraying the room to try to cover up the smoke (which was virtually billowing out the window). Ron snuck out the back door, and I was left alone, in a cold sweat, certain that my life was soon to be over.

I went downstairs, and my dad asked me the fated question. "Bart, were you and Ron smoking upstairs?"

I did what any self-respecting fourteen-year-old would do: I lied to his face. "No, dad, not me!" (The smoke was still heavy in the air as I spoke.)

His face softened, almost to a smile, and then he said something that stayed with me for a long time—forty years, in fact. "Bart, I don't mind if you sneak a smoke now and then. But don't lie to me."

Naturally I assured him, "I won't, dad!"

A Later Commitment to Truth

FIVE YEARS LATER, I was a different human being. Everyone changes in those late teenage years, of course, but I'd say my change was more radical than most. Among other things, in the intervening years I had become a born-again Christian, graduated from high school, gone off to a fundamentalist Bible college, Moody Bible Institute, and had two years of serious training in biblical studies and theology under my belt. At Moody we weren't allowed to smoke ("Your body is the temple of the Holy Spirit," the New Testament teaches, and you don't want to pollute God's temple!), drink alcoholic beverages ("Be ye not drunk with wine," says the Bible; it didn't occur to me that it might be okay to be drunk with bourbon)—or, well, do lots of other things that most normal human beings at that age do: go to movies, dance, play cards. I didn't actually agree with the "conduct code" of the school (there was also a dress code, and a hair code for men: no long hair or beards), but my view was that if I decided to go there, it meant playing by the rules. If I wanted other rules, I could go somewhere else. But more than that, I went from being a fourteen-year-old sports-minded, better than average student with little clue about the world or my place in it and no particular commitment to telling the truth to a nineteen-year-old who was an extremely zealous, rigorous, pious (self-righteous), studious, committed evangelical Christian with firm notions about right and wrong and truth and error.

We were heavily committed to the truth at Moody Bible Institute. I would argue, even today, that there is no one on the planet more committed to truth than a serious and earnest evangelical Christian. And at Moody we were nothing if not serious and earnest. Truth to us was as important as life itself. We believed in the Truth, with a capital T. We vowed to tell the truth, we expected the truth, we sought the truth, we studied the truth, we preached the truth, we had faith in the truth. "Thy Word is truth," as Scripture says, and Jesus himself was "the way, the truth, and the life." No one could "come to the Father" except through him, the true "Word become flesh." Only unbelievers like Pontius Pilate were confused enough to ask, "What is truth?" As followers of Christ, we were in a different category altogether. As Jesus himself had said, "You shall know the truth, and the truth shall make you free."

Along with our commitment to truth, we believed in objectivity. Objective truth was all there was. There was no such thing as a "subjective truth." Something was true or it was false. Personal feelings and opinions had nothing to do with it. Objectivity was real, it was possible, it was attainable, and we had access to it. It was through our objective knowledge of the truth that we knew God and knew what God (and Christ, and the Spirit, and everything else) was.

One of the ironies of modern religion is that the absolute commitment to truth in some forms of evangelical and fundamentalist Christianity and the concomitant view that truth is objective and can be verified by any impartial observer have led many faithful souls to follow the truth wherever it leads—and where it leads is often *away* from evangelical or fundamentalist Christianity. So if, in theory, you can verify the "objective" truth of religion, and then it turns out that the religion being examined is verifiably *wrong*, where does that leave you? If you are an evangelical Christian, it leaves you in the wilderness outside the evangelical camp, but with an unrepentant view of truth. Objective truth, to paraphrase a not so Christian song, has been the ruin of many a poor boy, and God, I know, I'm one.

Before moving outside into the wilderness (which, as it turns out, is a lush paradise compared to the barren camp of fundamentalist Christianity), I was intensely interested in "objective proofs" of the faith: proof that Jesus was physically raised from the dead (empty tomb! eyewitnesses!), proof that God was active in the world (miracles!), proof that the Bible was the inerrant word of God, without mistake in any way. As a result, I was devoted to the field of study known as Christian apologetics.

The term "apologetics" comes from the Greek word *apologia*, which does not mean "apology" in the sense of saying you're sorry for something; it means, instead, to make a "reasoned defense" of the faith. Christian apologetics is devoted to showing not only that faith in Christ is reasonable, but that the Christian message is demonstrably true, as can be seen by anyone willing to suspend disbelief and look objectively at the evidence.

The reason this commitment to evidence, objectivity, and truth has caused so many well-meaning evangelicals problems over the years is that they—at least some of them—really *are* confident that if something is true, then it necessarily comes from God, and that the worst thing you can do is to believe something that is false. The search for truth takes you where the evidence leads you, even if, at first, you don't want to go there.

The more I studied the evangelical truth claims about Christianity, especially claims about the Bible, the more I realized that the "truth" was taking me somewhere I very much did not want to go. After I graduated from Moody and went to Wheaton College to complete my bachelor's degree, I took Greek, so that I could read the New Testament in its original language. From there I went to Princeton Theological Seminary to study with one of the great scholars of the Greek New Testament, Bruce Metzger; I did a master's thesis under his direction and then a Ph.D. During my years of graduate work I studied the text of the New Testament assiduously, intensely, minutely. I took semester-long graduate seminars on single books of the New Testament, studied in the original language. I wrote papers on difficult passages. I read everything I could get my hands on. I was passionate about my studies and the truth that I could find.

But it was not long before I started seeing that the "truth" about the Bible was not at all what I had once thought when I was a committed evangelical Christian at Moody Bible Institute. The more I saw that the New Testament (not to mention the Old Testament, where the problems are even *more* severe) was chock full of discrepancies, the more troubled I became. At Moody, I thought that all discrepancies could be objectively reconciled. But eventually I saw that in fact they could not be. I wrestled with these problems, I prayed about them, I studied them, I sought spiritual guidance, I read all I could. But as someone who believed that truth was objective and who was unwilling to believe what was false, I came to think that the Bible could not be what I thought it was. The Bible contained errors. And if it contained errors, it was not completely true. This was a problem for me, because I wanted to believe the truth, the divine truth, and I came to see that the Bible was not divine truth without remainder. The Bible was a very human book.

But the problems didn't stop there. Eventually I came to realize that the Bible not only contains untruths or accidental mistakes. It also contains what almost anyone today would call lies. That is what this book is about.

Truth in the History of Christianity

ONE COULD ARGUE THAT the obsession with truth in parts of evangelical Christianity today was matched by the commitment to truth in the earliest years of Christianity. This is one of the features of Christianity that made it distinctive among the religions of antiquity.

Most people today don't realize that ancient religions were almost never interested in "true beliefs." Pagan religions—by which I mean the polytheistic religions of the vast majority of people in the ancient world, who were neither Jewish nor Christian—did not have creeds that had to be recited, beliefs that had to be affirmed, or scriptures that had to be accepted as conveying divine truth. Truth was of interest to *philosophers*, but not to practitioners of religion (unless they were also interested in philosophy). As strange as this may seem to us today, ancient religions didn't require you to believe one thing or another. Religion was all about the proper practices: sacrifices to the gods, for example, and set prayers. Moreover, because religion was not particularly concerned with what you believed about the gods and because all of these religions allowed, even encouraged, the worship of many gods, there was very little sense that if one of the religions was right, the others were wrong. They could *all* be right! There were many gods and many ways to worship the gods, not a single path to the divine.

This view—the dominant view of antiquity—stands completely at odds with how most of us think about religion today, of course. In our view, if Free-will Baptists are right, Roman Catholics are wrong; if Jews are right, Buddhists are wrong; if Muslims are right, Christians are wrong; and so on. But not in the ancient world. The worship of Zeus was no more "right" than the worship of Athena, Apollo, your city gods, or your family gods.

Another key difference between religions today and in antiquity is that the ancient polytheistic religions were not overly concerned with the afterlife. They were concerned about the present life, how to survive in a hard and capricious world, and how to live well: how to make sure the rain came and the crops grew; how to survive illness or combat; how to get enough to eat and drink; how to lead productive and fruitful lives; how to make the boy or girl next door fall madly in love with you.

Among the many things that made Christianity different from the other religions of the Roman Empire, with the partial exception of Judaism, is that Christians insisted that it did matter what you believed, that believing the correct things could make you "right" and believing the incorrect things could make you "wrong," and that if you were wrong, you would be punished eternally in the fires of hell. Christianity, unlike the other religions, was exclusivistic. It insisted that it held the Truth, and that every other religion was in Error. Moreover, this truth involved claims about God (there is only one, for example, and he created the world), about Christ (he was both divine and human), about salvation (it comes only by faith in Christ), about eternal life (everyone will be blessed or tormented for eternity), and so on.[1]

The Christian religion came to be firmly rooted in truth claims, which were eventually embedded in highly ritualized formulations, such as the Nicene Creed. As a result, Christians from the very beginning needed to appeal to authorities for what they believed. Do you believe that this view is true instead of that one? What is your authority for saying so? The ultimate authority was God, of course. But the majority of Christians came to think that God did not speak the truth about what to believe directly to individuals. If he did, there would be enormous problems, as some could claim divine authority for what they taught and others could claim divine authority for the completely opposite teaching. Thus most Christians did not stress personal revelation to living individuals. Instead, they insisted that God had revealed his truth in earlier times through Christ to his apostles. The apostles at the beginning of the church were authorities who could be trusted. But when the apostles died out, where was one to go for an authority?

One could claim—and many in fact did—that the leaders of the churches who were appointed by the apostles could pass along their teachings, so that these leaders had authority equal to God himself. God sent Jesus, who chose his apostles, who instructed their successors, who passed along the sacred teachings to ordinary Christians.[2] Several problems with this view arose, however. For one thing, as churches multiplied, each of them could no longer claim to have as its leader someone who had known an apostle or even someone who knew someone who once knew an apostle. An even bigger problem was the fact that different leaders of churches, not to mention different Christians in their congregations, could claim they taught the apostolic truths. But these "truths" stood at odds with what other leaders and teachers said were the teachings of the apostles.

How was one to get around these problems? The obvious answer presented itself early on in the Christian movement. One could know what the apostles taught through the writings they left behind. These authoritative authors produced authoritative teachings. So the authoritative truth could be found in the apostolic writings.[3]

Even though this might sound like a perfect solution to the problem, the solution raised problems of its own. One involves a reality that early Christians may not have taken into account, but that scholars today are keenly aware of. Most of the apostles were illiterate and could not in fact write (discussed further in Chapter 2). They could not have left an authoritative writing if their souls depended on it. Another problem is that writings started to appear that claimed to be written by apostles, but that contained all sorts of bizarre and contradictory views. Gospels were in circulation that claimed to be written by Jesus's disciples Peter, Philip, and Mary and his brothers Thomas and James. Letters appeared that were allegedly written by Paul (in addition to ones that he actually did write), Peter, and James. Apocalyptic writings describing the end of the world or the fate of souls in the afterlife appeared in the names of Jesus's followers John, Peter, and Paul. Some writings emerged that claimed to be written by Jesus himself.

In many instances, the authors of these writings could not actually have been who they claimed to be, as even the early Christians realized. The views found in these writings were often deemed "heretical" (i.e., they conveyed false teachings), they were at odds with one another, and they contradicted the teachings that had become standard within the church. But why would authors claim to be people they weren't? Why would an author claim to be an apostle when he wasn't? Why would an unknown figure write a book falsely calling himself Peter, Paul, James, Thomas, Philip, or even Jesus?

The answer should seem fairly obvious. If your name was Jehoshaphat, and no one (other than, say, your parents and siblings) had any idea who you were, and you wanted to write an authoritative Gospel about the life and teachings of Jesus, an authoritative letter describing what Christians should believe or how they should live, or an inspired apocalypse describing in detail the fate of souls after death, you could not very well sign your own name to the book. No one would take the Gospel of Jehoshaphat seriously. If you wanted someone to read it, you called yourself Peter. Or Thomas. Or James. In other words, you lied about who you really were.

It is often said—even by scholars who should know better—that this kind of "pseudonymous" (i.e., falsely named) writing in the ancient world was not thought to be lying and was not meant to be deceitful. Part of what I'll be showing in this book is that this view is flat-out wrong (see Chapter 4). Ancient authors who talked about this practice of writing a book in someone else's name said that it was both lying and deceitful and that it was not an acceptable practice.

Many early Christian writings are "pseudonymous," going under a "false name." The more common word for this kind of writing is "forgery" (I give more precise definitions of these terms in Chapter 1). In the ancient world forgery was a bit different from today in that it was not, technically speaking, against the law. But even though it was not an illegal activity, it was a deceitful one that involved conscious lying, as the ancients themselves said.

The crucial question is this: Is it possible that any of the early Christian forgeries made it into the New Testament? That some of the books of the New Testament were not written by the apostles whose names are attached to them? That some of Paul's letters were not actually written by Paul, but by someone claiming to be Paul? That Peter's letters were not written by Peter? That James and Jude did not write the books that bear their names? Or—a somewhat different case, as we will see—that the Gospels of Matthew, Mark, Luke, and John were not actually written by Matthew, Mark, Luke, and John?

Scholars for over a hundred years have realized that in fact this is the case. The authors of some of the books of the New Testament were not who they claimed to be or who they have been supposed to be. In some instances that is because an anonymous writing, in which an author did not indicate who he was, was later named after someone who did not in fact write it. Matthew probably did not write Matthew, for example, or John, John (see Chapter 7); on the other hand, neither book actually claims to be written by a person named Matthew or John. In other instances it is because an author lied about who he was, claiming to be someone he was not. As I have already intimated, some scholars have long been reluctant, and even opposed, to calling this authorial activity lying and to call the literary products that resulted forgeries. As I will explain at length in the following chapters, most of the scholars who have actually read what ancient authors say about the phenomenon have no such hesitancy.

It is true that the ancient authors who lied about their identity may well have felt they had a clear conscience, that what they did was completely justified, that they were ultimately in the right. They may have thought and believed, at least in their own minds, that they had very good reasons for doing what they did. But as we will see in later chapters, by ancient standards these authors engaged in fraudulent activities, and the books they produced were forgeries.

Let me conclude this introduction simply by saying that I have spent the past five years studying forgery in the ancient Greek and Roman worlds, especially but not exclusively within Christianity. My goal all along has been to write a detailed scholarly monograph that deals with the matter at length. The book you're reading now is *not* that scholarly monograph. What I try to do in the present book is to discuss the issue at a layperson's level, pointing out the really interesting aspects of the problem by highlighting the results of my own research and showing what scholars have long said about the writings of the New Testament and pseudonymous Christian writings from outside the New Testament. The scholarly monograph to come will be much more thoroughly documented and technically argued. The present book, in other words, is not intended for my fellow scholars, who, if they read this one, will be doing so simply out of curiosity. It is, instead, intended for you, the general reader, who on some level is, like me, interested in the truth.

CHAPTER ONE
A World of Deceptions and Forgeries

WHENEVER I TEACH ABOUT FORGERY, I think back to my first lecture on the subject, twenty-five years ago now, at Rutgers University. As odd as this might seem, forgery was on everyone's mind at the time. Only a few months earlier forgery had been front-page news for weeks in major newspapers around the world. The diaries of Adolf Hitler had been discovered, authenticated by one of the world's leading experts on the Führer, the British historian Hugh Trevor-Roper. The diaries had been purchased for millions of dollars, first by *Stern* magazine in Germany, then by Rupert Murdoch for English publishing rights. But just as they started to appear, they were shown to be worthless forgeries.[1]

The forger of the diaries was a West German named Konrad Kujau. Ironically, even before he perpetuated the biggest con job of modern times, his friends called him Connie. Kujau had grown up as a poor working-class fellow; at an early age he discovered an artistic ability that led him to a career of forgery. He spent some time in jail as a young adult, having been caught forging lunch vouchers. But he had a number of aliases, and the people to whom he sold the Hitler diaries were not assiduous in making a background check.

The Hitler diaries consisted of some sixty books of handwritten notes that Hitler himself had allegedly made during his time in power, from June 1932 to the very end in 1945. For collectors of Nazi memorabilia, such a discovery would be priceless. We have a number of documents and paintings that Hitler produced, but nothing like this, an account of his daily activities, encounters, successes, excesses, companions, loves, hates, and rambling thoughts. When *Stern* had come into possession of the books and decided to publish them in 1984, the publishers consulted with Trevor-Roper, who, despite an initial suspicion that they must be a hoax, became convinced of the authenticity of the books upon a quick perusal of some of their pages. The documents looked old; they contained numerous pieces of accurate data and lots of asides and irrelevancies that one would expect in a personal diary. And there were so many of them! What forger would go to that much trouble?

Moreover, there was a plausible explanation for how they had managed to survive the war. It was well known that when defeat was imminent, Hitler had several metal boxes filled with his personal effects flown out of Berlin; but the plane had been shot down and its pilot killed. Local villagers near the wreck site pillaged the plane, and the boxes ended up in private hands. Collectors of memorabilia later paid for the materials, and one such collector, named Konrad Fischer (an alias for Konrad Kujau), had ended up with the diaries. They had allegedly been smuggled out of the East by his brother, a general in the East German army.

But in fact it was all a hoax by Kujau himself, who had learned to imitate Hitler's handwriting, had read authoritative biographies of the Führer to get his facts more or less straight, and had painstakingly produced the accounts over a three-year period in the early 1980s. To make the pages look aged and worn, he blotted them with tea and repeatedly slapped them on the table. And he fooled the experts, long enough, at least, to be paid $4.8 million for his efforts.

The day before the diaries were to be released to the public, however, Trevor-Roper started having second thoughts. Over the course of the next few days, after *Stern* had announced the most significant historical find in decades, other specialists were brought in. The diaries were shown beyond any doubt at all to be fakes. Forensics experts found that the paper, the glue, and the ink were all of post-1945 vintage; historians showed that the diaries were filled with errors.

Kujau was convicted of forgery, a crime by modern standards, though, as we'll see, not by ancient ones, and spent several years in prison. He emerged unrepentant, however, and spent a good bit of the rest of his life painting forgeries of great art—imitations of Monet, Rembrandt, and van Gogh—and selling them precisely as imitations. This eventually created a market for other forgers to produce and sell replicas of Kujau's imitations. As a climax to this seemingly never ending story, at the end of Kujau's life he produced an autobiography, which was never published. Instead, a different book appeared in his name, called *Die Originalität der Fälschung* ("The Originality of Forgery"). Kujau claimed, evidently in all truthfulness, that he had not written a word of it.

Forgeries in the Ancient World

WHEN I GIVE PUBLIC lectures on forgery, I am often asked, "Who would do such a thing?" The answer is, "Lots of people!" And for lots of different reasons. The most common reason today, of course, is to make money. Konrad Kujau may be the most infamous and egregious case in point, but he has many hundreds of lesser-known colleagues and disciples. The forgery trade continues to thrive; forgeries in the names of George Washington, Abraham Lincoln, Lord Byron, Robert Frost, and many, many others continue to flood the market, as recent literature on modern forgery so aptly attests.[2] These forgeries are almost always produced in order to be sold as authentic. There was a good deal of that kind of activity in the ancient world as well (and far fewer forgery experts who could detect a forgery if they saw one), although it was not a major factor within early Christianity. This was for a simple reason: Christian books were not, by and large, for sale.

Other scoundrels today will occasionally forge a document just to see if they can get away with it. This too is something that occasionally happened in the ancient world. The most famous account is the well-known case of Dionysius the Renegade.

Dionysius was a literary scholar and philosopher of the third century BCE. He eventually earned the epithet "Renegade," because he had a falling out with his fellow Stoic philosophers when he came to realize that his philosophical views did not jibe with real life as he experienced it. Stoics taught that people should remove themselves, mentally and emotionally, from the pain and anguish of this life to experience inner tranquility of spirit. Dionysius for a long time subscribed to this view. But then he became very ill, experienced a good deal of pain, and started to think that his earlier philosophizing about pain was bogus in the face of pain itself. So he left the Stoics and was called by them a renegade.

What he is most famous for in the annals of history, however, is a ruse that he pulled on a fellow literary scholar, his former teacher but eventual opponent, Heraclides of Pontus. The ruse involved a forgery, and it was a pure set-up, produced to make Heraclides look bad.[3]

Dionysius wrote and put in circulation a tragic play he called the *Parthenopaeus*, claiming that it was the work of the famous Greek dramatist Sophocles. The play made its way into the hands of Heraclides, who had no reason to doubt its authenticity. Heraclides eventually quoted it to illustrate a point about Sophocles. This is just what Dionysius was hoping for, a chance to show up his opponent. He triumphantly confronted Heraclides and told him that the play was forged, that in fact he himself had written it. Heraclides, however, did not believe it and insisted that Dionysius was lying. But Dionysius had an ace or two up his sleeve. He showed Heraclides that if he took the first letter of a series of lines in the first part of the play and strung them together as an acrostic, they spelled the name Pankalos, which happened to be the name of Dionysius's male lover.

Heraclides was still not convinced, and so Dionysius showed him two other acrostics embedded in the lines of the text. The first formed a poetic couplet:

An old monkey is not caught by a trap;
Oh yes, he is caught at last; but it takes time.

The other line was completely decisive:

Heraclides is ignorant of letters and is not ashamed of his ignorance.

We find nothing quite so hilarious or outrageous in the writings of the early Christians. In fact, there is scant evidence to suggest that any Christian authors forged documents simply in order to see if they could get away with it. Even so, there were plenty of early Christian forgers who produced lots of forged documents, probably for lots of reasons. As I pointed out in the Introduction, we still have numerous forged documents that emanated from the early church, numerous Gospels, Acts, letters, and apocalypses (these are the four literary genres of the New Testament), all of them claiming to be written by apostles.

Many of these noncanonical books are fascinating and still worth reading.[4] Among the Gospels, for example, there is an account allegedly written by Peter that gives a detailed narration of the resurrection. This is striking because—most readers have never noticed this—the New Testament Gospels do not narrate the resurrection. They do say that Jesus was buried and indicate that on the third day his tomb was empty, but they do not narrate the account of his actually emerging from the tomb. There is such an account in the *Gospel of Peter*, however. In it Jesus walks out of the tomb supported by two angels who are as tall as mountains, although Jesus is taller still; behind them, out of the tomb, emerges the cross, which speaks out to God in heaven. Other "apostolic" Gospels tell yet other amazing stories about Jesus or record bizarre teachings supposedly spoken by him, Gospels allegedly written by Jesus's brother Thomas, his disciple Philip, and his female companion Mary Magdalene. All of these books claimed to be authentic, but each of them was classified as a "forgery" by other early Christians who did not believe the apostles had actually written them.

There are also noncanonical Acts, books that narrate the adventures of Jesus's apostles after his ascension, such as the *Acts of Paul*, in which Paul preaches that, to have eternal life, followers of Jesus must refrain from sex even if married and avoid marriage altogether if single. This book was fabricated by a church leader in Asia Minor (modern Turkey) in the second century. We know about it because a famous church father, Tertullian, indicates that the person was caught and put on trial in the church for producing the account and then unceremoniously removed from his leadership position.[5] Most church leaders did not appreciate fabricated documents. But there were plenty to go around. Today we still have extensive copies of Acts of John, Peter, Andrew, and Thomas as well as fragments of earlier works that no longer survive intact.

There were also forged letters, including a set of letters between Paul and the most famous philosopher of his day, Seneca, which showed not only that Paul was on intimate terms with the greatest minds of the empire, but also that he was respected and revered by them. Some later church leaders maintained that these letters were authentic, but others thought they had been forged for the purpose of making Paul look good. There were also debates over the authenticity of other letters of Paul, and of Peter, and even of Jesus. Some of these other writings still survive.

So too forged apocalypses dotted the Christian literary landscape, including a fascinating account discovered in 1886 in a tomb in Egypt, a firsthand account allegedly written by Peter in which he is given a personal guided tour, by Jesus himself, of heaven and hell and the respective blessings of the saved and the gruesome torments of the damned. This book, as it turns out, almost made it into the New Testament, as there were church leaders well into the fourth century who claimed that it was Scripture. Others, though, claimed it was forged.

These are just a few of the documents that were disputed in the ancient world. Some early Christians claimed they really were written by apostles and belonged in the New Testament. Others insisted that they were not written by apostles, but were forgeries. How many other such documents were there? We will never know. At present we know of over a *hundred* writings from the first four centuries that were claimed by one Christian author or another to have been forged by fellow Christians.[6]

Early Christian Forgeries

MOST OF THE INSTANCES I have just mentioned are forgeries from after the days of the apostles themselves, from the second, third, and fourth Christian centuries. Most of the books of the New Testament, on the other hand, were written during the first century. Is there any evidence that forgery was happening in this earlier period? In fact, there is very good evidence indeed, and it comes to us from the pages of the New Testament itself.

There are thirteen letters in the New Testament that claim to be written by Paul, including two to the Thessalonians. In the Second Letter to the Thessalonians we find a most intriguing verse in which the author tells his readers that they are not to be led astray by a letter "as if by us" indicating that the "day of the Lord" is almost here (2:2). The author, in other words, knows of a letter in circulation claiming to be by Paul that is not really by Paul. This other letter allegedly teaches an idea that Paul himself opposes. Who would create such a forged letter? Obviously someone who wanted to advance his own views about when the end would come and decided to do so with the authority of Paul, even though he was not Paul.

But there is a terrifically interesting irony connected with this passage. Second Thessalonians, in which the passage appears, is itself widely thought among scholars not to be by Paul, even though it claims to be written by him (we'll see the reasons for thinking this in Chapter 3). Is 2 Thessalonians itself a forgery in Paul's name? If so, why would it warn against a forgery in Paul's name? There can be little doubt about the answer: one of the "tricks" used by ancient forgers to assure readers that their own writings were authentic was to warn against writings that were not authentic. Readers naturally assume that the author is not doing precisely what he condemns.[7]

We have other interesting instances of this phenomenon in early Christian literature. Three hundred years later, at the end of the fourth century, there appeared a book that scholars have called the *Apostolic Constitutions*. This lengthy book, in eight volumes, gives instructions concerning how the church is to be organized and run by its leaders. The book claims to be written by a man named Clement, who was allegedly the fourth bishop of Rome (i.e., an early "pope"), appointed by the apostle Peter himself to lead the great church. But in reality the book was written three centuries or so after Clement himself was in the grave. That is, it is a forgery. More than that, the book is called "apostolic" Constitutions because it passes along the advice and instructions of the apostles of Jesus themselves, often in the first person: "I, Peter," say to you this; "I, John," say to you this; "I, James," say to you this; and so on. One of the most fascinating instructions of the real-life author of this book (we don't know who actually wrote it) comes at the end, where he warns his readers not to read books that *claim* to be written by the apostles, but are not. In other words, he's telling his readers not to read books such as the one they are reading, an apostolic forgery. Why insert this instruction? Once again, as with 2 Thessalonians, it is because by doing so he throws his readers off the scent of his own deceit.

With 2 Thessalonians we are presented with a particularly interesting situation. No matter how one understands the matter, the book shows that there were almost certainly forgeries in Paul's name in circulation all the way back during the time of the New Testament writings. If scholars who think that 2 Thessalonians was *not* written by Paul are wrong—that is, if Paul really wrote it—then it shows that Paul himself knew of a forgery in his name that had come to the Thessalonian church. But if the other scholars are right, that Paul did not compose 2 Thessalonians, then this book *itself* is a forgery in Paul's name that was floating around in the church. Either way, there must have been Pauline forgeries already in the first century.

Are there other forgeries from the earliest of Christian times? I deal with this question at length later in the book, looking into evidence that a number of the books of the New Testament were not written by the people who are claimed to be their authors. For now I'm interested in noting that this is not simply a finding of modern scholarship. A number of the books of the New Testament were disputed already in early Christianity, among the Christian scholars of the second to the fourth centuries, who were arguing over which books should be included in Scripture.

The most famous instance is the book of Revelation. A third-century Christian scholar of Alexandria, Egypt, named Dionysius, argued that the book was not actually written by Jesus's disciple John, the son of Zebedee. Dionysius's argument was compelling and continues to be compelling to scholars today. He maintained that the writing style of the book is so different from that of the Gospel of John that they could not have been written by the same person (modern scholars differ from Dionysius only in thinking that the Gospel too was probably not written by John). Dionysius thought there must have been two authors of the same name who later came to be confused as the same person. But it is interesting that Dionysius, according to the church father Eusebius, had a number of predecessors who had argued that Revelation was written not by a different man named John, but by a heretic named Cerinthus, who forged the account in order to promote his false teaching that there would be a literal future paradise of a thousand years here on earth.[8]

The small letter of Jude, allegedly written by Jesus's own brother, was also debated in the early church. Some Christians argued that it was not authentic, in part, according to the famous fourth-century Christian scholar Jerome, because the book quotes an apocryphal book called *Enoch* as if it were authoritative Scripture.[9] The book of 2 Peter was rejected by a number of early church fathers, as discussed by both Jerome and Eusebius, but none more straightforwardly than the notable Christian teacher of Alexandria Didymus the Blind, who argued that "the letter is false and so is not to be in the canon."[10] Peter, in other words, did not actually write it, according to Didymus, even though the author *claimed* to be Peter.

Other Christian teachers disputed whether 1 and 2 Timothy were actually by Paul, some claiming that their contents showed that he did not write them.[11] The book of Hebrews was particularly debated; the book does not explicitly claim to be written by Paul, but there are hints at the end that the author wants readers to *think* that he's Paul (see 13:22–25). For centuries its Pauline authorship was a matter of dispute. The book was finally admitted into the canon only when nearly everyone came to think Paul must have written it.

In short, there were long, protracted, and often heated debates in the early church over forged documents. Early Christians realized that there were numerous forgeries in circulation, and they wanted to know which books were written by their alleged authors and which were not. As we will see more fully later, practically no one approved of the practice of forgery; on the contrary, it was widely condemned, even in books that were themselves forged (such as 2 Thessalonians and the *Apostolic Constitutions*).

Most of this book will focus on examples of forgery in early Christianity. To make sense of the early Christian forgeries, however, we need to take a step back and consider the phenomenon of forgery in the ancient world more broadly. That will be the focus of the rest of this chapter. We begin with a very important discussion of the terms that I will be using.

The Terms of the Debate

THE FIRST TWO TERMS are especially technical and, although I won't be using them much, it is important to know what they mean. An "orthonymous" (literally, "rightly named") writing is one that really is written by the person who claims to be writing it. There are seven letters of Paul, out of the thirteen in the New Testament that bear his name, that virtually everyone agrees are orthonymous, actually written by Paul.

A "homonymous" (literally, "same named") writing is one that is written by someone who happens to have the same name as someone else. In the ancient world, the vast majority of people did not have last names, and a lot of people had the same first names. This was as true among Christians as it was for everyone else. Lots of people were named John, James, and Jude, for example. If someone named John wrote the book of Revelation and simply called himself John, he wasn't necessarily claiming to be anyone but himself. When later Christians assumed that this John must be the disciple John, the son of Zebedee, it wasn't really the author's fault. He just happened to have the same name as another more famous person. The book is not forged, then. It is simply homonymous, assuming that John the son of Zebedee did not write it, a safe assumption for most critical scholars. It was included in the canon because of this mistaken identity.

Other writings are "anonymous," literally, "having no name." These are books whose authors never identify themselves. That is, technically speaking, true of one-third of the New Testament books. None of the Gospels tells us the name of its author. Only later did Christians call them Matthew, Mark, Luke, and John; and later scribes then added these names to the book titles. Also anonymous are the book of Acts and the letters known as 1, 2, and 3 John. Technically speaking, the same is true of the book of Hebrews; the author never mentions his name, even if he wants you to assume he's Paul.[12]

The term "pseudonymous" (literally, "falsely named") is a little more slippery, and I need to explain how I will be using it. Technically it refers to any book that appears under the name of someone other than the author, but there are two kinds of pseudonymous writings. Sometimes authors simply take a pen name. When Samuel Clemens wrote *Huckleberry Finn* and signed it "Mark Twain," he was not trying to deceive his readers into thinking that he was someone famous; it was just a pen name to mask his own identity. So too when Mary Ann

Evans wrote *Silas Marner* and signed it "George Eliot." This use of a pen name did not happen a lot in the ancient world, but it did happen on occasion. The Greek historian Xenophon, for example, wrote his famous work the *Anabasis* using the pen name Themistogenes; and the Greek philosopher Iamblichus wrote his treatise *On the Mysteries* under the made-up name Abammon. In these instances there does not appear to have been any real attempt to deceive readers into thinking that the author was someone famous.[13]

The other kind of pseudonymous writing involves a book that is circulated under the name of someone else, usually some kind of authority figure who is presumed to be well known to the reading audience. For this particular kind of pseudonymous writing I will be using the technical term "pseudepigraphy" (literally, "written under a false name"). A pseudepigraphal writing, then, is one that is claimed to be written by a famous, well-known, or authoritative person who did not in fact write it.

But as it turns out, there are also two kinds of pseudepigraphal writings. Sometimes a writing was published anonymously, with no author's name attached, for example, the Gospel of Matthew. But later readers and copyists asserted that they knew who had written it and claimed it was by a well-known, authoritative person, in this case the disciple Matthew. In writings of this sort, which are *wrongly attributed* to a well-known person, the author is not trying to deceive anyone.[14] He or she remained anonymous. It is only later readers who claimed that the author was someone else. This kind of pseudepigraphy, then, involves a "false ascription"; a work is "ascribed" to someone who didn't write it.

The other kind of pseudepigraphy does involve a kind of intentional deceit by an author. This is when an author writes a work claiming to be someone else. This is what I am here calling forgery. My definition of a *forgery*, then, is a writing that claims to be written by someone (a known figure) who did not in fact write it.

Over the years I have had several people object to my use of the term "forgery," and I well understand the hesitancy of other scholars to use the term. In modern times, when we think of forgery, we think of highly illegal activities (forging precious stones, money, or books for profit) that can send a person to prison. Ancient forgers were not as a rule thrown in jail, because there simply weren't laws governing the production and distribution of literature. There were no copyright laws, for example. But ancient authors *did* see this kind of activity as fraudulent, they recognized it as deceitful, they called it lying (and other even nastier things), and they often punished those who were caught doing it. So when I use the term "forgery," I do mean for it to have negative connotations, in part because, as we will see, the terms used by ancient authors were just as negative, if not more so.

My use of the term "forgery," however, does not say anything about the legal status of the document in question or the criminal activity of the author. It is a technical term referring to one kind of pseudepigraphal writing, one in which an author knowingly claims to be someone else. One of the overarching theses of my book is that those who engaged in this activity in the ancient world were roundly condemned for lying and trying to deceive their readers.

Motivations for Forgery

IF, AS I SHOW later, forgery was widely condemned, why did people do it? And how did they justify what they were doing in their own eyes? Those will be two of the leading questions for the rest of this chapter. The question of "why" they did it is a bit complicated, and here I need to differentiate between two ideas that people sometimes confuse in their minds. These are the notions of "intention," on the one hand, and "motivation," on the other. I think the difference between the two can be easily explained.

If my wife asks me, "Why are you going to the store?" I could give a variety of answers. One answer might be, "To buy something for dinner." Another might be, "Because there is nothing in the fridge." These are actually two different kinds of answers. The first indicates what I *intend* to do once I'm at the store: I intend to buy some food for tonight. The second indicates what is *motivating* me to go to the store in the first place: I am motivated by the fact that there is no food in the house. Intentions are not the same as motivations. The "intention" is what you want to accomplish; the "motivation" is the reason you want to accomplish it.

This is also the case when it comes to forgers and their forgeries. There is a difference between a forger's intention and motivation. A forger's intention, in almost every instance, is to deceive readers about his identity, that is, to make readers believe that he is someone other than who he is. But he may have lots of different reasons (motivations) for wanting to do that.

Authors have always had numerous reasons for wanting to write a forgery. In the modern world, as we have already seen, the principal motivation is to make money, as in the case of Konrad Kujau and the Hitler diaries. This does not appear to be the main reason for forgeries back in antiquity. The market for such "original books" was limited then, because the book-selling industry was so modest—books could not be mass-produced and widely published. Still, there were instances in which forged books could turn a profit, as we learn from a famous author named Galen, a second-century physician who lived in Rome.

Galen was extremely learned and one of the most prolific authors from the ancient world. This was a world that did not, for the most part, have public libraries for people to use. But on occasion a local king would start up a library, principally for scholars, and there was sometimes competition among libraries to acquire greater holdings than their rivals as a kind of status symbol. The two most important libraries in antiquity were those of Alexandria in Egypt and Pergamum in Asia Minor. According to Galen, the kings who built these libraries were keen to increase their holdings and were intent on getting as many original copies as they could of such authors as Plato, Aristotle, Hippocrates, Aeschylus, Sophocles, and Euripides. Having original copies of these writings was important in an age when scribes could and did make mistakes when reproducing the text. If you had the original, you knew you had the author's own words, not some kind of error-ridden copy botched by the local scribe. So these two libraries were willing to pay cash on the barrelhead for original copies of their coveted authors' works.

You'd be amazed how many "original" copies of Plato, Aristotle, and Euripides start showing up, when you are willing to pay gold for them. According to Galen, forgeries started to appear by unscrupulous authors who simply wanted the money.[15]

We have seen another motivation, or combination of motivations, in the case of Dionysius the Renegade. One could argue that Dionysius perpetrated his fraudulent play, the *Parthenopaeus*, principally in order to see if he could get away with it. Or he may have done it to make a fool out of his nemesis, Heraclides. We have other instances in the ancient world of a similar motivation, to pull the wool over someone's, or everyone's, eyes. As it turns out, some such motivation may still be at work in our world today, as some scholars have thought that one of the most famous "discoveries" of an ancient Gospel in the twentieth century was in fact a forgery by the scholar who claimed to have discovered it. This is the famous *Secret Gospel of Mark* allegedly found by Morton Smith in 1958.[16]

Other authors forged documents for political or military ends. The Jewish historian Josephus, for example, reports that an enemy of Alexander, the son of King Herod, forged a letter in Alexander's name in which he announced plans to murder his father. According to Josephus, the forger was a secretary of the king who was "a bold man, cunning in counterfeiting anyone's hand." But the plan backfired; after producing numerous forgeries, the man was caught and "was at last put to death for it."[17]

Political forgeries were usually not treated kindly. But sometimes they worked. In the third century the Roman emperor Aurelian had a private secretary, named Eros, who had incurred his master's anger and was about to be punished. To forestall the outcome, he forged a list of names of political leaders whom the emperor had supposedly decided to have executed for treason and put the forged list into circulation. The men on the list rose up and assassinated the emperor.[18]

Sometimes the motivation for a forgery was less political than religious—to defend religious institutions or practices or to defend one's religious claims against those of opponents. One of the more humorous accounts occurs in the writings of the second-century pagan author Lucian of Samosata, a brilliant wit and keen critic of all things hypocritical. One of Lucian's hilarious treatises, *Alexander the False Prophet*, is directed against a man named Alexander, who wanted to set up an "oracle"—that is, a place where a god would communicate with humans—in the town of Abunoteichos. Alexander was a crafty fellow who knew that he had to convince people that the god Apollo really had decided to communicate through him, Alexander, at this newly founded place of prophecy, since he planned to receive payments for being able to deliver Apollo's pronouncements to those who would come to inquire. So, according to Lucian, Alexander forged a set of bronze tablets and buried them in one of the oldest and most famous of Apollo's temples, in the city of Chalcedon. When the tablets were then dug up, word got around about what was written in this "miraculous" find. On these tablets Apollo declared that he was soon to move to take up residence in a new home, in Abunoteichos. Alexander then established the oracle there and attracted a huge following, thanks in no small measure to the forged writings in the name of the god he claimed to represent.

An example of a Jewish forgery created to support Judaism can be found in the famous *Letter of Aristeas*.[19] Aristeas was allegedly a pagan member of the court of the Egyptian king Ptolemy II Philadelphus (285–246 BCE). In this letter "Aristeas" describes how the king decided to include a copy of the Jewish Scriptures in his expanding library, and so he made arrangements with the Jewish high priest in Israel to send scholars to Egypt who could translate the sacred texts from their original Hebrew language into Greek. Seventy-two scholars were sent, and through miraculous divine intervention they managed to produce, individually, precisely the same wording for their translations of the Scriptures. Since the *Letter of Aristeas* is allegedly by a non-Jew, giving a more or less "disinterested" account of how the Hebrew Bible was translated into Greek, it has all the appearance of stating the facts "as they really were." But in reality, the letter is a forgery, written by a Jew in Alexandria in the second century BCE. It was written, in part, in order to show the divine inspiration of the Jewish sacred texts, even in their Greek translation.

As already intimated in earlier examples, sometimes forgeries were created with the express purpose of making a personal enemy look bad (as with Dionysius the Renegade) or getting an opponent into serious trouble (as with the person who forged a letter to King Herod). As it turns out, this is one of the best-attested motivations for creating forgeries in the ancient world. The Roman poet Martial, author of a large number of witty and very funny poems, complains in several places that others have forged poems in his name that were either very bad or in very bad taste, precisely in order to make Martial himself look bad.[20] Even more slanderous is an episode reported by the historian of philosophy Diogenes Laertius, who indicates that an enemy of the famous philosopher Epicurus, a rival named Diotimus, forged fifty obscene letters in Epicurus's name and put them in circulation. Epicurus already had a problem with having a (totally undeserved) bad reputation as someone addicted to pleasure. These forgeries simply added fuel to the fire.[21]

Or consider the case of Anaximenes, as reported to us by a Greek geographer of the second century CE, Pausanias. Anaximenes was a clever but ill-natured fellow who had a quarrel with a famous public speaker named Theopompus. In order to strike out at his enemy, claims Pausanias, Anaximenes wrote a treatise in the writing style of Theopompus, naming himself as Theopompus. In this treatise he spoke abusively of the citizens of three chief Greek cities, Athens, Sparta, and Thebes. Once the treatise circulated in these cities, Theopompus became very much a persona non grata, even though he had nothing to do with it.[22]

Other forgers produced their work for more noble ends, for example, to provide hope for their readers. One of the most common forms of forgery in Jewish writings around the time of early Christianity is the literary genre known as the apocalypse. An apocalypse (from the Greek meaning a "revealing" or an "unveiling") is a text that reveals the truth of the heavenly realm to mortals to help them make sense of what is happening here on earth. Sometimes this truth is revealed through bizarre and highly symbolic visions that the author allegedly sees and that are explained by some kind of angelic interpreter. An example is in the book of Daniel in the Hebrew Bible. At other times the author is said to be taken up to heaven to see the ultimate truths of the divine realm that make sense of the horrible events transpiring here on earth. A Christian example is the book of Revelation in the New Testament.

These books are meant to inspire hope in their readers. Even though things seem to be completely out of control here on earth, even though there is rampant pain and misery and suffering, even though wars, famines, epidemics, and natural disasters are crushing the human race, even though things seem to be completely removed from God's hand—despite all this, everything is going according to plan. God will soon make right all that is wrong. If people will simply hold on for a little while longer, their trust in God will be vindicated, and he will intervene in the course of things here on earth to restore peace, justice, and joy forever.

Apocalypses are almost always written pseudonymously in the name of some renowned religious figure of the past.[23] In Christian circles we have apocalypses in the names of Peter, Paul, and the prophet Isaiah. In Jewish circles we have apocalypses in the names of Daniel, Enoch, Abraham, and even Adam! Scholars typically claim that these books cannot be considered forgeries, because writing them pseudonymously was all part of the task; the literary genre requires them, more or less, to be written by someone who would "know" such things, that is, someone highly favored by God. But I think this view is too simplistic. The reality is that ancient people really did believe that they were written by the people who claimed to be writing them, as seen repeatedly in the ancient testimonies.[24] The authors of these books knew it too. They assumed false names precisely because their writings would prove more effective that way.

This relates to the single most important motivation for authors to claim they were someone else in antiquity. Quite simply, it was to get a hearing for their views. If you were an unknown person, but had something really important to say and wanted people to hear you—not so they could praise you, but so they could learn the truth—one way to make that happen was to pretend you were someone else, a well-known author, a famous figure, an authority.

Thus, for example, if you wanted to write a philosophical treatise in which you dealt with some of the most confounding ethical problems facing the world, but you were not a famous philosopher, you might write the treatise and claim that you were, signing it Plato or Aristotle. If you wanted to produce an apocalypse explaining that suffering here on this earth is only temporary and that God would soon intervene to overthrow the forces of evil in this world, and you wanted people to realize this was a message that needed to be heard and proclaimed, you wouldn't sign it with your own name (the *Apocalypse of Joe*), but the name of a famous religious figure (the *Apocalypse of Daniel*). If you wanted to narrate a Gospel of Jesus's most important teachings, but in fact were living a hundred years after Jesus and didn't have any real access to what Jesus said, you would write down the sayings you found most compelling and claim to be someone who had actually heard Jesus speak, calling your book the *Gospel of Thomas* or the *Gospel of Philip*.

This motivation was at work in both Christian and non-Christian circles. We know this because ancient authors actually tell us so. For example, a commentator on the writings of Aristotle, a pagan scholar named David, indicated: "If someone is uninfluential and unknown, yet wants his writing to be read, he writes in the name of someone who came before him and was influential, so that through his influence he can get his work accepted."[25]

This is the case with the one instance we have of a Christian forger who was caught and who later explained in writing what he did. In the fifth Christian century, a church leader named Salvian lived in Marseille. As did many others in his day Salvian decided, with his wife, to express his devotion to God by renouncing the world and taking on an ascetic form of life. Salvian was outraged by the worldliness of the church and by church members who were more concerned with personal comfort and wealth than with the demands of the gospel. So he wrote a letter called *Timothy to the Church*. Written in an authoritative style, the letter seemed to its readers actually to have been written by Timothy, the famous companion of the apostle Paul four hundred years earlier. But somehow Salvian's bishop came to suspect that Salvian had written it. He confronted Salvian with the matter, and Salvian admitted that he had done it.

But Salvian was a defensive fellow, and so he wrote an explanation for why he had produced a pseudonymous letter. As defensive individuals often do, Salvian made lots of excuses. The name Timothy, for example, literally means "honored by God," and so, he said, he used that name to show that he wrote for the honor of God. His main defense, though, was that he was a nobody, and if he himself wrote a letter to the churches, no one would pay attention. Or as he put it in his written defense, the author had "wisely selected a pseudonym for his book for the obvious reason that he did not wish the obscurity of his own person to detract from the influence of his otherwise valuable book."[26]

By writing in the name of Timothy, on the other hand, he hoped to get a reading. His views were important enough for him to adopt a false name. There is nothing in the story to suggest that Salvian's bishop accepted this excuse with equanimity (the story is related to us by Salvian, not his bishop). On the contrary, if the bishop was like every other reader from the ancient world who comments on such things, he was not at all pleased that Salvian had lied about his identity.

Forgers' Techniques

WE ARE NEVER TOLD how Salvian's bishop came to realize that the letter allegedly by Timothy was in fact written by his presbyter, Salvian. But it is probably not too hard to figure out. The letter addressed major concerns that Salvian himself had had and that he no doubt had articulated repeatedly among his fellow churchgoers and the church leaders. Since he was a literate person, he may well have written other treatises on this and related subjects. If his bishop knew Salvian's ultimate concerns and had read his other writings, so that he was familiar with his writing style, he may have put two and two together and realized that this letter, which suddenly appeared out of nowhere, was a modern production written pseudonymously.

Very few forgers in the ancient world were actually caught red-handed.[27] The reasons should seem fairly obvious. For one thing, ancient scholars who were invested in detecting forgeries did not have the sophisticated methods of analysis that we have today, with our computers, databases, intricate analyses of writing style, and so on. An ancient scholar frequently *could* tell that a literary text was not by the same author who wrote another text (e.g., that the book of Revelation was not written by the same author who wrote the Fourth Gospel). But it's much easier to say who did *not* write a book (Paul did not write Hebrews) than who *did* write it (Ephesians, if not by Paul, was written by whom?).

Even more important, forgers went out of their way not to get caught. Most of the time, they were successful. In one of the fascinating modern discussions of forgery, Anthony Grafton, of Princeton University, shows that over the centuries the art of forgery became increasingly refined as the art of detecting forgery improved its methods. The better scholars became at recognizing a forgery, the better forgers got at avoiding detection. This compelled the scholars to refine their methods, which in turn drove the forgers to improve their craft.[28]

Ancient forgers typically used several methods to escape detection. First and most obviously, anyone forging a document in the name of a well-known author did his level best to imitate the author's writing style and vocabulary. Everyone has a distinctive style of writing, and every style, in principle, can be imitated. Less skillful imitators simply recognized unusual words commonly used by an author and used those words a lot (sometimes much more than the author being imitated). Others tried to imitate the distinctive ways the author used grammar: sentence length, use of participial phrases, use of sentence fragments, and so on. For highly educated authors, this matter of imitating writing style was almost second nature; in the advanced education of "rhetorical" schooling that the upper-class elite received, a regular exercise involved writing an account or a speech in the style of a famous author or speaker. The most highly educated people in the empire were trained to do this as a matter of course.[29] Most of those people, of course, were not involved in the business of forgery.

The fact that a forger tried to imitate an author's style can make it difficult to detect forgeries. But the reality is that some people were more skilled at it than others. Just as most people today couldn't forge a Rembrandt if their life depended on it, so too most people can't sound "just like" Aristotle, Plutarch, or Paul.

A second trick of forgers was to include verisimilitudes in their writings. The term "verisimilitude" refers to a statement, a comment, or an off-the-cuff remark that makes a writing look "very similar" to what you would expect the alleged author to have said. Forgers would make personal comments about the recipients of a letter, even if in fact they were not actually sending it to anyone. Why say you'll be praying for the letter's recipients during their time of persecution, if you're not actually sending it to people experiencing persecution? Because if you say that, it certainly *sounds* as though you're sending it to those experiencing persecution! Why ask for a personal favor from a person you're writing to, if you're not really writing to that person? ("Hey, James, be sure to say hello to your mother for me; and don't forget to bring that book that I left at your house.") Because there's no better way to make it look as if the letter is authentic. Why fabricate names of recipients, your past relationship with these recipients, remembered experiences you've shared, and so on? All of these add credibility to your writing, making it look as though you really are writing this person, at this time, in this situation, even if you're writing three hundred years later to no one in particular.

We've already seen one kind of verisimilitude in our earlier discussion. In both 2 Thessalonians from the first century and the *Apostolic Constitutions* three hundred years later, the pseudonymous author tells his readers not to read pseudonymous writings. Or to be more precise, the forger warns his readers not to read forgeries. Why? In part because it makes readers less likely to suspect that the book they have is itself a forgery. That is, it's a kind of verisimilitude.

One final technique used by some forgers involves a "discovery narrative." If a book shows up this week claiming to have been written two hundred years ago, one might well wonder where it has been all this time. Forgers sometimes begin or end their writing by describing what has led to the book's disappearance and discovery. For example, an author might begin a book by explaining that he had a dream, and in this dream he was told to dig a deep hole on the south side of the oak tree in the field across the stream from his farm. When he dug the hole, he found an ancient wooden box. Inside the box was a deteriorating manuscript. He has now copied this manuscript out by hand, and this is it, a revelation given directly by Christ to the apostle James and hidden from the world until now.

The book then claims to have been written by James, as "copied" by the discoverer of the manuscript. The book is not widely known, because it has been hidden all these years. But now it has come to light, and here it is. Except it's not really here. What is here is a book not written by James, but by a forger claiming to be James, who has conveniently included an explanation for why no one has ever heard of this book before.

Ancient Views of Forgery

I HAVE ALREADY INDICATED that scholars are sometimes loath to use the term "forgery" for pseudepigraphal writings in which an author claims to be someone else. Later, I deal at greater length with what some scholars have claimed about this phenomenon in order to avoid thinking of such books as forgeries. This will come in Chapter 4, after we have had two chapters of data to help us assess these claims. As it turns out, many New Testament scholars who make pronouncements on forgery ("It wasn't meant to be deceitful." "No one thought of it as lying." "It wasn't looked down upon.") simply haven't read what the ancient sources say about it. Throughout this book it will become quite clear from the ancient writings themselves that even though forgery was widely practiced, it was also widely condemned and treated as a form of lying. To get us started here, I want to give just a few examples, which could easily be multiplied, of how ancients thought and talked about the practice of forgery.

The first thing to note is that in virtually every instance in which an ancient author mentions forgery, he condemns it. There are a few exceptions, which I will discuss at greater length in Chapter 4. But these exceptions really are exceptional, for reasons we'll see. By far the dominant discourse in the ancient world opposed forgery and saw it as a deceitful and illicit practice. That doesn't mean that people didn't engage in the practice—adultery is usually seen as a deceitful and illicit practice today, but that doesn't stop a lot of people. Despite the condemnations of it, the practice of forgery thrived in antiquity.

One of the more famous stories of forgery involves the second-century Roman physician Galen, whom I mentioned earlier. In one of his surviving writings, Galen gives an autobiographical account in which he tells of detecting a forgery. As he relates it, he was one day walking down a street in Rome and was passing by a bookseller's shop. In the window were two men arguing about a book that was allegedly written by Galen! One man was heatedly arguing that Galen had in fact written the book; the other was insisting that the writing style was all wrong, that Galen could not have written it. This episode warmed the cockles of Galen's heart, since in fact he had *not* written the book. So he went home and wrote a book, which we still have today. Sometimes the book is called *How to Recognize Books Written by Galen*.

Did Galen think it was an acceptable practice for someone else to write in his name? Obviously not. Nor did anyone else who discovered forgeries in his own name. I earlier mentioned the poet Martial, who was incensed that other poets tried to pass off their own work (which he considered vastly inferior) as his. Among Christians we have outraged complaints about forgeries in the writings of Origen, Jerome, and Augustine. Forgery was so widely condemned in antiquity that even forgers condemned forgery—as we have seen in the case of 2 Thessalonians and the *Apostolic Constitutions*.

Some scholars have argued, strenuously, but without much evidence, that it was a common and accepted practice in schools of philosophy to write a philosophical treatise and sign your master's name to it (Plato, Pythagoras, etc.), rather than your own, and that no one looked askance at this practice. As we will see in Chapter 4, there is little evidence indeed that this happened. Ask a modern-day scholar who claims that in antiquity this was a widespread practice to cite an ancient source for it. In almost every instance, you will find a tongue-tied scholar.[30]

That forgery was widely condemned in antiquity can be seen by some of the terms that were used to describe the practice, most of which were at least as negative as the modern term "forgery." In Greek the two most common words to describe literary texts whose authors falsely claim to be a well-known figure are *pseudos*, which means "a falsehood" or "a lie," and *nothos*, which means "an illegitimate child," with connotations similar to our modern word "bastard."[31]

With respect to the first word, some scholars have stressed that *pseudos* does not have to have the negative connotation of a bald-faced lie, since it is sometimes used simply to indicate information that is incorrect, a falsehood. And that is certainly true, in some contexts. But it means that only in contexts in which those speaking the falsehood do not realize that what they are saying is an error. When a person speaks something that is false, knowing that it is false, *pseudos* always means what "lie" means in English: an intentional falsehood with the intent of deceiving hearers or readers into thinking that it is right. There can be no question which connotation applies to ancient forgeries. The person who wrote the *Gospel of Peter*, claiming to be Jesus's disciple Simon Peter, some sixty years after Peter's death—did he realize that he was not in fact Simon Peter? Unless he was a lunatic, then of course he did. He intentionally claimed to be someone he was not. In Greek that would be called a *pseudos;* in English we would call it a lie.

The other term, *nothos*, might seem a bit puzzling. It is often translated "spurious," which may be accurate enough, but does not carry the same connotations as the Greek word, which refers typically to a bastard child. The logic of the term in the context of forgeries is clear. If a child born out of wedlock is raised by his mother and her husband (who is not the child's father), then the child does not "belong," by blood, to his alleged father; they are not related. Moreover, in antiquity, the child had no legal rights. So too with a literary text. If it goes under the name of an author who did not in fact produce it, then it is not actually related or legally connected to that person, but derives from someone else. So it is called a *nothos*, an illegitimate child, a text that does not belong to the author claimed for it.

Both of these terms are negative, not neutral, and they show what ancients thought about the practice of forgery. An author who produces a writing in the name of someone else has produced a "false writing," "a lie," "an illegitimate child," or a "bastard." Similar words are used by Latin writers for the act of forgery, for example, words that mean "to lie," "to falsify," "to fabricate," "to adulterate," "to counterfeit."

Contrary to what some scholars have claimed (again, see Chapter 4) forgers in the ancient world typically wanted to deceive their readers by claiming to be persons of authority and standing. This has been long recognized by the real experts in ancient forgery.[32] And a moment's reflection shows why this must be the case. Consider the motivations for forgery mentioned earlier. Forgers who wanted to see if they could get away with it, to see if they could pull the wool over someone's eyes, would scarcely have tried to make their ploy transparent and obvious; they would have truly wanted to deceive people. If they wanted to make money by producing an "original" copy of, say, a dialogue of Plato, they wouldn't get very far if everyone knew who they really were. If they wanted to justify a political institution or religious practice by citing the views of an authority or wanted to have their own views accepted as authoritative even if they themselves were completely unknown, it would make no sense to claim to be someone else knowing full well that no one would believe you.

That forgery was not a transparent fiction is evidenced as well by the negative things people say about it in the ancient sources—the practice, as I have argued, is condemned in virtually every instance it is discussed. Moreover, the reactions to forgers when they are caught show quite clearly that they meant to deceive, that they were often successful, and that people were not at all pleased when they discovered the truth. Galen and Martial were incensed to find someone else claiming their name for writings they did not produce. And sometimes the reaction was even more hostile.

The first time we hear of a forger being discovered occurs all the way back in the fifth century BCE, in the writings of the famous Greek historian Herodotus.[33] In a puzzling and enigmatic passage, Herodotus speaks of Onomacritus of Athens, who had invented an oracle (i.e., a prophecy from a divine being) and ascribed it to the ancient bard Musaeus, a mythical figure thought to be able to predict the future. This oracle indicated that a certain group of islands would sink into the sea. It is hard to understand why Onomacritus forged the oracle or why people were upset by it. But they were. The ruler of Athens, Hipparchus, banished Onomacritus from the city; he fled Greece and ended up in Persia. On yet other occasions Onomacritus was thought to have forged other oracles and was roundly chastised for it by other ancient authors, such as Plutarch.[34]

Sometimes the punishment for forgery was even more harsh. Earlier I mentioned the fifty obscene letters that the philosopher

Diotimus forged in the name of Epicurus in order to sully his reputation. According to one ancient source, Epicurus's followers were not amused. One of them, a man named Zeno, tracked Diotimus down and murdered him for it.[35] This can be compared with the account already mentioned by the Jewish historian Josephus, who indicates that someone forged a letter in the name of Alexander, son of King Herod, indicating Alexander's plan to assassinate his father. As we have seen, the forger was the king's own secretary, who, according to Josephus, "was at last put to death for it."

From all of the discussions of forgeries in ancient sources, I think we can safely draw several major conclusions. Forgery was widely practiced in the ancient world, among pagans, Jews, and Christians. Forgers, motivated by a range of factors, intended to deceive their readers. Ancient authors who discuss the practice condemned it and considered it a form of lying and deceit. Forgers who were caught were reprimanded or punished even more severely.

Possible Justifications for Forgery

THE MOST THOROUGH STUDY of ancient forgery ever undertaken, by the Austrian classical scholar Wolfgang Speyer, maintains: "Every forgery feigns a state of affairs that does not correspond to the actual facts of the case. For this reason forgery belongs to the realm of lying and deception."[36] This view coincides perfectly well with the one I have been trying to make in this chapter, but it leaves us with a problem. When we are considering Christian forgeries, in particular, we are dealing with writings produced by followers of Jesus, who presumably ascribed to Jesus's ethical teachings and the moral norms set forth in the Hebrew Scriptures. Surely they knew that lying and deception were wrong. Why would they do what they knew was wrong? And surely the question applies to pagans and Jews as well, who as a whole were just as ethical as Christians. Why would any of them go against their own ethical views?

On one level, of course, the question is silly. All people do things they know are wrong. But I mean the question at a deeper level. Did the forgers who perpetrated their fraud think that they were justified in lying? Is lying ever justified? I return to this issue in Chapter 8, but for now I should at least set the stage by asking a more general question. What did people in antiquity think about lying and deceit?

Asking what ancient people thought about lying is like asking modern people—it depends completely on whom you ask. Some think lying is never acceptable under any circumstances; others think that in some circumstances it is the ethical thing to do. Yet others think nothing at all about lying whenever they feel like it, thank you very much!

Some ancient Greek philosophers, notably Aristotle, stressed the importance of normally being truthful.[37] But most philosophers thought there could be exceptions. Xenophon, for example, reports Socrates as saying it is a *good* thing to lie to a sick son or a friend who wants to commit suicide, if you can stop the person from doing so.[38] Socrates also said that it is useful for a field general to lie to his disheartened troops in battle, telling them that support troops are soon to arrive, in order to drive them to fight with greater valor; or for a parent to deceive a child into taking some unpleasant medicine that will be good for her. Plato taught that some lies can be useful, such as those doctors might tell patients for their own good or those rulers of a country might tell their people in order to ensure the healthy functioning of society. As one ancient writer, Heliodorus, put it: "A lie is good when it benefits the one who speaks it without doing harm to the one who hears."[39]

But what about Christians? Weren't they taught always to tell the truth? That is certainly what the great fifth-century church theologian Augustine taught in his two treatises devoted to "lying." It is never, ever, under any circumstances permissible to lie. This view of Augustine's was not based on a simplistic sense that it is always good to tell the truth, but on deep theological understandings about what it means to be truly human in relationship to the God of truth, who himself became fully human.[40]

But lots of other Christian thinkers, both before and after Augustine, thought otherwise. Some, such as the important Christian thinker Clement of Alexandria at the end of the second century, as well as his Alexandrian compatriot at the beginning of the third, Origen—arguably the most important theologian of the church before Augustine—agreed with Plato about the "medicinal lie": if a doctor's lie will impel a patient to take her medicine, it is ethically justified.[41] Both of them also pointed out that in the Old Testament, God himself appears to use deception at times. When God told Jonah to proclaim to the city of Nineveh that in forty days it would be overthrown, he obviously knew full well that the people would repent and that he would stay his hand of judgment. God never did plan, then, to overthrow the city, even though that's what he told his prophet to proclaim. Sometimes a deceptive statement can do a world of good.

There are plenty of other examples in Scripture in which the lies of God's chosen ones lead to good ends. If Abraham had not lied about his wife Sarah ("she's my sister"), he would have been killed, and the nation of Israel would never have come into existence (Gen. 12). Or if Rahab the prostitute had not lied about where the Israelite spies were hiding, they may have been killed and the children of Israel may never have been able to conquer the promised land (Josh. 2). Examples could be multiplied. Sometimes lying is the right thing to do.

Is that what forgers thought? That lying about who they were was worth it? That the good effects of their deception outweighed the bad? That the ends justified the means?

I'm afraid we may never know what drove these people to do what they did. We simply can't peer into their hearts and minds to see what they were thinking, deep down, when they decided to hide their own identity and to claim, deceitfully, that they were someone else. Their readers, had they known, would probably have called them liars and condemned what they did. But in their own eyes, their conscience may have been free from blame, and their motives may have been as pure as the driven snow. They had a truth to convey, and they were happy to lie in order to proclaim it.

CHAPTER TWO

Forgeries in the Name of Peter

UP TO THIS POINT IN my discussion of ancient lying, deception, and forgery I have been using the term "truth" in a very simple sense, to mean something like "correct information." In reality, though, truth and its opposite, falsehood, are complex. I think we all recognize this deep down, even if we haven't given it a good deal of thought. When we watch a movie, we often ask, "Is this a true story?" By that we mean, "Is this something that really happened?" If the answer is yes, then we somehow feel assured and comforted that the events took place, and so, as a story, it is "truer" than one that is just made up. But even then we never think that absolutely everything found in the movie—all of the characters, the dialogue, the individual scenes, and so on—is absolutely and completely the way it "really" happened. We allow for a kind of poetic license of distortion, even when acknowledging that the story is somehow "true."

One could easily make the case that a movie can be true in a deeper sense even if it is about something that never happened. This has been my view for many years, and it used to drive my kids crazy when they were young. We'd be watching a movie, and they'd say, "Dad, is this a true story?" And I'd almost always say yes. But then they'd remember that I tend to have a different view of things, and they'd ask the follow-up question, "No, Dad, I mean did this really happen?" I'd say no, and they'd continue to be puzzled.

As some of my readers may be. How can a story be "true" if it didn't happen? In point of fact, there are all sorts of true stories that didn't happen, as everyone will admit, I think, if they think about it a bit. When I try to illustrate this with my students, I usually rehearse for them the story of George Washington and the cherry tree.

True Stories That Didn't Happen

EVERY GRADE-SCHOOL KID IN the country knows the cherry tree story. As a young boy, George Washington, for unknown reasons, took a hatchet to his father's cherry tree. When his father came home, he saw the tree and asked, "Who chopped down my cherry tree?" Young George answered, "I cannot tell a lie. I did it." The way the story is normally told, we don't find out what happened afterwards— was young George taken out to the woodshed? The story ends with George's one-liner.[1]

We know that this story never happened, because the person who invented the tale later admitted to having done so. He was a Christian minister named Mason Locke Weems, usually known as Parson Weems. As a later biographer of Washington, Parson Weems confessed that he made up the story, even though he once had claimed that he received it from a credible eyewitness (a nice paradox: he "told a lie" in this story about not lying).

Here, then, is a story that we know is nonhistorical. But we still tell it to our children. Why? Not because we are trying to teach them about the facts of colonial history, but because we think the story conveys a "truth" that we want our children to learn. The truth claims of the story actually work on several levels. On one level the story is a good piece of political propaganda for the United States. Who was George Washington? He was the father of our nation. What kind of person was he? He was an honest man, a man who would never tell a lie. Really? How honest was he? Well, one day when he was a kid ... The conclusion is clear. This country is founded on honesty. This country is honest. This country cannot tell a lie. Or so the story goes.

But the story of George Washington and the cherry tree functions on another level as well, and this is probably why most parents are glad their kids learn it. This is a story about personal morality and responsibility. I told the story to my kids because I wanted them to be like young George. Even if they did something wrong, I wanted them to come clean and tell the truth about it. It is better to be truthful and face the consequences than to live a life of dishonesty. It is better not to tell a lie.

My point is that fiction, even historical fiction, can in some sense convey "truth" even if it is something that "didn't happen." Truth is more than simply correct information.

That does not mean, however, that there is no such thing as falsehood. Quite the contrary, there are plenty of kinds of falsehood: incorrect information, flat-out deception, stories that convey messages that we do *not* accept as "true" based on our understanding of the world.[2] If I were to read a story about the childhood of Joseph Stalin that stressed his inherently sweet disposition, his kind, gentle nature, and his deep concern for the well-being of others, I would say that the story is false.

Ancient people also had a more nuanced sense of truth and falsehood; they too had stories that they accepted as "true" in some sense without thinking that they actually happened.[3] Most scholars today recognize that the majority of educated people in ancient Greece and Rome did not literally believe that the myths about the gods had actually happened historically. They were stories intending to convey some kind of true understanding of the divine realm and humans' relationship to it. And ancients had their equivalents of modern fiction. It is true, as some scholars have emphasized, that modern notions of fiction are much more sophisticated and nuanced than anything you can find in antiquity. But in addition to myths ancient people had epic poems, legends, and novels (sometimes called "romances"), which correspond in many ways to the forms of fictional narrative that we have today. People didn't tell and retell, read and recite these forms of fiction simply because they thought they were literally true, but for much the same reason that we read fiction today: for entertainment, to learn something, to help them understand themselves and their world better.

The notion of "fiction" is very interesting. If we read a book that claims to be an authorized biography of Ronald Reagan, we expect it to stick to the facts and not to convey historically incorrect information. But if we read a novel about a president of the United States in the 1980s—a book that touts itself as pure fiction—we may expect some kinds of historical verisimilitude (the president would not be shown surfing the Internet or checking his wall on Facebook), but we do not expect to be given actual historical facts about an actual historical person. Ancient equivalents to modern fiction worked the same way. Readers expected the narrative to make some kind of historical sense—that is, to be plausible—but they did not expect the story to match up to the facts of historical reality.

The difference between a modern biography and a modern novel, of course, is a matter of literary genre. Scholars have long and protracted debates over what the notion of "genre" actually means, but for our purposes I think a fairly rough and ready description will suffice. A genre is a "kind" of writing that fits certain expected forms. A short story is short, for example; a novel is longer. Both have characters and plot and other shared features that make them different from a haiku. A limerick poem has clever rhymes and a surprising punch line. Free verse has neither, but relies on the depth of the language to convey meaning. And so on. The characteristics of each type of genre represent a sort of implied agreement between an author and readers. It is almost a contractual agreement in which the author provides what is expected for this kind of writing, and readers are not allowed to expect anything other than what typically happens in this kind of writing.

When it comes to fiction, in nearly all its forms, readers agree to suspend judgment on the historical accuracy of the details of the narrative, while expecting, nonetheless, that the account will be historically plausible.[4] The reason fiction works is that, for the sake of being entertained, readers are willing to make this tacit agreement with an author.

When it comes to biography or historical writing, however, readers do not make this agreement. In this case the author agrees to stick to the historical facts insofar as she can, and readers expect her to do so. Any breach of this contract is seen as a violation of the rules and is condemned.

In ancient historical writing the matter was a bit more complicated. In large part that was because in antiquity there simply weren't the research tools available that we have today: extensive access to reliable sources, copious written records, databases, data retrieval systems, the possibilities given us by mass media and electronic modes of communication. Ancient historians had to do their best to cobble together a plausible narrative of past events. It was very hard indeed to give an "accurate" account, though most historians tried. Nowhere was this more obviously a problem than in recording the actual words of someone who lived a long time ago. Some of the best histories from antiquity are chock full of speeches given by their main characters. But if the events took place decades or even centuries earlier, in an age before there were tape recorders, or even stenographers and same-day reporting, how was a historian to know what the character actually said? There was, in fact, no way to know.

For that reason, a superb historian such as the fifth-century BCE Thucydides explicitly states that he simply made up the speeches himself. What choice did ancient historians have? The best they could do was to invent a speech that seemed appropriate to the character of the speaker and the occasion and trust that it was a more or less close approximation of what was actually said. There was no way of showing whether the historian got it right. But educated readers realized that this is what the historians were doing, and so here again there was a kind of understood contract between author and readers; the author would come up with his best guess at what a speaker said and readers would accept it for what it was, a best guess.

Some scholars have thought that forgery was like that, a kind of fiction comparable to the invention of speeches in a history, in which the real author and the real readers agreed not to take seriously the false name attached to a writing. As I have shown, recent scholars who have actually studied the ancient discussions of forgery indicate that this view is not right at all. Forgeries were literary texts in which the author adopted a kind of fiction *without* the permission of readers. And readers, when they found out, did not appreciate it. Ancient people treated forged historical narratives, treatises, letters, and so on as "false writings" and "lies," not as some kind of harmless and innocent fiction. That is why the ancients were so interested in seeing whether books were "authentic children" of their named authors or "illegitimate" (*notha*), not really belonging to the person named as the author.

So too ancient people recognized the difference between fabricated fictional accounts and historical narratives. Some historians, such as Lucian of Samosata and Polybius, unlike Thucydides, were quite insistent that historical narratives should indicate only what actually happened. Historians should not make up stories or even the speeches delivered by the characters in their histories. As Polybius, a second-century BCE Greek historian who wrote about Rome's rise to power, succinctly states it: the historian should "simply record what really happened and what really was said." For Polybius, the historian is different from the "tragic poet" (i.e., the author of fictional drama): "The tragic poet should thrill and charm his audience for the moment by the verisimilitude of the words he puts into his characters' mouths, but it is the task of the historian to instruct and convince for all time serious students by the truth of the facts and the speeches he narrates."[5]

The reason a historian such as Polybius had to argue this point so strenuously, of course, is that other historians did precisely what he opposed, inventing speeches and even narratives as they saw fit for their "historical" accounts. It is certainly true that people in general, not just professional historians, made up a lot of stories about historical figures. In Christian circles this can be seen for nearly every historical figure of importance we know of: Jesus, Paul, Peter, and other members of the apostolic band. In this chapter, since I'm interested in books that claim to be written by Peter, but in fact were forged in his name, let us begin by considering some of the stories invented about him, before looking at books falsely attributed to him.

Stories About Peter

WE HAVE A NUMBER of books from early Christianity that tell stories about Peter. These were almost entirely "made up" by one Christian storyteller or another. By my definitions these stories are not forgeries; they are not accounts that falsely claim to be written by Peter. They, instead, might be called "fabrications," stories invented *about* Peter.[6]

One of the most interesting does happen to occur in a forged document. This forgery, however, is not in the name of Peter, but in the name of Titus, the companion of Paul. The New Testament contains a letter allegedly by Paul to Titus, which I argue in Chapter 3 is pseudonymous (i.e., a forgery). About four hundred years later another letter appeared, this one claiming to be written *by* Titus. It is an intriguing letter, because it argues vociferously that the only way to have eternal life is by living an ascetic, chaste life. Or to put it more bluntly, one can have salvation only by refraining from sex. In the context of the forger's discussion he cites a story about Peter that serves to illustrate his point.

A peasant brings his virgin daughter to Peter to be blessed. Peter says a prayer over the girl, asking that God do what is best for her. She drops down dead. The peasant is understandably distressed, but the author of the story calls him "distrustful," since he doesn't believe that what has happened is in the girl's best interest. He begs Peter to restore the girl to life, and Peter does so. But a few days later a visitor who claims to be a Christian comes to stay with the peasant and seduces his daughter. They run off together and are never seen again. And that's the end of the story. In its context the message is quite clear: it is far better to be dead than caught up in sexual desire.

A similar narrative can be found in a collection of stories about Peter's missionary activities, probably written in the second Christian century. The account, simply called the *Acts of Peter,* describes the great miracles Peter performed after Jesus's resurrection and ascension, as he demonstrates the power of his risen Lord and converts innumerable persons to the faith.

In one of the stories Peter is talking to a gathering of Christians in his home on a Sunday; they have brought a group of sick people for him to heal. But someone in the crowd asks Peter why he won't heal his own daughter, who is lying paralyzed in the corner. Peter assures his guests that God has the power to heal the girl, should he choose to do so. To prove his point, Peter orders the girl to arise and walk naturally. And she does so. But then he orders her to return to her corner paralyzed. The crowd is both amazed and distraught.

Peter then tells the story of his daughter. When she was young, Peter learned in a vision from God that if she remained healthy, she would lead many astray; she apparently was beautiful as a child, and as an adult she would entice men to sleep with her. When she was ten, a next-door neighbor attempted to seduce her, but before he could sleep with her, she became paralyzed, by the mercy of God. The neighbor went blind for his troubles, until healed by Peter and converted to faith in Christ. But the girl had to remain paralyzed, lest she lead others astray. Here again the point is perfectly clear: sex is dangerous and to be avoided at all costs, even if it means being an invalid for life.

The *Acts of Peter* is chiefly built around a series of contests between Peter, the representative of the true God, and a heretic named Simon, a magician empowered by the devil. Each of them can do miracles, and each tries to convince the crowds that he, not the other, stands for the truth. One of the miracles involves Peter and a smoked tuna. We are told that Peter has been trying to convince the crowds and is having little success. But he is standing by a fishmonger's shop and sees a smoked tuna hanging in the window. He asks the crowds if they will believe if he can make the dead fish come back to life. Yes, they reply, then they will believe. So he removes the tuna from the hook, throws it into a nearby pond, and orders it to come back from the dead. The fish comes to life—not for just a few minutes, but for real. The crowd rejoices and comes to believe.

Greater miracles are yet in store. Peter and Simon the Magician are called by the local Roman official into the arena to compete in order to see who is the true spokesperson for God. A slave boy is ordered into the arena. Simon is instructed to kill the boy, and Peter to raise him from the dead. Simon speaks a word in the boy's ear, and he falls down dead (it is the heretic who speaks the word of death). But Peter tells the boy's master to take his hand and raise him up, and the boy is immediately restored to life (the man of God has the word of life).

A wealthy woman then comes up to Peter and cries out for him to help her as well. Her son has died, and she desperately wants Peter to raise him back to life. Peter challenges Simon to a duel to see who can raise the man. While the crowd looks on, Simon goes through several shenanigans: standing next to the dead body, he stoops down three times and stands up three times, and lo and behold, the dead man raises up his head. The crowds are convinced that Simon is the true power of God, and Peter must be an impostor. They prepare to burn him at the stake. But Peter shouts them down and points out that the man has not actually been raised from the dead; he has simply moved his head. If Simon is truly from God, he will be able to raise him up and make him talk. When Simon is unable to do so, Peter then has his chance. He speaks a word, raises the man fully from the dead, and has him speak. From that hour on, the people "venerated Peter as a god."

The climax of the story comes when the heretic Simon announces to the crowds that he will prove his superior power by flying like a bird over the hills and temples of Rome. When the day of his feat arrives, he is true to his word and takes off, flying like a bird. Peter, not to be outdone, calls out to God and deprives Simon of his power in mid-flight. He crashes to the ground and breaks his leg. The crowds converge on him and stone him to death as an impostor. It is Peter who has the true power of God.

Stories like this can easily be multiplied. In fact, they *were* multiplied as Christian storytellers fabricated legendary accounts of the great heroes of the faith in the second and third Christian centuries. So they made up stories *about* Peter. Did they also make up writings *by* Peter? There seems to be no doubt about that either. Nor are there many doubts about why they invented such writings. In no small measure it is for the reason we have seen. Different Christians had competing assumptions, outlooks, practices, and theologies, all of which needed apostolic "authority" behind them. A writing in the name of Peter could authorize one set of views in the name of a great "authority," named as its "author."

Noncanonical Writings Forged in the Name of Peter

THE GOSPEL OF PETER

One of the most significant Gospels to be rediscovered in modern times is the so-called *Gospel of Peter*. I say that it has been rediscovered, because we actually knew of its existence for centuries, before it turned up in an archaeological dig near the end of the nineteenth century. Our earlier source of information was Eusebius. Eusebius is often called the "father of church history," since his ten-volume book, *The Church History*, was the first narrative account of the early Christian church. In this account Eusebius traces the spread of the Christian movement from the time of Jesus down to his own day, the early fourth century. Eusebius is an invaluable source of information for Christianity's first three hundred years. For many of his narratives, his *Church History* is the only source we have. It is true, as scholars have increasingly recognized, that Eusebius very much puts his own slant on his accounts, that he has personal views, theological perspectives, and hidden agendas that dictate how he tells his narrative. He often needs to be taken with a pound of salt. But he is especially valuable when he quotes verbatim from the earlier sources that were available to him. In those cases we get primary sources preserved for us from authors living before his time, direct access to earlier Christian authors whose writings have otherwise been lost.

In Book 6 of his *Church History* Eusebius tells the story of an important bishop of the large church in Antioch, Syria, near the end of the second century, a man named Serapion. The story concerns a *Gospel of Peter*, and luckily this is one of those instances in which Eusebius actually quotes a primary source, a writing of Serapion himself.[7] As bishop of one of the largest communities in Christendom, Serapion had under his jurisdiction the churches in the villages and towns of the surrounding area, including the church in the town of Rhossus. Serapion indicates that while making the rounds of his churches, he visited Rhossus and found there was a division in the congregation. He attributed the division to petty squabbling and learned that it may have had its roots in the Gospel that was being used in the church. It was not Matthew, Mark, Luke, or John (Gospels that he doesn't mention), but a *Gospel of Peter*. Serapion's response was that Peter, of course, was a disciple of Jesus; any Gospel that he wrote must be perfectly acceptable. On these grounds he allowed the parishioners in Rhossus to continue using it.

But he did so without reading the book himself. When he returned to Antioch, he learned from several informers that the Gospel in fact was a problem—it contained heretical teachings. In particular, it was used by a group of Christians known as docetists. Docetists (from the Greek word *dokeo*, "to seem" or "to appear") maintained that since Christ was fully divine, he could not have been fully human and could not have really suffered (people suffer, God doesn't suffer). Why then did Christ "seem" to be human? For docetists, it was all an appearance. Christ didn't have a real flesh-and-blood body and didn't really suffer and die. He only seemed to do so.

Docetists maintained that Christ was not a real human being in two different ways. Some docetists claimed that Christ's body only seemed to be human, because it was, in fact, phantasmal (like Casper the Friendly Ghost). The other docetic view is a bit more complicated. It maintained that there was a real man Jesus (flesh and blood like the rest of us), but there was also a different being known as the Christ. The Christ was a divine being who descended from heaven and came into Jesus at his baptism (the dove that descended on him and went into him), empowering him to perform miracles and deliver his divine teachings. Then, before Jesus died, the Christ left him to return to its heavenly home. So some people might have mistakenly thought that the Christ was a human who really died; but that was only Jesus. The Christ was divine and could not suffer.

When Serapion received word that the Gospel he had previously approved might contain docetic teachings, he was naturally disturbed, and so he procured a copy to read. Sure enough, he came to think that even though most of the account was perfectly "orthodox" (a "right teaching"), some parts were not. Serapion decided that the book was forged, and he wrote a letter to the Christians of Rhossus disallowing its use. In a kind of appendix he gave a list of the offensive passages.

Eusebius quotes from the letter in his *Church History*, but unfortunately he does not include the appendix with the portions that Serapion found objectionable. That is very much to be regretted, for a *Gospel of Peter* has been discovered in modern times, and without knowing what Serapion's book said, it is difficult to know if what we now have is the same book he had.

The modern discovery occurred in 1886 or 1887, during an archaeological dig near the city of Akhmim in Upper Egypt. To the northeast of this city are three cemeteries, and during the winter months of 1886–87 a French archaeological team working out of Cairo was digging in the tombs. They uncovered the tomb of a person they took to be a monk, because he was buried with a sacred book (modern scholars are less sure that he was a monk; almost anyone could have been buried with an important book). The book itself was highly significant. It is sixty-six pages in length, written in Greek on vellum (pages made out of animal skin), and it contains a small anthology of four texts. The first of these, occupying the first ten pages, is a Gospel that was previously unknown.[8]

The Gospel is not a complete text, with beginning, middle, and end. It starts in the middle of a story, " . . . but none of the Jews washed his hands, nor did Herod or any of his judges. Since they did not wish to wash, Pilate stood up." What follows is an alternative account of the trial, crucifixion, and resurrection of Jesus—alternative in that the story differs in remarkable ways from the accounts in the New Testament Gospels. One key difference can be seen already in this opening verse. In the New Testament, it is only in the Gospel of Matthew that we have a story of Pilate washing his hands at Jesus's trial, declaring himself "innocent of this man's blood" (27:24). Matthew says nothing about anyone else washing or refusing to wash his hands. But that is stressed here. And who does not wash their hands? "The Jews," Herod (the Jewish king), and his (Jewish) judges.

This Gospel maintains even more emphatically than the Gospels of the New Testament that the blame for Jesus's death falls squarely upon the Jewish people and their leaders. This anti-Jewish emphasis is part of a trend we can see developing throughout the early Christian tradition. With the passing of time, the fact that the Romans killed Jesus retreats into the background, and the Jewish leaders and Jewish people are made increasingly culpable. That can be seen simply by looking chronologically at the Gospels of the New Testament.

Our earliest Gospel, Mark, seems to suggest that the decision to have Jesus killed is shared by the Jewish leaders and the Roman governor Pilate (although even here Pilate's hand seems to be forced). When we come to the Gospel of Luke, written later, Pilate actually declares Jesus innocent three times—so that the fault for his death falls on the Jewish leaders who demand it. The Gospel of Matthew, written at about the same time as Luke, has Pilate wash his hands to declare that he is innocent in the shedding of Jesus's blood. Somewhat notoriously the Jewish people (this is only in Matthew) cry out,

"His blood be upon us and our children" (27:25). In other words, for Matthew, the Jewish people are willing to accept the responsibility and consequences of Jesus's death and to pass the responsibility on to their descendants. This verse, of course, came to be used for horrible acts of Christian anti-Semitism down through the Middle Ages, and even today.

The Gospel of John, the last of our canonical Gospels, goes a step farther. Here we are told that the Jewish people rejected Jesus as their king and declared that "we have no king but Caesar" (even though God himself was to be the king over his people). And then John says that Pilate "handed Jesus over to them to be crucified" (19:16). In this distortion of historical reality, it is the Jews themselves who actually kill Jesus.

And so, as time goes on, within the Christian tradition Pilate becomes increasingly innocent in the death of Jesus, and the Jewish people and their leaders become increasingly guilty. The *Gospel of Peter* is even later than John, and here Jewish responsibility is heightened further. Now it is not even the Roman governor Pilate who orders Jesus crucified; it is the Jewish king Herod: "Then King Herod ordered the Lord to be taken away and said to them, 'Do everything that I ordered you to do to him'" (v. 2).

In other verses of this account the Jewish mistreatment of Jesus is intensified. The Jewish authorities crucify Jesus and take him off the cross. The author is quite clear that they are the ones who are at fault: "They brought all things to fulfillment and completed all their sins on their heads" (v. 17). More significant still, the Jewish people realize that what they have done is wrong and that they will be punished for it: "Then the Jews, the elders, and the priests realized how much evil they had done to themselves and began beating their breasts, saying, 'Woe to us because of our sins. The judgment and the end of Jerusalem are near'" (v. 25). This is a reference to the view, found among Christians in the second century and later, that when the Roman armies destroyed Jerusalem in 70 CE after a Jewish uprising, it was not for political or military reasons, but religious ones. Jerusalem was destroyed and the Jewish Temple burned to the ground as divine retribution against the Jews for their sinful act of killing God's messiah. Here in the *Gospel of Peter* the Jewish people themselves recognize their guilt and their imminent punishment.

In addition to the anti-Jewish character of this account, there are a number of other interesting legendary features. In the Gospels of the New Testament Jesus is crucified with two others, as happens here. But in this Gospel there is a curious incident. When those who crucify Jesus gamble for his clothes, one of the "evildoers" being crucified with him maligns them: "We have suffered like this for the evil things we did; but this one, the Savior of the people, what wrong has he done you?" The soldiers get angry at the man and order "his legs not be broken, so that he would die in torment" (vv. 14–15).[9] The idea is that a crucified man would die more quickly if he could not push up with his legs to relieve the pressure on his lungs and breathe. By *not* breaking the criminal's legs they prolong his torment.

One of the big questions of this Gospel is whether Jesus himself experiences any torment. In v. 11 we are told that Jesus was "silent, as if he had no pain." Is it possible that this is one of the verses that Serapion found potentially objectionable? That Jesus appeared not to have pain, because in fact he did not have any pain? That his body was a phantasm?

A later verse is equally puzzling. When Jesus is about to die, rather than crying out, "My God, my God, why have you forsaken me?" as, say, in the Gospel of Mark (15:34), he instead cries, "My power, O power, you have left me behind!" And then we are told, "When he said this, he was taken up." Doesn't this sound like the other kind of docetism, the kind where the divine Christ leaves the human Jesus to die alone?[10]

The most striking passage of the Gospel comes at the very end, a passage that provides us with something we never find in the New Testament Gospels: an actual account of the resurrection. As I pointed out in Chapter 1, the canonical Gospels do not narrate the resurrection of Jesus. In their stories, Jesus is crucified, dies, and is buried, and on the third day the women go to the tomb and find it empty. But there is no story in the Gospels of the New Testament about Jesus coming out of the tomb alive. The *Gospel of Peter*, however, does have such a story.

As happens in the Gospel of Matthew, but in none of the other canonical Gospels, a guard is posted at the tomb of Jesus to make sure that no one comes to steal the body. But unlike in Matthew, in the *Gospel of Peter* a very peculiar sequence of events occurs while the guards are looking on. The heavens open up and two "men" descend, while the stone in front of the tomb rolls aside. The two heavenly men enter the tomb.

Terrified, the soldiers go off to wake the centurion to tell him what has happened. But while they are talking, they look up and see three figures emerge from the tomb. Two of them are so tall that their heads reach up to the sky. The one they are supporting—Jesus obviously—is taller still; his head reaches above the sky. And then, behind them, the cross itself emerges from the tomb. And a voice comes from heaven asking, "Have you preached to those who are asleep?" And the cross replies, "Yes." So, at the resurrection, we have a giant Jesus and a walking, talking cross.

The narrative is meant, of course, to be highly symbolic. Divine beings are often portrayed as gigantic in ancient texts. Jesus is the tallest since he is the most divine. And the cross is said to have proclaimed its message, the news of the salvation brought to those who are "asleep," that is, to those who are already dead and waiting for the salvation to come.

The Gospel continues by indicating that the Jewish authorities go to Pilate and urge him to cover up the story by ordering the soldiers not to breathe a word of what they have seen. Then comes an account of the women going to the tomb to anoint the body of Jesus, only to learn that he has been raised. The disciples are still grieving over what has happened, not knowing yet about the resurrection. Then we have the concluding sentences of the Gospel: "But we, the twelve disciples of the Lord, wept and grieved; and each one returned to his home, grieving for what had happened. But I, Simon Peter, and my brother Andrew, took our nets and went off to the sea. And with us was Levi, the son of Alphaeus, whom the Lord . . . (vv. 59–60). And there it ends, right in the middle of a sentence.

The reason the account seems to start in the middle of a thought and definitely ends in the middle of a sentence is that the person who created this book of sixty-six pages—probably in the sixth century—had only a fragmentary account in front of him. It is impossible to say whether the complete *Gospel of Peter* included stories of Jesus's birth, life, ministry, teachings, miracles, and so on before the account of his Passion and resurrection. What is clear, from the final verse, is that this Gospel, unlike the Gospels of the New Testament, is written in the first person. The author claims to be Peter. But there is no way he was Peter. This is an author claiming to be someone he is not. This is a forgery.

The reason Simon Peter could not have written this account is that it almost certainly dates to the second century, at least sixty years after Peter had died. Virtually all scholars agree on this, for compelling reasons. For one thing, the heightened anti-Judaism fits better with the second century, when it became common, for example, for Christians to blame the destruction of Jerusalem on the Jews themselves for killing Jesus. Moreover, there are the highly legendary aspects of the story, such as the robber whose legs were not broken, the giant Jesus, and the talking cross. These too suggest it is a later account. Scholars debate whether the author of this Gospel had access to the stories of Matthew, Mark, Luke, and John; there are numerous parallels with one or the other of the Gospels throughout. If he did use them, then he was obviously writing after them, that is, no sooner than the beginning of the second century.

Scholars also debate whether this is the *Gospel of Peter* that was known to Serapion. In part the debate has been over whether this is really a docetic account, as the Gospel described by Serapion evidently was, at least in his eyes. Some scholars have their doubts. When it says that Jesus was silent on the cross "as if" he felt no pain, that isn't really the same thing, it is often argued, as saying that he did *not* feel pain. And to say that "he was taken up" may not mean that the Christ had left Jesus. Jesus still has a miraculous body and divine power at the resurrection, for example. So the phrase about being taken up may simply be a euphemism for "he died."

My own view is that the Gospel would not need to be actually docetic in order to be the Gospel mentioned by Serapion. Serapion admitted that most of the Gospel was perfectly orthodox, but he found some "additions" that were troubling and that could be used by docetic Christians. And certainly this Gospel fits that bill. It is by and large perfectly acceptable from an orthodox perspective, but several verses might easily lend themselves to a docetic reading. This would include the major account of Jesus emerging from the tomb, where he looks as if he has anything *but* a real body that has just suffered the agonies of crucifixion!

Whether or not this is Serapion's Gospel, it is certainly *a Gospel of Peter.* It claims its authority in the name of Jesus's closest disciple, in part, no doubt, to make its incredible and anti-Jewish narratives seem completely credible. But Peter didn't write it. This is a forgery in the name of Peter. And it's not the only one.[11]

THE EPISTLE OF PETER

Many scholars have thought of the early Christian church as seriously divided. On one side were the Jewish followers of Jesus, such as his brother James, who was the head of the church in Jerusalem, and the disciple Peter. On the other side were people like the apostle Paul, who focused on converting Gentiles (non-Jews). In this modern schema, James and Peter are often thought to have been more "true" to Jesus's original message, that it was the God of Israel who had brought salvation to those who kept his teachings, as found in the Jewish law. For these early Christians, Jesus was the Jewish messiah sent from the Jewish God to the Jewish people in fulfillment of the Jewish law. Naturally, to be a follower of this Jewish savior, a person had to be Jewish. Gentiles were, of course, welcomed into the community with open arms, but only if they converted to Judaism. For men that meant getting circumcised, and for both men and women it meant observing the Sabbath, keeping kosher, and following the other Jewish laws.

Paul, in this understanding, taught something quite different, that believing in the death and resurrection of Christ was the only way to have a right standing before God. Moreover, this salvation applied equally to Jews and Gentiles, so that one did not have to be a Jew to be a follower of Jesus. For Paul, according to this view, the law had passed away; Jews could keep it if they chose (and as a Jew he himself kept it), but Gentiles were not supposed to keep it. This was the national law for Israel, and it had nothing to do with salvation. Only Jesus's death and resurrection could bring salvation. Through Paul, then, the church largely filled up with Gentiles who did not see themselves as Jewish and who worshiped the God of Israel without following his law.

It is not necessary here for me to evaluate this common understanding of the relationship of Paul to the apostles before him, particularly James and Peter. But I do want to say that this idea that there was a split between their views is not just a modern notion. It goes way back to earliest Christianity. Historically speaking, it is true that Paul established churches made up of Gentiles and that he insisted that these converts not keep the Jewish law. This is a case he makes quite strenuously, for example, in the (orthonymous) letter to the Galatians. For Paul, any Gentile who tried to keep the law completely misunderstood that salvation comes from Christ's death alone, to be received by faith. Keeping the law was worse than irrelevant; it was an admission that Christ's death was insufficient for salvation (see 2:15–16, 21).

Other Christians did indeed disagree. Many of them were Paul's opponents in his various churches. Later, in the second Christian century, there continued to be groups of Jewish Christians who insisted that the law certainly had to be followed by anyone who wanted to belong to God's people. God had given the law, and he never changed his mind. This was the law that told people how to live, it was the law that Jesus himself taught and fulfilled, and it was the law that was to be followed, *especially* by followers of Christ.

This split in the early church between the (now) minority of Jewish Christians and the dominant majority of Gentiles can be seen nowhere more clearly than in a writing forged in Peter's name called the *Epistula Petri*, or the *Epistle of Peter*.[12] This book is not to be confused with 1 Peter or 2 Peter in the New Testament. It was written later, years after the New Testament writings had been completed.

The *Epistle of Peter* is found as a kind of introduction to group of writings that scholars call the *Pseudo-Clementines*. As implied by its scholarly name, this group of writings falsely claims (hence "Pseudo") to be written by Clement, who, as we saw earlier, was widely thought to have been the fourth bishop of Rome (or pope), appointed to his position by none other than Peter. The *Pseudo-Clementines* have a highly complicated literary history. For over a century scholars have strenuously debated what sources the books used, how the various writings are related to each other, and other technical questions. But the basic character of the writings is clear. These are accounts of the travels and adventures of Clement, especially as he converts to Christianity through Peter's preaching and then journeys with Peter as the apostle spreads the gospel, gives speeches, and performs miracles. These include miracle contests with the archheretic Simon the Magician, whom we saw earlier. The *Acts of Peter* may have been one of the sources for these stories.

The Clementine books clearly were not written by the historical Clement, but long after his death, even though they are (allegedly) narrated by him in the first person. They are, therefore, forged. In one set of these writings the adventures of Clement are prefaced by the *Epistle of Peter*, a letter supposedly written by Peter to the brother of Jesus, James, head of the church in Jerusalem. The letter instructs James not to allow Peter's writings to be handed over to just anyone, because they might be misinterpreted or altered, but only to a select group of trustworthy people. The author, "Peter," attacks Christians who interpret his message as saying that the Jewish law is no longer in force. That is completely false, says the author, for Jesus himself had indicated that "not one jot or tittle will pass away from the law" and that it would be eternally valid (see Matt. 5:17–20). According to this letter, one of Peter's opponents in particular has led "the Gentiles" to reject Peter's "lawful preaching" and, instead, to prefer "a lawless and absurd doctrine of the man who is my enemy."

It does not take a lot of thought to realize who the enemy is whom "Peter" is opposing. It is someone who preaches to the Gentiles, insists on a gospel apart from the Jewish law (a "lawless doctrine"), and claims that Peter himself subscribes to that view (see Gal. 2). Without naming him, this author is talking about Paul.

Here we have a view of Peter and Paul very much at odds with what we find in some of the writings of the New Testament.[13] In the history of the early church found in the book of Acts, for example, Peter and Paul see eye to eye, they agree on every major point, they stand arm in arm in the mission to spread the gospel, and most important, they wholeheartedly concur that Gentiles do not need to be Jews to be followers of Jesus (see Acts 10–11; 15). This is not the case, however, for the author of the *Epistle of Peter*. Here there is a clear split between Peter, Jesus's closest disciple, and Paul, an interloper who has misinterpreted Peter. Paul has misrepresented the gospel.

This, then, is an author who saw Paul as the enemy and his "lawless and absurd" doctrine as heresy. For this author, Paul not only disagreed with Peter; he was wrong. And on what authority does the author claim this? On the authority of Peter himself. The author forged the letter in Peter's name in order to make his point.

THE APOCALYPSE OF PETER

I will not be talking at length in this book about how we got our twenty-seven books of the New Testament, that is, how the canon was formed and how some writings came to be included and others left out. Plenty of other books describe this process at length.[14] I can say, though, that there were some writings that were a "close call," that nearly made it in but did not, just as there were others that nearly were left out, but finally made it in. One of the books that nearly made it in is called the *Apocalypse of Peter*.[15]

From authors such as Eusebius, we know that there were Christian communities as late as the fourth century who thought that the *Apocalypse of Peter* should be included in the canon, either in place of the Apocalypse of John (i.e., the book of Revelation), which obviously ended up being included, or alongside it.[16] The *Apocalypse of Peter* is very different from the Apocalypse of John, however. Both books are apocalypses, in which an author is given a secret revelation about the divine, heavenly mysteries that can make sense of the mundane, earthly realities. In the New Testament Apocalypse of John, these mysteries have to do with the future course of history to be unfurled on earth, as has been decided already in heaven. In the noncanonical *Apocalypse of Peter*, these mysteries have to do with the fate of souls in life after death. This book describes a personal tour that Peter is given of the realms of the blessed and of the damned.

Most readers are familiar with the idea of a tour of heaven and hell from Dante's *Divine Comedy*. Dante did not invent the idea, however. He stood in a long line of Christian authors who used the motif of a tour of the afterlife in order to make whatever important points they wanted to stress about life here on earth. Our earliest example of this kind of writing is the *Apocalypse of Peter*.

Here again we knew about the book for centuries before it was available. As it turns out, it was another of the four texts found in the sixty-six-page book uncovered by archaeologists near Akhmim, Egypt, in 1886–87. Since then an Ethiopic version has been found, which gives an even fuller account.

The narrative begins with Peter and the disciples talking with Jesus on the Mount of Olives (see Mark 13). They ask Jesus about what will happen when the world comes to an end, and he provides them with a brief account. But then the discussion shifts to a description, given in some graphic detail, of what happens to souls after they die, either in the place of torment or the place of eternal bliss. As sometimes happens in these personal tours of heaven and hell, the description of the realms of the blessed is a bit stereotyped and brief. There are, after all, only so many ways you can describe eternal, ecstatic joy. It's *fantastic*! What more can one say? The realms of the damned, however, are a different matter altogether. Anyone with any creativity and imagination can invent lurid and detailed descriptions of the torments of sinners.

In Peter's vision, a number of the damned are tortured in ways that befit their characteristic sins, so that the punishment fits the crime. Those who have blasphemed against the ways of God, for example—that is, sinned by what they've said—are hanged by their tongues over eternal flames. Women who have braided their hair in order to make themselves attractive to men so as to seduce them are hanged by their hair over eternal flames. The men they seduced are hanged by a *different* body part over the flames. In this case, the men cry out, as you might imagine, "We didn't know it would come to *this*!"

The overarching message of this book is quite clear and not altogether subtle: if you want to enjoy the amazing blessings of paradise and avoid the horrific torments of hell, don't sin! This message conveys a reliable and incontrovertible truth: those who fail to follow God's will face eternal torture. How do we know? Because someone who has observed the realms of the damned has told us, Jesus's right-hand man, Peter himself. In order to get his point across, the author writes in the first person—not in his own name, but in the name of the chief disciple. Here again we have a forgery in the name of Peter.

"Petrine" Writings in the New Testament

THE BOOKS I HAVE talked about here at some length—the *Acts of Peter*, the *Gospel of Peter*, the *Pseudo-Clementine Writings*, the *Epistle of Peter*, the *Apocalypse of Peter*—are not the only fabrications *about* Peter and forgeries allegedly written *by* Peter from the early church. There were others: other "Acts" of Peter, a collection called the "Preaching" of Peter, two other apocalypses of Peter. And these are just the ones that we still have today. No one knows how many once existed. Producing books in the name of Peter was a virtual cottage industry in the early church.

Is it possible, in light of this extensive use of Peter's name to authorize others' views, that any forgeries in the name of Peter made it into the New Testament? As it turns out, two books bear Peter's name there as well, the letters of 1 Peter and 2 Peter. Both claim to be written by Peter, but there are solid reasons for thinking that Peter did not write either one.

1 Peter

The book of 1 Peter is allegedly written by "Peter, an apostle of Jesus Christ," to Christians whom he calls "exiles" in five provinces in the western part of what is now Turkey.[17] There is no doubt that the author is claiming to be Jesus's closest disciple, Peter. "Peter" was not a personal name before Peter was given it as a nickname by Jesus himself. According to the Gospels, this disciple's real name was Simon. But Jesus indicated that he would be the "rock" (Greek *petros*) on whom the church would be founded. So he called him "Rocky," or "Peter" (see Matt. 16:13–18).[18] So far as we know, there were no other persons named Peter until later times when Christians started naming their children after the great apostle. So the author of 1 Peter is certainly claiming to be "that" Peter. This is borne out by his comment in 5:1, that he was personally a "witness of the sufferings of Christ."[19]

This matter of suffering is the key theme of the book. In fact, the word "suffering" occurs more often in this short five-chapter letter than in any other book of the entire New Testament, including the Gospels, which are much, much longer. The author assumes that his readers themselves are undergoing persecution and that they will be experiencing yet more in the future. "Now for a little while," he tells them, they "have had to suffer various trials." But that is all to the good, because through being "tested" their faith will be refined and become "more precious than gold that is . . . tested by fire" (1:6–7). They should not therefore be "surprised at the fiery ordeal that is coming . . . , as if something strange were happening," but they are to "rejoice," because they "share in the sufferings of Christ" (4:12–13).

Scholars have long debated what kind of suffering the author has in mind. The older view was that the author was dealing with official state persecutions, such as happened when the emperor Nero imprisoned and then executed Christians in the city of Rome in 64 CE, blaming them for starting the horrible fire that destroyed much of the city, a fire that his own arsonists may have set. But over the past twenty years or so scholars have begun to stress that the book of 1 Peter never says much about "official" persecution, where Christians are arrested, put on trial for their faith, and martyred. Instead, the opposition seems to come from former friends and neighbors who do not understand or appreciate the Christians' new lifestyle, which is removed from the joyful celebrations of pagan religions (4:1–5). That is to say, Christians stopped attending pagan festivals to form their own secret societies, and pagans became upset, suspicious, and hateful, leading to local opposition to Christians that could at times turn nasty.

If this is the case, it makes sense that the author stresses to his readers that it is important for them to be obedient to the government and governing officials (2:13–15), to show good conduct among outsiders (2:12), to be devoted slaves, wives, and husbands (2:18–3:7), to do nothing to warrant any opposition, but to suffer only for doing what is right (2:20). A good deal of the exhortation and encouragement to his readers is based on a sophisticated interpretation of key passages in the Old Testament, quoted, of course, in Greek, the so-called Septuagint (the legendary origins of which are described in the forged *Letter of Aristeas* discussed in Chapter 1), as can be seen, for example, in 1:24–25; 2:3, 6–9, 22, 24–25; 3:10–12.

The author ends his exhortation to be steadfast in the face of adversity by indicating that he has written his letter "through Silvanus, a faithful brother" (i.e., a true Christian) and by sending greetings from "she who is in Babylon, who is also chosen" (5:13). Scholars have long realized what this last bit means. Babylon was the city that was seen as the ultimate enemy of God among Jews, since it was Babylon that had defeated Judah and destroyed Jerusalem and its Temple in the sixth century BCE. By the end of the first century, Christians and Jews had started using the word "Babylon" as a code word for the city that was the enemy of God in their own day, the city of Rome, which also destroyed Jerusalem and its Temple, in the year 70 (see, e.g., Rev. 14:8; 17:5). The author, then, is claiming to be writing from the city of Rome. This makes sense, given the later traditions that associated Peter with the city of Rome, in fact as its first bishop—the first pope.

But tradition also indicates that Peter was martyred in Rome under Nero in 64 CE. Would it make sense that he would be calling Rome "Babylon" before the Romans had destroyed Jerusalem in the year 70? By the time that catastrophe hit, Peter was long dead. As it turns out there are other, very good grounds for thinking that Peter did not actually write this book. It was written by someone *claiming* to be Peter. Before explaining some of those grounds, we should first look at the second letter in the New Testament written in Peter's name.

2 PETER

There is less debate among scholars of the New Testament about the authorship of 2 Peter than for any of the other books sometimes considered forgeries. Whoever wrote 2 Peter, it was not Simon Peter.[20] The author certainly *claims* to be Peter, even more explicitly than in the case of 1 Peter. He introduces himself as "Simeon Peter,[21] a slave and apostle of Jesus Christ." But more than that, he claims personally to have been present at the "transfiguration" scene narrated in the Gospels, where Jesus was transformed before the eyes of his disciples Peter, James, and John and began speaking with Moses and Elijah, before a voice came from heaven saying, "This is my beloved son in whom I am well pleased" (see Matt. 17:1–8). The author insists that he himself was there to hear these words, brought to him by the "voice . . . of the majestic glory" (1:17). The author wants there to be no doubt: he is Peter.

His chief concern is that there are false teachers in the community who have twisted the true message of the gospel. Most of chapter 2 is devoted to maligning these persons, without ever explaining what, exactly, they teach. This highly vituperative attack calls their teachings "destructive heresies" and says that they, the opponents, are licentious, greedy, and exploitative. The author indicates that they will suffer like the people of Sodom and Gomorrah and like the inhabitants of the entire world in the days of Noah. That is to say, they too will be destroyed. He calls them ignorant and says they are "blots and blemishes, reveling in their dissipation, carousing." He says they have eyes that are "full of adultery, unslakable for sin." And on and on.

This assault on his opponents, the "false prophets," contains numerous verbal similarities to what can be found in the New Testament book of Jude. The parallels are so numerous that scholars are virtually unified in thinking that the author has taken Jude's message and simply edited it a bit to incorporate it into his book.

In addition to the false teachers, "scoffers" have appeared who mock the Christian view that Jesus is soon to return from heaven in judgment on the earth. If he was supposed to come soon, say these skeptics, why hasn't he come? A lot of time has passed, and everything goes on just the same as before! The author replies that these unbelievers are ignorant and deceived, having forgotten that "with the Lord one day is as a thousand years and a thousand years are as one day" (3:8). In other words, even if Jesus waits another three thousand years, he still is coming "soon." Jesus has in fact delayed returning simply to give people a chance to repent before the coming destruction. Paul himself, the author tells us, taught such things in "all his letters, which the ignorant and unstable people twist, as they do with all the other Scriptures, to their own destruction" (3:16).

One of the reasons virtually all scholars agree that Peter did not actually write this letter is that the situation being presupposed appears to be of much later times. When Peter himself died—say, the year 64 under Nero—there was still eager expectation that Jesus would return soon; not even a full generation had passed since the crucifixion. It was only with the passing of time that the Christian claim that all would take place "within this generation" (Mark 13:30) and before the disciples had "tasted death" (9:1) started to ring hollow. By the time 2 Peter was written, Christians were having to defend themselves in the face of opponents who mocked their view that the end was supposed to be imminent. So "Peter" has to explain that even if the end is thousands of years off, it is still right around the corner by God's calendar; everything is still on schedule.

Moreover, the author of 2 Peter is writing at a time when there was already a collection of Paul's letters in circulation, and these letters were being considered on a par with the Old Testament "Scriptures" (3:16). This could not have been during Paul's lifetime,[22] and early church tradition indicates that both Peter and Paul were killed during the reign of Nero.

These are among the reasons for thinking that 2 Peter almost certainly could not have been written by Peter.[23] And there is one more compelling reason. There are excellent grounds for thinking that Peter could not write.

Simon Peter, Ancient Palestine, and Literacy

WHAT DO WE KNOW about literacy and the ability to write in the ancient world, especially in rural Palestine, where Simon Peter was born and raised? Scholars of antiquity have been diligent over the past twenty-five years or so in trying to understand every aspect of ancient literacy and education. In what is now the classic study, the

1989 book *Ancient Literacy*, William Harris, professor of ancient history at Columbia University, shows that modern assumptions about literacy simply are not applicable to ancient times.[24] Today, in modern America, we live in a world where nearly every child goes to school and learns to read and write. Just about everyone we know can read the sports page and copy out a page of a novel if they choose. But the phenomenon of massive and widespread literacy is completely modern. Before the industrial revolution, societies had no compelling reasons to invest enormous amounts of money and other resources into creating a literate population. It was only with the development of the industrial world that such a thing became both desirable and feasible.

Harris argues that in the ancient world, at the very best of times, only about 10 percent of the population was reasonably literate. By the "best of times" he means Athens, a center of learning, at the height of its intellectual power, during the days of Socrates and Plato (fifth–fourth century BCE). Most of these 10 percent were men, as might be expected in a highly patriarchal society. And all of them were in the upper classes, the social and economic elite, who had the leisure and the money (well, their parents had the money) to afford an education. Lower-class people did not learn how to read, let alone write. And the vast majority of people in the ancient world were in the lower classes (to the surprise of many, the "middle class" is another invention of the industrial revolution; in the ancient world virtually everyone was high or low, or very, very low). The only notable exceptions were slaves, who were naturally a very low class indeed, but who were sometimes educated at their masters' expense, so that they could carry out household duties that required literacy skills, such as taking care of the household finances, helping with correspondence, or teaching the children.

When I say that few people could read, "let alone write," I mean to signal something else quite significant about the ancient world. When upper-class people were educated, reading and writing were taught as two different skills.[25] Today we learn reading and writing together, and we naturally assume that if people can read, they can also write—not necessarily write a novel, but at least a letter. But that's because of the way we have set up our educational system. There is nothing inherent in learning to read that can necessarily teach you how to write. I know this full well personally. I can read Greek, Hebrew, French, German, and a range of other languages, but I cannot compose a letter in any of these languages. I learned how to read all of them in graduate school, so I could read ancient documents in their original languages and modern scholarship in the languages of Europe. But I never learned how to write them.

Most people in the ancient world could not read. And those who could read often could not write. And in this case by "write" I mean that most people—even if they could copy down words—could not compose a sentence, let alone a well-argued treatise. On the contrary, the people who could compose an ethical essay, a learned philosophical discussion, or an involved religious treatise were highly educated and highly exceptional. And that was in the very best of times. Very, very few people indeed were able to perform these skills in a language other than the one they were raised with. I'm not saying that just 1 percent of the population could do such a thing. I'm saying that far fewer than 1 percent of the population could do it.

It is sometimes thought that Palestine was an exception, that in Palestine Jewish boys all learned to read so that they could study the Hebrew Scriptures, and that since they could read, they could probably write. Moreover, it is often argued that in Palestine most adults were bilingual or even trilingual, able to read Hebrew, speak the local language, Aramaic, and communicate well in the language of the broader empire, Greek. Recent studies of literacy in Palestine, however, have shown convincingly that none of these assertions is true.

The fullest, most thoroughly researched, and most widely influential study of literacy in Palestine during the period of the Roman Empire is by Catherine Hezser.[26] After examining all of the evidence, Hezser concludes that in Roman Palestine the best guestimate is that something like 3 percent of the population could read, and that the majority of these would have been in the cities and larger towns. Most people outside of the urban areas would scarcely ever even see a written text. Some smaller towns and villages may have had a literacy level of around 1 percent. Moreover, these literate people were almost always the elite of the upper classes. Those who learned to read learned how to read Hebrew (not Greek).

And what is more, once again, far more people could read than could write. The people who knew how to write were primarily men who were priests. In fact, for the entire first century CE (the time of Jesus and Simon Peter), we know for certain of only two authors in Palestine who produced literary works (i.e., educated compositions other than tax documents, land deeds, or marriage certificates, etc.): the Jewish historian Josephus and a man named Justus of Tiberius. We still have Josephus's writings, but Justus's don't survive. Both of these men were in the upper echelons of society, and both were inordinately well educated. We know of no other literary authors for the entire century. Was Peter in Josephus's and Justus's class? No, not even close.

What about Greek education in the land of Peter's birth and upbringing? It is sometimes assumed that since Galilee, the northern part of what we think of as Israel, was occasionally called "Galilee of the Gentiles," it was overrun by Gentiles in Jesus and Peter's day. And according to a common kind of logic, if there were lots of Gentiles in Galilee, they would have spoken Greek; so to get along, everyone must have spoken Greek. As it turns out, that's not true either.

The most recent thorough studies of Gentiles in Galilee have been undertaken by the American scholar Mark Chancey.[27] Chancey has studied every archaeological find from Galilee from around the time of the first century, has read every single piece of writing from the period of any relevance, and draws a decisive conclusion: the Gentiles in Galilee were almost exclusively located in the two major cities, Sepphoris and Tiberias. All the rest of Galilee was predominantly Jewish. And since most of Galilee was rural, not urban, the vast majority of Jews had no encounters with Gentiles. Moreover, Greek was not widely, let alone normally, spoken. The vast majority of Jews spoke Aramaic and had no facility in Greek.

How do all these findings affect our question of whether Peter wrote 1 and 2 Peter or any other books? Was Peter among the very upper echelons of the educated elite of Palestine who could compose letter-essays in Greek? Apart from the legendary accounts I have mentioned, all we know about Peter's life comes to us from the New Testament. What we principally learn about him is that before he was a follower of Jesus he was a fisherman from Capernaum in Galilee.

In order to evaluate Peter's linguistic abilities, the place to begin, then, is with Capernaum. A full summary of what we know about Capernaum from Peter's day is provided by an American archaeologist of Palestine, Jonathan Reed.[28] On the basis of archaeological digs and historical sources, it is clear that Capernaum was a historically insignificant village in rural Galilee. It is never mentioned in any ancient source prior to the Gospels. It is scarcely mentioned by any sources after that. It was discovered by archaeologists in the nineteenth century and has been excavated since then. In the time of Jesus it may have had anywhere between six and fifteen hundred inhabitants, so say a thousand.

The archaeological digs have revealed no evidence of any public buildings whatsoever, such as shops or storage facilities.[29] The market for buying food and other necessities must have been held in tents or booths in open unpaved public areas. The town is on none of the major international trade routes. The Roman roads in the area date from a hundred years after Peter's life. There is no trace of any pagan or Gentile population in the town. There are no inscriptions of any kind on any of the buildings. Reed concludes that the inhabitants were almost certainly "predominantly illiterate." Archaeologists have found no building structures or materials associated with social elites from the first century (e.g., plaster surfaces, decorative frescoes, marble, mosaics, red ceramic roof tiles). The houses were roughly constructed out of stone basalt, and mud or clay was used to fill in the gaps; they probably had thatched roofs.

In short, Peter's town was a backwoods Jewish village made up of hand-to-mouth laborers who did not have an education. Everyone spoke Aramaic. Nothing suggests that anyone could speak Greek. Nothing suggests that anyone in town could write. As a lower-class fisherman, Peter would have started work as a young boy and never attended school. There was, in fact, probably no school there; if there was a school, he probably didn't attend; if he did attend, it would have been in order to receive rudimentary training in how to read Hebrew. But that almost certainly never happened. Peter was an illiterate peasant.

This should come as no surprise, really. As it turns out, there is New Testament evidence about Peter's education level. According to Acts 4:13, both Peter and his companion John, also a fisherman, were *agrammatoi*, a Greek word that literally means "unlettered," that is, "illiterate."

And so, is it possible that Peter wrote 1 and 2 Peter? We have seen good reasons for believing he did not write 2 Peter, and some reason for thinking he didn't write 1 Peter. But it is highly probable that in fact he could not write at all. I should point out that the book of 1 Peter is written by a highly literate, highly educated, Greek-speaking Christian who is intimately familiar with the Jewish Scriptures in their Greek translation, the Septuagint. This is not Peter.

It is theoretically possible, of course, that Peter decided to go to school after Jesus's resurrection. In this imaginative (not to say imaginary) scenario, he learned his alphabet, learned how to sound out syllables and then words, learned to read, and learned to write. Then he took Greek classes, mastered Greek as a foreign language, and started memorizing large chunks of the Septuagint, after which he took Greek composition classes and learned how to compose complicated and rhetorically effective sentences; then, toward the end of his life, he wrote 1 Peter.

Is this scenario plausible? Apart from the fact that we don't know of "adult education" classes in antiquity—there's no evidence they existed—I think most reasonable people would conclude that Peter probably had other things on his mind and on his hands after he came to believe that Jesus was raised from the dead. He probably never thought for a single second about learning how to become a rhetorically skilled Greek author.

Some scholars have suggested that Peter did not *directly* write 1 Peter (as I've indicated, almost no one thinks he wrote 2 Peter), but that he *indirectly* wrote it, for example, by dictating the letter to a scribe. Some have noted that the letter is written "through Silvanus" (5:12) and thought that maybe Silvanus wrote down Peter's thoughts for him. I deal with this question of whether scribes or secretaries actually ever composed such letter-essays in Chapter 4. The answer is, "Almost certainly not." But for now I can say at least a couple of words about the case of 1 Peter.

First off, scholars now widely recognize that when the author indicates that he wrote the book "through Silvanus," he is indicating not the name of his secretary, but the person who was carrying the letter to the recipients. Authors who used secretaries don't refer to them in this way.

But why not suppose that Peter used someone else, other than Silvanus, as a secretary? It would help to imagine how this theory is supposed to work exactly. Peter could not have *dictated* this letter in Greek to a secretary any more than he could have written it in Greek. That would have required him to be perfectly fluent in Greek, to have mastered rhetorical techniques in Greek, and to have had an intimate familiarity with the Jewish Scriptures in Greek. None of that is plausible. Nor can one easily think that he dictated the letter in Aramaic and the secretary translated it into Greek. The letter does not read like a Greek translation of an Aramaic original, but as an original Greek composition with Greek rhetorical flourishes. Moreover the letter presupposes the knowledge of the Greek Old Testament, so the person who composed the letter (whether orally or in writing) must have known the Scriptures in Greek.

Is it possible, then, that the historical Peter directed someone to write a letter, basically told him what to say, and let him produce it?

To that there are two responses. First, it would seem that if someone else actually composed the letter, it would be *that* person, not Peter, who was the author. But the other person is never named. Even in Paul's letters that are coauthored (almost all of them) he names the others, even though he probably wrote them himself. In this case, Peter would not have even written the thing. And it should be remembered that there are good grounds for thinking that the letter was written after Peter had died, since it alludes to Rome's destruction of Jerusalem in the year 70.

But even more compelling is this. Where in the ancient world do we have anything at all analogous to this hypothetical situation of someone writing a letter-essay for someone else and putting the other person's name on it—the name of the person who did *not* write it—rather than his own name? So far as I know, there is not a single instance of any such procedure attested from antiquity or any discussion, in any ancient source, of this being a legitimate practice. Or even an illegitimate one. Such a thing is never discussed.

There are plenty of instances of another phenomenon, however. This is the phenomenon of Christian authors writing pseudonymous works, falsely claiming to be a famous person. Ancient scholars would have called a book like that a "falsely inscribed" writing, a "lie," an "illegitimate" child. Modern people would simply call it a forgery.

CHAPTER THREE

Forgeries in the Name of Paul

WHEN I BECAME A BORN-AGAIN Christian in 1971, I was eager to read and learn all I could about the Scriptures. I had no idea at the time that there was such a thing as biblical scholarship, or that there were books written by real experts who had mastered the relevant ancient languages—Greek and Hebrew, for example—and plumbed all the ancient sources for years on end in order to provide historically accurate accounts. I was just as happy with a good novel about, say, Jesus or Paul as with something serious. And novels, of course, make for easy reading, just the sort of thing I liked.

During the preceding year one of the best-selling biblical novels of all time had appeared, Taylor Caldwell's *Great Lion of God*, a fictional account of the life of the apostle Paul. For eight months it had been on the *New York Times* bestseller list, and as far as I was concerned, if that many people read it, it must be accurate and informative. So I devoured it. It was only later in life that I realized just how much fiction there was in this "historical" novel. I remember, years after, fervently hoping that I hadn't gotten too much of my "common knowledge" about Paul from this fantastical account.

The one episode that stuck with me over the years involved Caldwell's attempt to explain why Paul was so ripe for conversion to become a follower of Jesus after being such a violent persecutor of the church. The way she mapped out the scenario, roughly, was this. As a very young teenager Paul was extremely zealous for his Jewish faith and strove mightily to keep the Jewish law. But at one point he succumbed to an irresistible temptation. It involved a tryst out at the local lake with a dark-haired slave girl. This sexual encounter created an enormous burden of guilt in the young Paul, which he tried to assuage by becoming even more hyperreligious. As a young man, he heard of the followers of Jesus, who were preaching that salvation can come to people who do *not* keep the law. Salvation comes simply through faith in Christ. Paul became incensed and got official permission to oppose and persecute them. This was a further way of working out his own personal guilt; by engaging in religious zeal he assuaged his conscience. But he found that the harder and harder he pressed for keeping the Jewish law in all its rigorous details, the more overwhelmed he was with guilt for having broken it.

Then he had a vision of Jesus on the road to Damascus. He realized for the first time both that he could not really keep the law and that he did not need to. Jesus brought a release from the deeply hidden guilt within him, and out of profound gratitude he threw himself with equal zeal into being a missionary for the church rather than its persecutor.

Caldwell's long book was a compelling read, especially for an eager teenager wanting to know more about the truth of his newfound faith. As it turns out, though, the entire plot is a fiction. There is no historical record of Paul's sexual fling at the local pond and no indication that he felt tremendous guilt over being unable to keep the law, even though a lot of Christians continue to misinterpret Paul that way. We have a reasonable understanding of what Paul thought, since he has left us some letters (all in the New Testament). When he talks about his Jewish life before Jesus, even though he does indicate that he was extremely zealous for the law, he makes it quite clear that it was not because of guilt over being unable to keep it. On the contrary, Paul indicates that as a faithful Jew he was "blameless" in keeping the law (Phil. 3:6). When he became a follower of Jesus, it was not to resolve internal conflict and guilt. It was because he came to realize that Christ's death was the only thing important for salvation, and everything else, even the law, was as worthless as "garbage" (as he puts it in Phil. 3:8)

Taylor Caldwell, of course, had access to Paul's own writings and could have known what he actually said about his life before Jesus. But probably the reality of his life didn't make as good a story as the idea of the tryst with the slave girl. Having the true account from the horse's mouth (or in this case the Great Lion's) has never stopped people from telling fictional accounts about Paul.

Ancient Fictions About Paul

OF ALL THE CHRISTIANS who have ever lived, probably no one has had more stories told about him than Paul. We still have a number of ancient legendary accounts, just as we have for Peter. In the case of Paul we have a record of someone actually being caught red-handed fabricating stories about him and being punished for it. Ancient people saw fabrications about historical figures (i.e., made-up stories) much as they saw forgeries (false authorial claims): they were *pseuda*, "falsehoods" or "lies," and they normally were not tolerated.

Many of the ancient fabricated accounts can be found in a book that has survived the ravages of time only in bits and pieces, called the *Acts of Paul*. The narrative describes the missionary activities of Paul, his preaching, and his amazing miracles. Probably the most famous part of the story involves Paul's conversion of a wealthy young woman named Thecla, who abandons her fiancé to become Paul's devoted follower.

Paul is said to have arrived in the city of Iconium and to have been welcomed into the house of a Christian named Onesiphorus. There he preaches a sermon. But it is a sermon quite unlike anything Paul himself teaches in his own letters in the New Testament, where his message always concerns the need to believe in Jesus's death and resurrection for salvation. Here, in the *Acts of Paul*, the apostle's message is one of sexual abstinence. Only the pure in heart and body, preserved through remaining sexually chaste, can inherit the kingdom. This applies not only to single people, but also to those who are married. Sex is forbidden.

Thecla, who lives next door, happens to be sitting in her second-floor window and overhears the sermon. She is engaged to a wealthy and prominent man, but decides on the basis of what she has heard to abandon her wedding plans and follow Paul. Her mother and her aggrieved fiancé try to dissuade her, but to no avail. Rejected and angry, they turn her over to the authorities to be burned at the stake for violating social custom. She miraculously escapes and becomes Paul's follower. The rest of the story is about her adventures with Paul and her persecutions.

In another city she resists the sexual advances of an aristocrat and once more is condemned to death. This time she is to be thrown to the wild beasts. She is upset, though, that she might die before she has been baptized into her new faith. Seeing a vat of water filled with man-eating seals (whatever those might be), she throws herself in and declares herself baptized. God performs another miracle, and Thecla escapes intact. Finally she reunites with the apostle Paul, informs him of her desire to spread the word of the gospel, and is authorized by him to do so.

I've given just a brief sketch here of this fairly long and interesting story. The full account was very popular among some Christian groups in the early centuries. And it caused quite a stir among church leaders who were offended by the significant role it gave to Thecla as someone who could baptize (herself!) and preach the gospel, even though she was a woman. By the second century, most churches reserved such ministerial duties for men. But these stories, through no less significant a figure than Paul, seemed to authorize women to engage in them. Moreover, the "gospel" of Paul in this text is all about sexual abstinence and the avoidance of marriage. In other churches it was taught that the family was important, that the male leaders of the churches should be married, that their wives should have babies and be submissive to their husbands in all things. The alternative perspective of the Thecla story led to some serious divisions in the church.[2]

We know this because the first time an ancient author mentions the story, it is in order to oppose it. The writer was the famous Christian theologian, defender of the faith, and misogynist Tertullian, who around 200 CE wrote a treatise on baptism. In this treatise he attacks women who used the story of Thecla as a justification for practicing baptism since, for Tertullian, only men should be allowed to baptize. Tertullian argues that this story of Thecla was fabricated and had no historical value. In fact, he says the author of the story was an elder ("presbyter") in a church of Asia Minor. He was caught fabricating the account, was put on trial in the church, and was relieved of his duties. Thus, for Tertullian, the story cannot be used to authorize women's baptism practices.[3]

Scholars frequently cite this brief but fascinating passage from Tertullian in order to show that forgers were not welcomed in the church. I wish that were the point of the story, since I think it is true that forgers were not welcome. But unfortunately, the story is not about a forger. It is about a fabricator. This Asia Minor presbyter did not write a book claiming to be Paul; he wrote a book with fabricated stories *about* Paul. At the same time, it is true to say that he was treated as forgers were also generally treated. He was severely reprimanded for not speaking the truth.

With good reason a number of scholars have argued that the presbyter did not actually invent these stories about Thecla, but simply retold them, editing them for his own purpose. In other words, the stories were floating around in the oral tradition for a long time before the end of the second century, when he produced his account. This may well be the case, as we will see later in this chapter when we return to the stories. But in any event, *somebody* made up the stories, since they are not historical. The author or editor who wrote them down was found out. And the consequences were not good.

Noncanonical Writings Forged in the Name of Paul

IF CHRISTIANS MADE UP stories *about* Paul, did they also make up writings allegedly *by* Paul? This is the question we asked about Peter in Chapter 2, and the answer here will be the same. There are numerous forgeries in the name of Paul from the early church, all of them, so far as we can tell, written to "authorize" certain views in the name of this great author. Some of these forgeries survive; we know of other forgeries that once existed, but have since been lost.

FORGERIES PERPETRATED BY MARCION

You might think that someone of Paul's stature would have been a unifying influence on the early church. As it turns out, nothing could be farther from the truth. At about the time the presbyter of Asia Minor was propounding stories about Paul that led to splits over the role of women in the church, an even bigger menace to the church's unity was coming from a completely different direction. It involved the teachings of one of Paul's greatest early admirers, the second-century teacher and theologian Marcion.[4]

It is unfortunate that we no longer have any of Marcion's own writings. They were deemed heretical ("false teachings") and destroyed. What we do have are the writings of his opponents, including especially the already-mentioned Tertullian, who wrote a five-volume refutation of Marcion's teachings. We still have this work, and it is a gold mine of information about one of the most divisive persons in the history of the early church.

Marcion came from the city of Sinope on the southern coast of the Black Sea. His father was reportedly a bishop of the local church, and so Marcion was raised, in the early second century, in a Christian household. His family was from the upper class, and he himself became an entrepreneur as a young man, apparently in the shipbuilding business. After he amassed a good deal of wealth, he left Asia Minor for the capital city of the empire, Rome, where he joined the church and participated actively in its ministry. Scholars have traditionally dated Marcion's time in Rome as 139–144 CE.

It was in Rome that Marcion developed his distinctive theological ideas. Marcion was especially attracted to Paul's idea that a person is made right with God not by doing the requirements of the Jewish law (the "works of the law," as Paul puts it), but only by having faith in Christ's death and resurrection. Paul, in such books as Galatians and Romans in the New Testament, emphasizes that no one can be right with God through the works of the law. He preached his "gospel" (literally, the "good news") to Gentiles, telling them that Christ's death could bring a reconciliation with God for all who have faith.

Marcion saw this contrast between the law of the Jews and the gospel of Christ in extreme terms and pushed the contrast to what he saw as its logical consequences. Where there is law, there is no gospel. The law and the gospel are fundamentally distinct. They are contrary things. The Old Testament has nothing to do with the gospel of Paul. The necessary conclusion, for Marcion, was that the God who gave the Jewish law must not be the God who saved people from their sins, which they incurred by breaking the law. In other words, the Old Testament God was not the same as the God of Jesus and his apostle Paul. There were literally two Gods.

Marcion argued that the God of the Old Testament was the Jewish God who created this world, chose Israel to be his people, and then gave them his law. No one was able to keep this law, however. So the Old Testament God was perfectly justified in condemning everyone to damnation. He was a just, wrathful God—not evil, just ruthlessly judicial. The God of Jesus, on the other hand, was a God of love, mercy, and forgiveness. This good God, superior to the God of the Jews, sent Jesus into the world in order to die for the sins of others, to save people from the wrathful God of the Old Testament. Salvation comes, then, by believing in Jesus's death.

Marcion set out to prove his doctrine of the two Gods by writing a book called the *Antitheses* (i.e., the "contrary statements"). In it he showed that there were severe inconsistencies between the Old

Testament and the teachings of Jesus and Paul. The God of the Old Testament, for example, orders the Israelites to take over the promised land, first by destroying the city of Jericho (Josh. 6). He instructs them to go into the city and slaughter every man, woman, and child in it. Is this the same God, asks Marcion, who says, "Love your enemies," "Turn the other cheek," and "Pray for those who persecute you"? It doesn't *sound* like the same God. Because it's not.

The God of the Old Testament sent his prophets, one of whom was Elisha. One day, we are told in the Old Testament, Elisha was verbally harassed by a group of boys making fun of his bald head. Elisha called the wrath of God down upon the boys, and two she-bears came out of the woods and mauled forty-two of them to death (2 Kings 2). Is this the same God who said, "Let the little children come unto me"? No, there are two different Gods.

Since the God of Jesus is not the God of the Old Testament and is therefore not the creator of the world, Jesus could not belong to this created order. He could not be born into this world as a flesh-and-blood being; otherwise he would belong to the God of the Jews, just as every other created being does. Jesus must have come from heaven, from the true God, directly. For that reason he was not an actual, physical human being. He only seemed to be. In other words, Marcion was a docetist (see Chapter 2). For this view he could again appeal to the writings of Paul, who stated that Jesus came into this world "in the *likeness* of sinful flesh" (Rom. 8:3). For Marcion, it was all an appearance.

Marcion is the first Christian of record to have insisted on a distinct canon of Scripture, that is, a collection of books he considered sacred authorities. Marcion's canon was remarkably short by most standards. Since the Jewish God was not the true God, his book was not part of the Christian Scriptures. There was no Christian Old Testament. The canon, instead, was made up of two sections. One part consisted of Paul's letters. Marcion apparently knew ten of these, all the ones in the New Testament except 1 and 2 Timothy and Titus, the so-called pastoral letters. Moreover, in his letters Paul constantly refers to his "gospel." So Marcion included, as the other part of his canon, a Gospel account of the life of Jesus. This was apparently a version of the Gospel of Luke.

The problem with this eleven-book canon is that even these books quote the Old Testament as an authority and seem to affirm the creation as coming from the true God. How could that be, if Marcion's views of Paul and Jesus were right? Marcion had an easy answer to that. He believed that after Jesus left this earth, his followers, the disciples, changed his teachings and went back to their old Jewish ways, misinterpreting his gospel message and turning it around to affirm the goodness of the creator God and his creation. They never fully understood Jesus's teaching that the creator was not the true God. That is why Paul had to be called to be an apostle. The apostles before him had altered Jesus's teachings, and so Paul was commissioned to set things straight. According to Marcion, this wide misinterpretation of Jesus's message had affected lots of other Christians, including the scribes who copied the writings of Paul and Luke. These eleven books had in fact been miscopied over the years. Scribes who did not understand the truth—that there are two Gods, that Jesus was not really born and is not really human, and so on—altered the texts and inserted false views into them. Marcion then edited his eleven books, eliminating from them portions that seemed too Jewish.

In addition to these eleven books, Marcion and his followers had other books forged in Paul's name. We know this from a fragmentary text that comes to us from the second century, a text that discusses which books belong in the true cannon of Scripture, as opposed to the canons of Marcion and other heretics. This text is called the Muratorian Canon, named after the Italian scholar, Muratori, who discovered it.[5] Among other things the Muratorian Canon indicates that the Marcionites, the followers of Marcion, had forged two books in the name of Paul, a letter to the Christians in the city of Alexandria and a letter to those in the town of Laodicea. These letters to the Alexandrians and Laodiceans, regrettably, no longer survive. But we can be relatively certain that if they ever turn up, they will represent even more forcefully than the books of Marcion's canon his distinctive views about the two Gods, the non-human Jesus, and the salvation he brought.

3 CORINTHIANS

It was quite common for "orthodox" Christians (i.e., Christians who accepted the theological views that eventually became widely accepted throughout Christianity) to charge "heretics" (those who taught "false teachings") with forging documents in the names of the apostles in order to support their views. We will see much more of this phenomenon in Chapter 6. The *Gospel of Peter*, for example, was charged with being heretical, as teaching a docetic view of Jesus. But orthodox Christians forged documents of their own. We have far more of this kind of forgery, since orthodox writings were more likely to be preserved for posterity, even if they were not actually written by their alleged authors.

Everyone familiar with the New Testament knows that it contains two letters by Paul to the church in Corinth, called 1 and 2 Corinthians. What most people do not know is that outside of the New Testament is a book called *3 Corinthians*. It is a fascinating book, penned in the name of Paul to oppose heretics like Marcion. But Paul did not write it. It is an orthodox forgery of the second century.[6]

Like the stories of Thecla, *3 Corinthians* is now found in the *Acts of Paul*. According to the account, two heretics came to Corinth propounding their false views, Simon the Magician, whom we have met before, and Cleobius. The Corinthian Christians were disturbed by what they were hearing and wrote to Paul asking him to correct the heretical teachings and to come in person to straighten out those who had succumbed to them.

This letter to Paul, forged in the name of the Corinthians, is the first part of *3 Corinthians*. It sets out the claims of the two false teachers, namely, that it is wrong to appeal to the Old Testament prophets, that God is "not almighty" (i.e., that the creator God is not God over all), that there will be no future resurrection of the flesh, that the world was not created by God, that Christ did not come to earth bearing real flesh, that he was not born of Mary, and that the world was not created by God, but by angels.

Much of this sounds like the teaching of Marcion. As we have seen, Marcion devalued human "flesh," because he rejected the idea that the creator of this world is the true God. And the creator, of course, is the one who made fleshly beings. As a consequence, the followers of Marcion did not believe that the afterlife would be lived "in the flesh"; there would be no physical resurrection at the end of time. So too Christ could not have had real flesh and was not actually born. Since the Old Testament is not part of the Christian Bible, for Marcion, one cannot appeal to the prophets, and the creator God is not the true God.

At least one aspect of the alleged teachings of Simon and Cleobius, however, does not sound like Marcion, their teaching that the world was created "by angels." Marcion maintained that it was created by the God of the Old Testament. Either some of Marcion's followers thought that the Jewish God had created the world through powerful angelic intermediaries, or the fictitious opponents of the Corinthians are not followers of Marcion per se, but are "heretics" with views very similar to Marcion's.

The rest of *3 Corinthians* is Paul's letter in response. This letter is much longer than the one from the Corinthians, and in it "Paul" argues strongly against the heretical views being propounded by the false teachers. Paul stresses that the message he preaches is the one that he received from the other apostles, "who were together with the Lord Jesus Christ at all times." In other words, his message is not unique to him. This stands in contrast to Marcion, who saw Paul as the apostle par excellence, who opposed the false teachings of the other apostles who corrupted Jesus's message. Paul goes on to stress that Jesus really was born of Mary and came in the flesh in order to redeem all flesh and to raise people from the dead in the flesh. The true God is the creator, and the prophets were his spokespersons.

This emphasis on the "flesh" is very interesting, but also a bit ironic. One recent study of *3 Corinthians* has shown that the forger, who was intent on opposing the false teachings of the heretics, does so by teaching ideas about the flesh that are contrary to what the real, historical Paul taught.[7] Paul himself certainly believed that God had created this world and that at the end of time he would redeem it. Paul, like most Jews and Christians in his day, thought that at the end of this age there would be a bodily resurrection. That is to say, humans would face judgment, either reward or punishment, in their own bodies, which had been raised from the dead (see, e.g., 1 Cor. 15). But Paul did not call the body the "flesh." On the contrary the "flesh" meant something completely different for Paul. It meant that part of human nature that is controlled by sin and is alienated from God (see, e.g., Rom. 8:1–9). For Paul, the "flesh" needed to be overcome, since it was controlled by sin. The human *body* would be raised from the dead, but the flesh had to die.

This somewhat technical understanding of the term "flesh" came to be lost in later orthodox Christianity, when theologians began thinking that flesh and body were the same thing. And that has happened here in *3 Corinthians*. Unlike Paul, this author emphasizes the importance of flesh as a creation of God that will be raised. In other words, this is an instance in which a forger claiming to be Paul represents a point of view that is contrary to Paul's, even though he is trying to correct, in Paul's name, teachings he thinks are false.

THE LETTERS OF PAUL AND SENECA

A completely different agenda is found in a much later forgery of Pauline letters that was destined to become quite influential on later Christian thinking about Paul. By the end of the second century, many Christians—not just Marcion—considered Paul to be the most important figure in the religion after Jesus. Paul was understood as the great apostle, the great spokesperson, the great theologian of the church. His writings were widely read, and his thought was deeply appreciated. But over the years Christians wondered why, if Paul was such a brilliant and astute thinker, none of the other great thinkers of his day mentions him. Why does he appear to have been a great unknown in the Roman Empire, outside of the Christian church itself?

Sometime in the fourth century an unknown author sought to address the issue and did so by forging a series of fourteen letters between Paul and the Roman philosopher Seneca.[8] Seneca was widely recognized as the greatest philosopher of his day, one of the real intellectual giants of the early Roman Empire. He was in the upper crust of elite and powerful society, as he was the tutor and later the adviser of the emperor Nero. A number of Seneca's philosophical writings were widely read in antiquity, and a good number of them survive today. But nowhere in these writings does he mention the existence of Christianity or refer to Jesus or any of the great leaders of the new faith.

These fourteen letters repair the damage. Eight of the fourteen are allegedly Seneca's letters to Paul; the other six are Paul's responses. Modern readers of these letters are often a bit disappointed that their contents are so meager. One would hope for some good juicy gossip between the greatest thinker of the first century and the greatest apostle of the church. But with one exception the letters are not meant to provide fabricated stories about life in the imperial palace, for example. They are meant to show that Paul was well placed and well respected by intellectuals of his time.

"Seneca" in his first letter praises Paul for his "wonderful exhortations to the moral life" and indicates that these are divine teachings not spoken so much by Paul as *through* him by God. Paul, in his response, simply indicates that, yes, Seneca has spoken the truth! In another letter Seneca praises Paul's "sublime speech" and his "most venerable thoughts" and indicates that the emperor Nero himself has read the letters and has been moved by Paul's sentiments. All of this, of course, is historically bogus. Seneca had almost certainly never heard of Paul. But it makes for a good story three hundred years later.

In only one letter is there any historical reference of interest. In Letter 11 (sometimes numbered 14, since it appears to be the last one chronologically) Seneca expresses his sincere regret that Paul has been condemned to death even though he is innocent. This is a reference to the tradition that Paul was among the Christians martyred by Nero, who blamed them for starting the fire that burned the city of Rome, which he himself may have had started. Seneca states that the fire burned for six days, destroying 132 palaces and 4,000 apartment buildings. And he indicates his distress that Christians and Jews were being executed because of it by Nero, an unjust ruler "who takes pleasure in murder and uses lies as a disguise." But the emperor's days were numbered, and he would pay the penalty by enduring eternal torment: "This accursed one will be burned in the fire for all."

Here we have, then, not just a set of forgeries written in the names of Paul and Seneca centuries after they were dead, but also a fabricated account of how such an eminent philosopher both appreciated Paul and held him and his fellow Christians innocent of the charges of arson brought against them in 64 CE. Christians of later centuries took these writings with extreme seriousness. It later became a commonplace that Seneca knew the apostle Paul and his Christian message, and that the famous philosopher, the greatest mind of his day, was entirely open to the gospel of Christ.

"Pauline" Writings in the New Testament

AS WITH PETER, so with Paul. Outside of the New Testament there are numerous fabricated stories told about him and a number of writings only allegedly by him. All of the writings attributed to Paul from outside the New Testament were forged. Are there any Pauline forgeries within the New Testament?

Here again there is a broad scholarly consensus. There are thirteen letters that claim to have been written by Paul in the New Testament, nearly half of the New Testament books. But six of these were probably not written by Paul. Scholars have called these six the "deutero-Pauline" letters, meaning that they have a "secondary" standing in the corpus of Paul's writings.

Virtually all scholars agree that seven of the Pauline letters are authentic: Romans, 1 and 2 Corinthians, Galatians, Philippians, 1 Thessalonians, and Philemon. These seven cohere well together and appear stylistically, theologically, and in most every other way to be by the same person. They all claim to be written by Paul. There is scarce reason to doubt that they actually were written by Paul.

The other six differ in significant ways from this core group of seven. Three of them—1 and 2 Timothy and Titus—are so much alike that most scholars are convinced that they were written by the same person. The other three are usually assigned to three different authors. There is greatest scholarly agreement about the first group of three, and so I begin by discussing why scholars have long considered them to be forgeries.

THE PASTORAL LETTERS: 1 AND 2 TIMOTHY AND TITUS

The letters of 1 and 2 Timothy and Titus have been grouped together and called the "Pastoral epistles" since the eighteenth century. The name derives from the subject matter; the author, who claims to be Paul, is allegedly writing to church leaders, his companions Timothy and Titus, to instruct them on their pastoral or ministerial duties in their respective churches. The three letters have many striking similarities to one another, as I show in a moment; but they are also three distinct letters with, probably, three distinct purposes, just as the authentic letters of Paul each has a distinct purpose. Before showing why most scholars consider them to be written by someone other than Paul, I should give a brief summary of each letter.

Summary of the Letters

First Timothy claims to be a letter from Paul to his junior colleague Timothy, whom he has left behind to be the leader of the church in the city of Ephesus. In the letter "Paul" gives Timothy instructions pertaining to how to run and organize the church. He is to oppose groups of false teachers who propound wild theories involving "myths and genealogies" and who promote a kind of rigorous ascetic activity as a spiritual exercise, in which, for example, marriage is forbidden and certain strict dietary restrictions must be observed. He is to make sure that only the right kind of person is appointed to the church offices of bishop and deacon. In particular, the offices are to be occupied only by men who are married, are not recent converts, and live upright lives. Most of the letter provides instruction on how Christians are to conduct themselves and interact with one another, for example, how to pray, how to behave toward the elderly and widows, and how to relate to material wealth.

Among the sundry problems addressed by the author of 1 Timothy is the role of women in the church. In a strident passage the author indicates that women are to be submissive and not to exercise any authority over a man, for example, through teaching. They, instead, are "to keep silent." This, for the author, is how things simply ought to be, as seen from the very beginning in the Garden of Eden, when the first man, Adam, was deceived by his wife, Eve, and ate the forbidden fruit. It was all the woman's fault. But she, the woman, can still be saved, assures the author, by "bearing children" (2:11–15). In other words, women are to be silent, submissive, and pregnant.

Even though 2 Timothy is addressed to the same person, it is written to a different situation. In this case Paul is allegedly writing from prison in Rome (we're never told where 1 Timothy was written); he has been put on trial and is expecting a second trial soon in which he will be condemned to death. He writes Timothy to encourage him in his ongoing pastoral duties and his rooting out of the false teachers who have infiltrated the church. "Paul" expresses a good deal of love and concern for Timothy in this letter; it is far and away the most personalized of the Pastorals. And he hopes that Timothy will be able to join him in Rome soon, bringing some of his personal possessions.

The book of Titus sounds very much like the book of 1 Timothy, almost as if it is a *Reader's Digest* version of the longer letter. But it is addressed by Paul to Titus, a different companion, who is allegedly the pastor of the church on the island of Crete. Paul writes to have his representative correct those who are delivering false teachings, which again involve "genealogies" and "mythologies." He also gives instructions to various groups within the church: older men, older women, younger women, younger men, and slaves.

The First Scholarly Suspicions About the Letters

These three letters are particularly significant for our discussion, because they were the first books of Paul that, in the history of modern scholarship, were extensively argued to be forgeries. The big moment came in 1807 with the publication of a letter by the German scholar Friedrich Schleiermacher. Schleiermacher was one of the most important Christian theologians of the nineteenth century. He was famous for defending the Christian faith against its "cultured despisers" and for developing distinct theological views that influenced theologians well into the twentieth century. There are still scholars today who specialize in studying the works and teaching of Schleiermacher. Among his many writings is an open letter sent to a pastor in 1807 in which he tried to demonstrate that 1 Timothy was not written by Paul.

Schleiermacher argued that 1 Timothy used words and developed ideas that were at odds with those in the other letters of Paul, including 2 Timothy and Titus. Moreover the false teachings attacked in the letter do not sound like anything we know about from Paul's day. Instead, they sound like heresies of the second century generally called "Gnostic."

Like Marcion, Gnostic Christians maintained that this world is not the creation of the one true God. But unlike Marcion, Gnostics did not believe there were just two Gods. They maintained that there were many divine beings in the divine realm that had all come into existence at some point in eternity past, and that this world was created when one of the divine beings fell from the divine realm and came to be entrapped in this miserable world of matter.[9] The Gnostic religions taught that some of us have a spark of the divine trapped in our bodies. Salvation will come to the spark only when it learns the truth of where it came from and who it really is. In other words, the inner element of the divine within us needs to acquire the true and secret "knowledge" that can set it free. In Greek, the word for "knowledge" is *gnosis*, and so this kind of religion is called Gnosticism. According to Gnostic Christians, Christ brings salvation by providing the secret knowledge, not, for example, by dying on the cross. And since the goal of salvation was to escape the trappings of the human body, many Gnostics were rigidly ascetic, urging their followers to treat the body severely, for example, in what was eaten and in avoiding the pleasures of sex.

Schleiermacher argued that the "myths and genealogies" opposed in 1 Timothy sound like the mythologies propounded by these later, second-century Gnostics. In connection with the other problems of the book, such as the non-Pauline vocabulary, this shows that it was a later production, forged in the name of Paul. Soon after Schleiermacher wrote his open letter-essay, other scholars came forward arguing not only that he was right about 1 Timothy, but also that the other two pastoral letters were written by the same person. All three were forged.

Current Scholarship: Are the Letters Forged?

An incredible amount of scholarship has been devoted to the pastoral letters just in the past thirty or forty years, two centuries removed from Schleiermacher. Much of it is tedious to normal human beings, but fascinating to those of us who are abnormal scholars. I can't summarize it all here. Instead, I simply give a few reasons for thinking that all three letters were written by the same person, and that this person was not Paul.[10]

I should admit at the outset that some recent scholars have argued strenuously that 2 Timothy is so different from the other books that it should be considered separately, as by a different author from the others, possibly Paul himself.[11] For about a year or so before I started writing this book, I myself began to be increasingly inclined to take this view. But then I did some further serious research on the matter and am now thoroughly persuaded that whoever wrote 1 Timothy must have written 2 Timothy. The reason is that they share way too many verbal connections and similarities for these to be accidental. Just consider how they begin:

1 Timothy: *"Paul, an apostle of Christ Jesus . . . to Timothy . . . grace, mercy, and peace from God the Father and Christ Jesus our Lord."*

2 Timothy: *"Paul, an apostle of Christ Jesus . . . to Timothy . . . grace, mercy, and peace from God the Father and Christ Jesus our Lord."*

They are virtually the same. And even more important, there is no other letter of Paul that begins this way. Either these are by the same author, or one author is copying the writing of another. But there are reasons for thinking it is not the work of a copyist. For one thing, there are tons of verbal agreements of a similar sort. Both letters have words and phrases in common not found in any of the other letters attributed to Paul: the "promise of life"; "with a pure conscience"; "from a pure heart"; "guard the deposit (of faith)"; Paul is an "apostle, herald, and teacher." And on and on and on. What is striking is not only that these phrases and many others like them are found in these two letters, but that they are found *only* in these two letters.

That's why one of the letters isn't being written by a copyist using the other as his model. To do so would have required the copyist not only to know which words and phrases were important in the first letter, but also which of these words and phrases were, simultaneously, ones that Paul himself never used. I suppose it is theoretically possible that a very astute student of Paul in the first century read through all of Paul's letters, made a list of words that occurred in them, then read 1 Timothy, made a list of important words there, compared the two lists, and decided to write another letter to Timothy using lots of words and phrases that occurred in the second list, but not the first. But it really stretches the imagination. It is much easier to believe that whoever wrote the one letter had his favorite terms and used them in the other letter as well. It's just that those terms were not terms used by Paul.[12]

That is one of the reasons scholars from the nineteenth century on have been convinced that Paul did not write the letters. The vocabulary and the writing style are very different from those of the other Pauline letters. In 1921 the British scholar A. N. Harrison wrote an important study of the pastoral letters in which he gave numerous statistics about the word usage in these writings. One of his most cited set of numbers is that there are 848 different words used in the pastoral letters. Of that number 306—over one-third of them!—do not occur in any of the other Pauline letters of the New Testament. That's an inordinately high number; especially given the fact that about two-thirds of these 306 words are used by Christian authors living in the second century. That suggests that this author is using a vocabulary that was becoming more common after the days of Paul, and that he too therefore lived after Paul.[13]

A number of scholars have called Harrison's use of statistics into question, since, as we all know, you can make statistics say just about anything you want them to say. But the arguments over word usage have gotten increasingly refined over the ninety years since he wrote, and in almost every study done, it is clear that the word usage of the Pastorals is different from that in Paul's other letters.[14] At the same time, probably not too much stock should be placed in mere numbers. Everyone, after all, uses different words on different occasions, and most of us have a much richer stock of vocabulary than shows up in any given letter or set of letters we write.

The problem is that a large number of factors all seem to point in the same direction, showing that this author is not Paul. For one thing, sometimes this author uses the same words as Paul, but means something different by them. The term "faith" was of supreme importance to Paul. In books such as Romans and Galatians faith refers to the trust a person has in Christ to bring about salvation through his death. In other words, the term describes a *relationship* with another; faith is trust "in" Christ. The author of the Pastorals also uses the term "faith." But here it is not about a relationship with Christ; faith now means the body of teaching that makes up the Christian religion. That is "the faith" (see Titus 1:13). Same word, different meaning. So too with other key terms, such as "righteousness."

Even more significant, some ideas and concepts in the pastoral letters stand at odds with what you find in the letters that Paul certainly wrote. For example, we have seen that Paul was highly concerned with arguing that performing the "works of the law" could not contribute to one's right standing before God. It was not the Jewish law that could bring salvation, but the death and resurrection of Jesus. When Paul talks about "works," that is what he means: doing the things that the Jewish law requires, such as getting circumcised, keeping kosher, and observing the Sabbath. In the Pastorals, however, the Jewish law is no longer even an issue, and the author speaks of works as "good works," that is, doing good deeds for other people. The term occurs this way six times in 1 Timothy alone. This author is concerned to show that by being a morally good person you cannot earn your salvation. That may be true, but it is a completely different idea from Paul's; Paul was concerned about whether you kept the Jewish law as a means to salvation (you should not), not if you did good deeds for it.

Or take a completely different idea, marriage. In 1 Corinthians 7 Paul is insistent that people who are single should try to remain single, just as he is. His reason is that the end of all things is near, and people should devote themselves to spreading the word, not to establishing their social lives. But how does that square with the view in the Pastorals? Here the author *insists* that the leaders of the church be married. In Paul's letters it is better not to be married; in the Pastorals it is required that people (at least church leaders) be married.

Or think about the basic issue of how a person is "saved." For Paul himself, only through the death and resurrection of Jesus can a person be saved. And for the Pastorals? For women, at least, we're told in 1 Timothy 2 that they will "be saved" by bearing children. It is hard to know what that means, exactly, but it certainly doesn't mean what Paul meant!

Probably the biggest problem with accepting the Pastorals as having come from Paul involves the historical situation that they seem to presuppose. Paul, like Jesus before him, thought he was living at the very end of time. When Jesus was raised from the dead, that was the sign that the end had already started and that the future resurrection of the dead was about to take place. According to Jewish thinking the resurrection was to arrive when this age had come to an end. That's why Paul called Jesus the "first fruits of the resurrection" in 1 Corinthians 15:20. This is an agricultural metaphor. The farmhands celebrate the first day of harvest by throwing a party that night; this commemorates the "first fruits" of the harvest. And when do they go out to get the rest of the harvest? The next day—not twenty or two thousand years later. Jesus is the first fruits, because with him the resurrection has started, and very soon everyone—all the dead—will be raised for judgment. That is why Paul thinks he himself will be alive when Jesus returns from heaven (see 1 Thess. 4:14–18).

In the meantime, though, the church has to grow and survive in the world. Paul thought that in this short interim period between the resurrection of Jesus and the end of time, the Spirit of God had been given to the church and to each individual making up the church. When a person was baptized, he or she received the Spirit (1 Cor. 12:13), and the Spirit gave the person a spiritual "gift." Some of the baptized were given the gift of teaching, others of prophecy, others of healing, others of speaking in angelic tongues, others of interpreting those tongues. All of these gifts were meant to help the

Christian community function together as a unit (1 Cor. 12–14). None of the gifts was paltry or insignificant. They all mattered. Everyone in the church was equally endowed with a gift, so that in the church all were equals. Slaves were on the same level as masters, women were equal with men. That's why Paul could say, "In Christ there is neither slave nor free, neither male nor female" (Gal. 3:28). There was equality.

When problems arose in one of Paul's churches—for example, the church of Corinth, for which we have the best documentation—he wrote to deal with them. It is interesting to read his correspondence with the Corinthians. The church was in a mess. There were divisions and episodes of infighting, some members were taking others to civil court, the worship services were chaos, and there were harsh disagreements over major ethical issues, such as whether it was right to eat meat that had been sacrificed to pagan idols. Some people denied that there was to be a future resurrection, and there was gross immorality—some men were visiting prostitutes and bragging about it in church, and one fellow was sleeping with his stepmother.

To address these severe problems, Paul appeals to the church as a whole and to the individuals in it. He urges them to use their spiritual gifts for the mutual good. He appeals to them to act as a unit. He exhorts them to begin behaving in an ethical fashion. He chastises them for not accepting the proper teaching, for example, about the future resurrection.

The one thing Paul does not do is write to the leaders of the church in Corinth and tell them to get their parishioners in order. Why is that? Because there *were* no leaders of the church in Corinth. There were no bishops or deacons. There were no pastors. There was a group of individuals, each of whom had a gift of the Spirit, in this brief time before the end came.

Contrast that with what you have in the Pastorals. Here you do not have individuals endowed by the Spirit working together to form the community. Here you have the pastors Timothy and Titus. You have the church leaders: bishops and deacons. You have hierarchy, structure, organization. That is to say, you have a different historical situation than you had in the days of Paul.

If you expect Jesus to come back soon—say, sometime this month—there is no real need for a hierarchical system of organization and leadership. You simply need to get along for the short term. But if Jesus does not return, and you need to settle in for the long haul, things will be different. You have to get organized. You have to have leadership. You have to have someone run the show. You have to have teachers who can root out the false teaching in your midst. You have to specify how people should relate to one another socially: masters to slaves, husbands to wives, parents to children. In a hierarchical system there is no equality; there is leadership. That's what you find in the pastoral letters—churches settling in for the long haul. But that's not what you find in the historical Paul. For the historical Paul, there was not going to *be* a long haul. The end was coming soon.

As I said at the outset of this discussion, some scholars have been willing to concede that 1 Timothy and Titus, which is closely tied to 1 Timothy, are pseudepigraphal, but that 2 Timothy may stem from Paul. I've tried to show that this view can't work, because whoever wrote 1 Timothy also wrote 2 Timothy. If the one is forged, so too is the other. That doesn't mean the two letters are addressing the same concerns or were written for the same purpose; it just means the same author wrote them. But one point sometimes raised is that there is so much personal information in 2 Timothy, it is hard to see how it could be forged. Why, for example, would a forger tell his alleged reader (who was not actually his reader!) to be sure to bring his cloak to him when he comes and also the books he left behind (2 Tim. 4:13)?

This objection has been convincingly answered by one of the great scholars of ancient forgery, Norbert Brox, who gives compelling evidence that this kind of "verisimilitude" (as I called it in Chapter 1) is *typical* for forgeries. Making the letter sound "homey" removes the suspicion that it's forged. The personal notices in 2 Timothy (there are fewer in Titus and fewer still in 1 Timothy) serve, then, to convince readers that this really is written by Paul, even though it is not.[15] But why does an author forge letters like this?

Why Were the Pastoral Letters Forged?

The most obvious answer is that the author is someone facing new problems in a generation after Paul, problems that Paul himself never addressed, and he wants to deal with them in the name of an authority who will be listened to. And who in Paul's churches has greater authority than Paul himself? So the author dealt with the problem of false teachings, for example, of those propounding "myths and genealogies" in 1 Timothy and of other false teachers who claimed that the resurrection "had already happened" in 2 Timothy. He also dealt with problems involving church leadership and with problems over with the roles of women in the church. He did all this by pretending to be Paul.

Some scholars have thought that something even more precise may have occasioned these forgeries. In a very interesting and influential study, the American scholar Dennis MacDonald argues that the pastoral letters were written to oppose the views that were in circulation in the stories connected with Thecla.[16] It is true that the *Acts of Paul*, where the Thecla stories are now found, were probably written later than the Pastorals by as much as seventy to eighty years. But the stories recorded in the *Acts of Paul* had been circulating for a very long time before the presbyter in Asia Minor fabricated his account. And in remarkable ways, the views found in the Thecla stories contrast with the views advocated in the Pastorals. Could one of them have been written to authorize a contrary view under the authority of Paul?

In the *Acts of Paul*, marriage is disparaged. In the Pastorals marriage is encouraged; church leaders in fact are *required* to be married. In the *Acts of Paul* sexual activity is condemned; only by remaining chaste can you enter the kingdom of heaven. In the Pastorals sexual activity is urged; women will be saved only by having babies. In the

Acts of Paul women—specifically Thecla—are allowed to teach and exercise authority. In the Pastorals women are to be silent and submissive; they are not allowed to teach or exercise authority. Since the pastoral letters are directly opposing the views found in the stories incorporated into the *Acts of Paul*, MacDonald argues that the letters were forged by someone who had heard the stories about Thecla and wanted to set the record straight from Paul's "true" point of view.

This is a very appealing argument, and it may be right. But for many scholars the biggest problem with it has to do with the dates of the materials. The *Acts of Paul* was probably written by the presbyter of Asia Minor some decades after the Pastorals were produced. The stories the presbyter used may have been much older, but without corroborating evidence, it is hard to say. So a different historical reconstruction may be more plausible.

It goes like this. Paul's churches were split in lots of ways, as we have seen. One of the splits involved issues of sex, sexuality, and gender. Some Pauline Christians thought that women should be treated as equals and given equal status and authority with men, since Paul did say that "in Christ there is neither male nor female" (Gal. 3:28). Other Pauline Christians thought that women were equal with men only "in Christ," by which they meant "in theory," not in social reality. These Christians were keen to tone down Paul's own emphasis on women, and one of them decided to write a set of letters, the Pastorals, that authorized his view in Paul's name. He had other issues he wanted to address as well: the nature of the leadership in the church, the need to suppress false teaching, the relations of slaves and masters, parents and children, and so on. He packaged all of these sundry issues in a set of letters and wrote them in the name of Paul, forging them to provide them with the authoritative voice they needed.

But not everyone was convinced and not everyone accepted these letters as coming from Paul. Remember that Marcion, for example, did not have them (it is hard to know if he was aware of them). Moreover, the other side of the split over the role of women was not destroyed by the appearance of the pastoral letters. It lived on, seeing

Paul as an opponent of marriage and of sex, but as a proponent of women. This other side told stories about Paul that supported their views, and these stories eventually came to center on one of Paul's key converts, Thecla. At one time in the second century both sets of documents were in wide circulation, the fabricated stories about Paul and Thecla and the forged letters of Paul that eventually came to be included in the New Testament.

2 THESSALONIANS

When I was a conservative evangelical Christian in my late teens and early twenties, there were few things I was more certain of, religiously, than the fact that Jesus was soon to return from heaven to take me and my fellow believers out of the world, at the "rapture" before the final tribulation came. We read all sorts of books that supported our view. Few people today realize that *the* bestselling book in English in the 1970s, apart from the Bible, was *The Late, Great Planet Earth*, written by the fundamentalist Christian Hal Lindsey. Based on a careful (or careless, depending on your perspective) study of the book of Revelation and other biblical books of prophecy, Lindsey wrote with assurance about what was about to transpire in the Middle East as the superpowers of the Soviet Union, China, the European Union, and finally the United States converged in a massive confrontation leading to an all-out nuclear holocaust, right before Jesus returned. All of this, we were told, had to happen before the end of the 1980s, as Scripture itself taught.

It obviously never happened. And now there *is* no Soviet Union. But that hasn't stopped people from writing about how the end will come very soon now, in our own day, at any time. On the recent bookselling front, dwarfing the sales of the Harry Potter books has been the multivolume *Left Behind* series, about those who will not be taken in the imminent rapture. These books were coauthored by Jerry Jenkins and Timothy LaHaye, the latter of whom previously enjoyed a career writing books with his wife, Beverly, about sex for Christians.

What most of the millions of people who believe that Jesus is coming back soon, in our lifetime, don't realize is that there have always been Christians who thought this about their own lifetimes. This was a prominent view among conservative Christians in the early twentieth century, in the late nineteenth century, in the eighteenth century, in the twelfth century, in the second century, in the first century—in fact, in just about every century. The one thing that all those who have ever thought this have had in common is that every one of them has been demonstrably and irrefutably wrong.

Paul himself thought the end was coming in his lifetime. Nowhere is this more clear than in one of the letters we are sure he wrote, 1 Thessalonians. Paul wrote the Christians in Thessalonica, because some of them had become disturbed over the death of a number of their fellow believers. When he converted these people, Paul had taught them that the end of the age was imminent, that they were soon to enter the kingdom when Jesus returned. But members of the congregation had died before it happened. Had they lost out on their heavenly reward? Paul writes to assure the survivors that, no, even those who have died will be brought into the kingdom. In fact, when Jesus returns in glory on the clouds of heaven, "the dead in Christ will rise first; then we who are alive, who remain, will be caught up together with them to meet the Lord in the air" (4:17). Read the verse carefully: Paul expects to be one of the ones who will still be alive when it happens.

He goes on to say that it will be a sudden, unexpected event. That day will come "like a thief in the night," and when people think that all is well, "sudden destruction will come upon them" (5:2–3). The Thessalonians should be alert and prepared, because, as with the labor pains of a pregnant woman, it is possible to know that it will come very soon, but you can't predict the exact moment.

It is precisely this emphasis on the suddenness of the reappearance of Jesus, which will catch people by surprise, that makes the *second* letter that Paul allegedly wrote to the Thessalonians so interesting. This too is a book written about the second coming of Jesus, but now a completely different problem is being addressed. The readers have been "led astray" by a letter that has apparently been forged in Paul's name (2:2) saying that "the day of the Lord is at hand." The author of 2 Thessalonians, claiming to be Paul, argues that the end is not, in fact, coming right away. Certain things have to happen first. There will be some kind of political or religious uprising and rebellion, and an Antichrist-like figure will appear who will take his seat in the Temple of Jerusalem and declare himself to be God. Only then will the "Lord Jesus" come to "destroy him with the breath of his mouth" (2:3–8).

In other words, the Thessalonians can rest assured they are not yet at the final moment of history when Jesus reappears. They will know when it is almost here by the events that transpire in fulfillment of Scripture. But can this be by the same author who wrote the other letter, 1 Thessalonians? Compare the scenario of Jesus's appearance in 2 Thessalonians, according to which it will be a while yet and preceded by recognizable events, with that of 1 Thessalonians, when the end will come like a "thief in the night," who appears when people least expect it. There seems to be a fundamental disparity between the teachings of 1 and 2 Thessalonians, which is why so many scholars think that 2 Thessalonians is not by Paul.[17]

It is particularly interesting that the author of 2 Thessalonians indicates that he taught his converts all these things already, when he was with them (2:5). If that's the case, then how can one explain 1 Thessalonians? The problem there is that people think the end is supposed to come any day now, based on what Paul told them. But according to 2 Thessalonians Paul never taught any such thing. He taught that a whole sequence of events had to transpire before the end came. Moreover, if that is what he taught them, as 2 Thessalonians insists, then it is passing strange that he never reminds them of this teaching in 1 Thessalonians, where they obviously think that they were taught something else.

Paul probably did not write 2 Thessalonians. That makes one feature of the letter particularly intriguing. At the end of the letter the author insists that he is Paul and gives a kind of proof: "I Paul write this greeting with my own hand. This is the mark in every letter of mine; it is the way I write" (3:17). This means that "Paul" had been dictating his letter to a scribe who had written it all down, until the end, when Paul signed off with his own hand. Readers of the letter could see the change of handwriting and recognize Paul's, authenticating this letter as really his, as opposed to the forged one mentioned in 2:2. What is peculiar is that the author claims that this is his invariant practice. But it is not how most of the undisputed letters of Paul end, including 1 Thessalonians. The words are hard to account for as Paul's, but they make sense if a forger is trying to convince his readers that he really was Paul. But perhaps the queen doth protest too much.

Some scholars have taken the question of forgery a bit farther and suggested that when the author, claiming to be Paul, tries to soothe his readers not to be led astray by a forged letter ("as if by us,"), which maintains, in Paul's name, that the end is right around the corner, the forger is actually referring to 1 Thessalonians! That is, someone living later wanted to disabuse readers of the message Paul himself had taught about the imminent end, since it did not, after all, come, and Paul and everyone else had died in the meantime. So an author provided some reassurance by forging a letter claiming that the authentic letter was a forgery. Whether or not that is right, what seems relatively certain is that someone after the time of Paul decided that he had to intervene in a situation where people were eagerly anticipating the end, so eagerly, he suggests, that they were neglecting the duties of daily life (3:6–12); he did so by penning a letter in Paul's name, knowing full well that he was someone else living later. Second Thessalonians, then, appears to be another instance of a Pauline forgery.

EPHESIANS

When I was teaching at Rutgers in the mid-1980s, I regularly offered a course on the life and teachings of Paul. One of the textbooks for the course was a book on Paul by the conservative British scholar F. F. Bruce.[18] I used the book because I disagreed with just about everything in it, and I thought it would be a good idea for my students to see a different side of the story from the one I told in class. One of the things F. F. Bruce thought about the writings of Paul was that Ephesians was the most Pauline of all the Pauline letters. Not only did he think Paul wrote it; he thought it encapsulated better than any other letter the heart and soul of Paul's theology.

That's what I once thought too, years earlier, when I was just starting out in my studies. Then I took a course on the New Testament at Princeton Theological Seminary with Professor J. Christiaan Beker. Beker was a formidable scholar of Paul. In the late 1970s he wrote a massive and influential study of Paul's theology, one of the truly great studies ever to be published on the matter.[19] Beker was thoroughly convinced that Paul had not written Ephesians, that in fact Ephesians represents a serious alteration of Paul's thought.[20]

At the time, when I took the course, I wasn't so sure. But the more I studied the matter, carefully comparing what Ephesians says with what Paul himself says in his undisputed letters, I became increasingly convinced. By the time I was teaching at Rutgers, I was sure Paul had not written the letter. Today the majority of biblical scholars agree. Ephesians may sound like Paul, but when you start digging a bit deeper, large differences and discrepancies appear.

Ephesians is written to Gentile Christians (3:1) to remind them that even though they were once alienated from both God and his people, the Jews, they have now been reconciled; they have been made right with God and the boundary that divided Jew from Gentile—the Jewish law—has been torn down by the death of Christ. Jews and Gentiles can now live in harmony with one another, in Christ, and in harmony with God. After laying out this theological set of ideas in the first three chapters (especially chapter 2), the author turns to ethical issues and discusses ways that followers of Jesus must live in order to manifest the unity they have in Christ.

The reasons for thinking Paul did not write this letter are numerous and compelling. For one thing, the writing style is not Paul's. Paul usually writes in short, pointed sentences; the sentences in Ephesians are long and complex. In Greek, the opening statement of thanksgiving (1:3–14)—all twelve verses—is one sentence. There's nothing wrong with extremely long sentences in Greek; it just isn't the way Paul wrote. It's like Mark Twain and William Faulkner; they both wrote correctly, but you would never mistake the one for the other. Some scholars have pointed out that in the hundred or so sentences in Ephesians, 9 of them are over 50 words in length. Compare this with Paul's own letters. Philippians, for example, has 102 sentences, only 1 of which is over 50 words; Galatians has 181 sentences, again with only 1 over 50 words. The book also has an inordinate number of words that don't otherwise occur in Paul's writings, 116 altogether, well higher than average (50 percent more than Philippians, for example, which is about the same length).[21]

But the main reason for thinking that Paul didn't write Ephesians is that what the author says in places does not jibe with what Paul himself says in his own letters. Ephesians 2:1–10, for example, certainly looks like Paul's writing, but just on the surface. Here, as in Paul's authentic letters, we learn that believers were separated from God because of sin, but have been made right with God exclusively through his grace, not as the result of "works." But here, oddly, Paul includes himself as someone who, before coming to Christ, was carried away by the "passions of our flesh, doing the will of the flesh and senses." This doesn't sound like the Paul of the undisputed letters, who says that he had been "blameless" with respect to the "righteousness of the law" (Phil. 3:4). In addition, even though he is talking about the relationship of Jew and Gentile in this letter, the author does not speak about salvation apart from the "works of the law," as Paul does. He speaks, instead, of salvation apart from doing "good deeds." That simply was not the issue Paul addressed.

Moreover, this author indicates that believers have already been "saved" by the grace of God. As it turns out, the verb "saved" in Paul's authentic letters is always used to refer to the future. Salvation is not something people already have; it's what they *will* have when Jesus returns on the clouds of heaven and delivers his followers from the wrath of God.

Relatedly, and most significantly, Paul was emphatic in his own writings that Christians who had been baptized had "died" to the powers of the world that were aligned with the enemies of God. They had "died with Christ." But they had not yet been "raised" with Christ. That would happen at the end of time, when Jesus returned and all people, living and dead, would be raised up to face judgment. That's why in Romans 6:1–4 Paul is emphatic: those who are baptized "have died" with Christ, and they "will be raised" with him, at Jesus's second coming.

Paul was extremely insistent on this point, that the resurrection of believers was a future, physical event, not something that had already happened. One of the reasons he wrote 1 Corinthians was precisely because some of the Christians in that community took an opposing point of view and maintained that they were already enjoying a resurrected existence with Christ now, that they already were enjoying the benefits of salvation. Paul devotes 1 Corinthians 15 to showing that, no, the resurrection is not something that has happened yet. It is a future physical event yet to occur. Christians have not yet been raised with Christ.

But contrast this statement with what Ephesians says: "Even when we were dead through our trespasses, God made us alive together with Christ . . . and raised us up with him and seated us with him in the heavenly places" (2:5–6). Here believers *have* experienced a spiritual resurrection and are enjoying a heavenly existence in the here and now. This is precisely the view that Paul argued against in his letters to the Corinthians!

In point after point, when you look carefully at Ephesians, it stands at odds with Paul's own work. This book was apparently written by a later Christian in one of Paul's churches who wanted to deal with a big issue of his own day: the relation of Jews and Gentiles in the church. He did so by claiming to be Paul, knowing full well that he wasn't Paul. He accomplished his goal, that is, by producing a forgery.

COLOSSIANS

Much the same can be said about the book of Colossians. On the surface it looks like Paul's work, but not when you dig deeply into it. Colossians has a lot of words and phrases that are found in Ephesians as well, so much so that a number of scholars think that whoever forged Ephesians used Colossians as one of his sources for how Paul wrote. Unfortunately, he used a book that Paul almost certainly did not write.[22]

Colossians has a different agenda and purpose from Ephesians. This author is especially concerned with a group of false teachers who are conveying some kind of "philosophy." Unfortunately the author does not detail what this philosophy entailed and leaves only hints. Evidently the false teachers urged their listeners to worship angels and to follow Jewish laws about what to eat and what special days to keep as religious festivals. One reason the author does not explain in detail what these false teachers taught may be that the people reading the letter knew full well whom he had in mind and what they were saying.

The author opposes them by emphasizing that Christ alone, not angelic beings, is a divinity worthy of worship and that his death put an end to the need to keep the law. In fact, for him, believers in Christ were already above all human rules and regulations, because they were already raised with Christ in the heavenly places, experiencing some kind of mystical unity with Christ in the here and now. This does not mean, however, that Christians could live just any way they please. They were still responsible for living moral lives. So the final two chapters outline some of the ethical requirements of the new life in Christ.

The reasons for thinking the book was not actually written by Paul are much the same as for Ephesians. Among other things, the writing style and the contents of the book differ significantly from those in the undisputed letters of Paul. Far and away the most compelling study of the writing style of Colossians was done by the German scholar Walter Bujard nearly forty years ago now.[23] Bujard analyzed all sorts of stylistic features of the letter: the kind and frequency of conjunctions, infinitives, participles, relative clauses, strings of genitives, and scores of other things. He was particularly interested in comparing Colossians to Paul's letters that were similar in length: Galatians, Philippians, and 1 Thessalonians. The differences between this letter and Paul's writings are striking and compelling. Just to give you a taste:

How often the letter uses "adversative conjunctions" (e.g., "although"): Galatians, 84 times; Philippians, 52; 1 Thessalonians, 29; Colossians, only 8.

How often the letter uses causal conjunctions (e.g., "because"): Galatians, 45 times; Philippians, 20; 1 Thessalonians, 31; Colossians, only 9.

How often the letter uses a conjunction (e.g., "that," "as") to introduce a statement: Galatians, 20 times; Philippians, 19; 1 Thessalonians, 11; Colossians, only 3.

The lists go on for many pages, looking at all sorts of information, with innumerable considerations all pointing in the same direction: this is someone with a different writing style from Paul's.

And here again, the content of what the author says stands at odds with Paul's own thought, but is in line with Ephesians. Here too, for example, the author indicates that Christians have already been "raised with Christ" when they were baptized, despite Paul's insistence that the believers' resurrection was future, not past (see Col. 2:12–13).

What we have here, then, is another instance in which a later follower of Paul was concerned to address a situation in his own day and did so by assuming the mantle and taking the name of Paul, forging a letter in his name.

Conclusion

WE HAVE SEEN THAT there were a number of Pauline forgeries floating around in the early church, letters claiming to be written by Paul, but in fact written by someone else. Some of these letters are acknowledged as forgeries by everyone on the planet, such as the *Letters of Paul and Seneca*, for example. Others are a matter of serious scholarly discussion. But the majority of scholars acknowledge that, whereas there are seven letters in the New Testament that Paul certainly wrote, six others are probably (or for some scholars, certainly) not by Paul, for some of the reasons I have laid out here. There are plenty more reasons, but the arguments can get a bit dull after a while.

Some scholars, though, have been reluctant to call these deutero-Pauline letters forgeries. Some have argued that they differ from Paul's own letters, because they were given by Paul to a secretary to write, who used a different writing style from Paul's. Others have suggested that since Paul in some of his letters mentions coauthors, possibly these other authors were responsible for writing the letters, accounting for their differences. And yet others have claimed that it was common in philosophical schools for disciples of a teacher to write treatises and sign them in the name of their teacher, as an act of humility, since all the ideas originated with the teacher himself.

These are all interesting proposals. But I think they are all wrong. I try to show why in the next chapter.

CHAPTER FOUR

Alternatives to Lies and Deceptions

WHEN I WAS A GOOD conservative evangelical Christian at Moody Bible Institute in my late teen years, I knew for a fact that there could not be any forgeries in the New Testament. My view of Scripture was deeply rooted in Scripture itself and above all in that classic statement of the Bible's own inspiration, 2 Timothy 3:16: "All Scripture is inspired by God [literally, is God-breathed] and is profitable for teaching, for reproof, for correction, and for training in righteousness." If Scripture is "breathed out," or inspired, by God, then it obviously cannot have anything wrong in it, let alone anything approaching a lie. In no small measure that is because God himself, who breathed forth the text, does not lie.

For this, we knew all the key verses, including the following:

God is not a human being, that he should lie. (Num. 23:19)

The Glory of Israel [i.e., God] will not deceive. (1 Sam. 15:29)

In hope of eternal life, which God, who never lies, promised . . . (Titus 1:2)

He guaranteed it by an oath, so that by two unchangeable matters, in which God cannot lie . . . (Heb. 6:18)

Scripture says that it is inspired or breathed out by God. God does not and cannot lie. Therefore Scripture does not and cannot contain lies. Forgery, on the other hand, involves lying. For that reason there can be no forgeries in the Bible.[1]

This conservative evangelical view is still very much held by some scholars today, at least by conservative evangelical scholars. But I should emphasize it is a view that is built on theological premises of what *has* to be true, not on the grounds of what actually is true.[2] For conservative evangelicals, the Bible has to be without mistake, error, or lie. And if it has to be that way, well then, it is that way!

Can the Bible Contain Lies?

I OBVIOUSLY CHANGED MY view on the matter. Three years after I graduated from Moody, I was studying in a master's program at Princeton Theological Seminary, a mainline Presbyterian school that stresses critical scholarship more than uncritical dogmatism. It was at Princeton Seminary that I came to think that I had previously been approaching the Bible in precisely the wrong way. As a conservative evangelical I had come to the Bible assuming certain things about it even before reading it. I claimed it couldn't have mistakes. And if it couldn't have mistakes, then it obviously didn't have mistakes. Anything that looked like a mistake, therefore, couldn't really be a mistake, because the Bible couldn't have mistakes. And how did I know that the Bible couldn't have mistakes? Not on the basis of any examination or investigation of the Bible, but simply on the basis of what other people had told me, backed up by a few proof texts. I brought the belief in an error-free text to the Bible, and so naturally I found no mistakes, because there couldn't be any.

But why should I have believed this view was true? There were plenty of other Christians who believed other things, especially at a place like Princeton Theological Seminary. It was there that I realized that since the Bible is a book, it makes better sense to approach it the way one approaches books. There are certainly books in the world that don't have any mistakes in them. But no one would insist that a particular phone book, chemistry textbook, or car instruction manual has absolutely no mistakes in it before reading it to see whether it does or not. Rather than thinking that the Bible cannot have mistakes, before looking to see if it does, why not see if it does, and only then decide whether it could?

I know that many evangelical Christians think that this is backwards and wrong, that questioning the Bible is questioning God. But I don't see it that way. If God created an error-free book, then the book should be without errors. If what we have is not an error-free book, then it is not a book that God has delivered to us without errors.

Moreover, as I studied the Bible I began to see the errors, here and there. And then they started to multiply. And eventually they came to involve not just little details, but very big questions and issues of real importance. I came away convinced that the Bible, whatever else it might be, is a very human book.

Human books from the ancient world sometimes contained forgeries, writings that claim to be authored by someone who did not write them. This is certainly true of the Hebrew Bible, the Christian Old Testament. The book of Daniel claims to be written, in part, by the prophet Daniel during the Babylonian captivity in the sixth century BCE. But there is no way it was written then. Scholars for over a hundred years have shown clear and compelling reasons for thinking that it was written four hundred years later, in the second century BCE, by someone falsely claiming to be Daniel. So too the book of Ecclesiastes. The author of this book does not come out and say his name is Solomon, but he does say that he is the son of David, who is the king in Jerusalem, and that he is fantastically rich and wise. In other words, he is claiming to be Solomon without using his name. But there is no way he was Solomon. This book could not have been written until six hundred years after Solomon's death, as critical biblical scholars today agree.[3]

Whereas there are a couple of forgeries in the Old Testament, there are numerous instances in the New Testament. So far we have considered two books that falsely claim to have been written by Peter and six that falsely claim to have been written by Paul. It is a striking phenomenon that even though scholars far and wide agree that these books were not actually written by their alleged authors, many scholars are reluctant to call the books what they are: literary forgeries meant to deceive their readers. Sometimes I think it is a bit strange that when some scholars refer to books with false authorial claims *outside* the New Testament, they have no qualms calling them "forgeries," but when they refer to such books *within* the New Testament, they call them "pseudepigrapha." Maybe it is better to use the more antiseptic, technical term when dealing with the Bible? Or maybe, instead, it is better to call a spade a spade. We are dealing with precisely the same phenomenon whether a book came to be included in the canon or not.

In this chapter I deal with the ways some scholars have tried to get around the problem that the New Testament contains forgeries. Sometimes they do so with explanations that have become extremely common and widespread, so much so that they sound like common sense to some people. Among other things, it is widely claimed that the practice of making false authorial claims was acceptable in philosophical schools in antiquity and so was excusable for a follower of Peter or Paul. Or it is stated that allegedly pseudepigraphal letters can be explained by thinking that Peter and Paul used secretaries to produce these writings. As we will see, there is very little evidence to support either view.[4] Before dealing with such explanations, I need to address another point of view often asserted by scholars, that ancient authors who assumed a false identity were not actually trying to be deceitful.

Is Forgery Deceitful?

A MISTAKEN SCHOLARLY COMMONPLACE

A surprising number of scholars have claimed that even though the Bible may contain forgeries, these forgeries were never meant to deceive anyone. According to this view, ancient authors who assumed a false name were not trying to lead their readers astray. They were not lying, they were not being deceitful, and they were not condemned.

It is hard to understand how anyone who has actually read any of the ancient discussions of forgery can make such claims. But this view is so widespread that it has become a complete commonplace in New Testament scholarship. Let me give several examples of scholars who make statements of this sort, along with some interspersed comments, before emphasizing just how wrong this view is.

One highly respected author of the 1920s, in a classical study of the pastoral letters, claimed that the author, who called himself Paul even though he was someone else, "was not conscious of misrepresenting the Apostle in any way; he was not consciously deceiving anybody; it is not, indeed, necessary to suppose that he did deceive anybody."[5] What evidence does this scholar provide for these claims? None at all. And what a remarkable statement! If the author did not want to deceive anyone and in fact did not deceive anybody, why is it that every known interpreter of these letters for over seventeen hundred years was deceived, as many continue to be today, when they assume that the author who claims to be Paul really was Paul?

Or consider the statement of an author from the 1970s who tells us: "Pseudonymity was a frequent feature in early literature. There was nothing immoral about it; it was simply the equivalent of modern anonymity. It was a mark of humility; the author, being too diffident to write under his own name, took shelter under a better-known name."[6] This author is at least right about one thing: forgery is frequent in ancient literature. But is it like "modern anonymity"? This is a rather odd thing to say about the practice. Why not say it is like "ancient" anonymity? Books were written anonymously in the ancient world as well as in the modern one, more often in fact. But this raises an enormous question that this scholar can't answer. If an author who was writing out of humility did not want to mention his own name, why didn't he simply write anonymously? Why did he attach a false name to his work, misrepresenting himself as someone else?

Or take this comment from a scholar writing in the 1990s about the pseudonymous authorship of 2 Thessalonians: "This kind of pseud-onymity should not be labeled as 'forgery.' This latter qualification implies a negative moral judgment, and we shall see that in all prob-ability the author of 2 Thessalonians, and the authors of comparable pseudonymous documents, did not consider their writings as prod-ucts of fraud. We should try to assess such writings by the standards that were accepted in the environment in which they originated."[7] This sounds like a sensible approach indeed, to evaluate the writings by ancient rather than modern standards. But this scholar never does so. He never looks at what ancient people called this practice or con-siders what they had to say about it. It is important to remember what ancient people called "this kind of pseudonymity"—they called books like this "falsely inscribed writings," "lies," and "bastards"!

Representative of this same line of thought is the work of a recent scholar who is dealing with the fact that the author of Ephesians falsely claimed to be Paul. This scholar states that such a false claim "was a widespread and accepted literary practice in both Jewish and Greco-Roman cultures. . . . There is no reason to think of the device of pseudonymity in negative terms and to associate it necessarily with such notions as forgery and deception."[8] Once again, critical readers want to know what *evidence* the author cites that the practice was "ac-cepted" and that it was not associated with "forgery and deception." But he cites none. Why? Either because the author—even though he's an otherwise reputable New Testament scholar—is not familiar with what ancient people actually said about forgery or because he doesn't dare cite what they said, since what they said runs counter to what he says.

Other scholars have allowed their theological views to cloud their historical judgment. Consider one of the most recent commentators on Colossians, who sees the work as a forgery, but maintains it is an "honest forgery" (as opposed to a dishonest one):

> The evidence from the ancient world makes it necessary to distinguish dishonest forgery, undertaken for nefarious and malicious ends, and what might be described, paradoxical as it may appear, as honest forgery. . . . It should be emphasized once again that the last option [that Colossians was not written by Paul] does not necessarily carry with it the stigma of fraud or forgery. That might apply in the case of a work written to propound some heretical doctrine, and as noted above many such works were later to be stigmatized as apocryphal or heretical, and therefore rejected. In the case of New Testament pseudepigrapha, however, the situation is somewhat different: these works came to be recognized by the Church as valid and authentic witnesses to the genuine Christian faith. . . . They witness to what the Church believed.[9]

In other words, if later, second-, third-, or fourth-century orthodox Christians agreed with the views found in the book of Colossians and decided that it should be included in the Bible, then its author was an honest forger. Other authors, however, who espoused views that later Christians rejected, were dishonest forgers. And how would the authors themselves know that centuries later their views would be accepted or not? Well, obviously, they'd have no way of knowing. So their honesty or dishonesty is rooted in circumstances completely outside of their own control.[10]

AN ALTERNATIVE PERSPECTIVE

All of the scholars I have just quoted have three things in common. All of them maintain that what I'm calling forgery—the claim of an author to be someone other than who he really is—was not a deceptive practice; all of them base their views on statements to that effect by earlier scholars rather than on an examination of the ancient sources; and all of them choose not to provide a single stitch of evidence.

That these views are wrong should be clear even from my brief examination of the ancient evidence in Chapter 1. If forgery was never thought of as wrong, why is it that in every known instance of a person being caught he is either reprimanded, abused, or punished? And if the purpose was not to deceive readers, what exactly was the purpose?

Just consider the motivations that drove authors to claim to be someone else. Some forgers did it to see if they could get away with it. Well, if no one was deceived, then how would they get away with it? Some did it to make money. But if no one was fooled, who would pay the money? Others used forgery to cast aspersions on the character of another, the person who allegedly wrote the text. But if readers knew that the alleged author wasn't the real author, how could this tactic possibly work? Some authors forged documents for military or political ends, to convince people in the name of an authority to engage in some kind of violent action or coup. But what would be convincing if the authority turned out not to be the person he claimed to be? Other forgers, probably the majority among Christians, produced their work in the name of someone else in order to make sure that their views would get a wide circulation. But if it was *known* that the alleged author didn't actually write the book—if it *wasn't* really written by Plato or Peter or Paul—why would anyone bother to read the book?

You can go through all the motivations I have documented from the ancient sources. None of them makes sense if the forgery didn't "work," that is, if no one was fooled. And as I've said, the fact that people were fooled can explain the negative and sometimes violent reactions by readers who realized they had been fooled.

This is why there is another set of scholars who talk about forgery and call it what it is—an intentional deceit. These other scholars have actually read what ancient sources say about the practice. My own teacher, Bruce M. Metzger, who knew the ancient sources like the back of his hand, asked the rhetorical question of the first group of scholars I mentioned: "How can it be so confidently known that such productions 'would deceive no one'? Indeed, if nobody was taken in by the device of pseudepigraphy, it is difficult to see why it was adopted at all."[11]

One of the finest German scholars to discuss forgery in the ancient world, Norbert Brox, after having surveyed all the ancient discussions, states explicitly: "Contemporary scholarship on forgery shows beyond any doubt that literary forgery even at that time raised the question of its own morality and was not at all tolerated as a common, purely routine and acceptable practice."[12] And the leading authority of forgery in modern times, the Austrian scholar Wolfgang Speyer, indicates plainly at the very beginning of his massive study of the phenomenon: "Every kind of forgery misrepresents the facts of the case, and to that extent forgery belongs in the realm of lying and deception."[13]

Pseudepigraphy as an Accepted Practice

OTHER SCHOLARS WHO DO not want their readers to think badly about forgeries (especially the ones in the Bible) do more than simply make blanket statements that forgers were not being deceitful. These other scholars, instead, give reasons and special circumstances under which the use of a false name was an acceptable practice in antiquity. Scholars who do so can be grouped into three major schools of thought.

PSEUDEPIGRAPHY IN THE SPIRIT

One view that was popular among scholars for years was that when an early Christian author wrote a book in someone else's name, it was because he had been inspired to do so by the Spirit of God.

When stated baldly, this sounds very much like a theological claim (and possibly not a very good one); but it is not necessarily that. You do not have to think that the Holy Spirit literally inspired a person to write this way; you could simply think that the person *believed* he was moved by the Spirit to write in the name of an early Christian authority. For this person who believed he was inspired, the words he wrote came from an impeccable authority (e.g., an apostle).

One of the chief proponents of this view was the German scholar Kurt Aland, who claimed that the earliest Christian "prophets" believed they were inspired by the Spirit and so spoke forth a kind of "prophetic word" whose authority was not themselves, but the Holy Spirit. Eventually Christian "authorities" began writing down these prophetic words. But an author could not write in his own name, as if his personal authority could back up an idea or words provided by the Spirit. The author, instead, was a kind of tool used by the Spirit (in the author's belief) to convey its own message. Aland claimed:

> Not only was the tool [i.e., the human author] by which the message was given irrelevant, but . . . it would have amounted to a falsification even to name this tool, because . . . it was not the author of the writing who really spoke, but only the authentic witness, the Holy Spirit, the Lord, the apostles.

As a result:

> When pseudonymous writings of the NT claimed the authorship of the most prominent apostles only, this was not a skillful trick of the so-called fakers, in order to guarantee the highest possible reputation and the widest possible circulation for their work, but the logical conclusion of the presupposition that the Spirit himself was the author.[14]

Despite the one-time popularity of this view among some scholars, it has never really caught on widely. For one thing, it doesn't make sense to say that in the earliest Christian tradition authors refused to use their names, because it was the Spirit who was speaking through them. Our very first author was Paul, and he uses his own name.

Second, if authors wanted to claim that it was the Spirit speaking through them, that is, that they were not grounding their message on their own authority, why wouldn't they simply say, "Thus says the Lord," or "Thus says the Spirit"? Why would they claim to be some other human—Peter, or Paul, or James—knowing full well that was not who they were? That is to say, this view can explain early *anonymous* writings, but it doesn't explain the one thing that it is trying to explain: early *pseudonymous* writings. In particular, it doesn't explain why an author would falsely claim one name instead of another for himself. If it was the Spirit that inspired the writer, why would he call himself Peter? Why not John, or Paul, or James? Or, as I suggested, why not give no name at all? As a result, this explanation, although interesting, is simply not convincing.

REACTUALIZING THE TRADITION

The next explanation of how pseudepigraphal authorship could be seen as an acceptable practice is a bit more complicated. In a nutshell, it argues that if an author understood himself to be a later representative of points of view held by a famous earlier author (who since had died, for example), he could write a document in that person's name. The purpose was not to claim that he really was that person, but to suggest that the views represented in the document were those of this older authority. Or at least they would be that authority's views, if he were still living to deal with the new situation that had arisen since his death.

A technical term for this kind of procedure is "reactualizing the tradition." A "tradition" is any point of view, teaching, or story that is passed down in writing or by word of mouth. A tradition is "reactualized" when it is made actively relevant (reactuated) to a new situation.

Suppose a highly influential author in 1917 condemned Christians who drank alcohol, on the grounds that doing so made them leave their senses and behave irresponsibly. Fifty years later, a different problem has arisen—people have started using hallucinogenic drugs. A new author wants to tell Christians that they are not to do any such thing. The new author, living in 1967, writes an essay claiming to be the famous and respected author from 1917, condemning not just alcohol consumption, but also the use of drugs. This new author stands in the tradition of the older author and makes the tradition applicable to the "actual" situation he is addressing. In other words, he has "reactualized" the tradition. By claiming the name of the author from 1917, he is not so much claiming to *be* that person as to be *continuing the tradition* of that person.

That at least is the theory, and it has been applied by some scholars to the phenomenon of pseudepigraphy in the New Testament. As one British scholar has argued, pseudonymity was "an acceptable practice, not intended to deceive," because a pseudepigraphal author continuing an older author's tradition "could present his message as the message of the originator of that stream of tradition, because in his eyes that is what it was. . . . There was no intention to deceive, and almost certainly the final readers were not in fact deceived."[15]

You can probably see one of the key problems with this view. If the people who forged the New Testament letters of, say, Peter and Paul had no "intention to deceive" and did "not in fact" deceive anyone, we again are left with the problem of why everyone (for many, many centuries) was in fact deceived. For seventeen hundred years, everyone who read these letters thought that Peter and Paul wrote them. And here again we're left with the question: What is the *evidence* that "reactualizing the tradition" by assuming a false name was a widely followed and acceptable practice?

The chief proponent of this view is the American scholar David Meade, who published his Ph.D. dissertation on the topic.[16] Meade argues that the evidence for this practice comes from the Hebrew Bible. It was customary, he says, for writings of various authors to be passed along under the name of the person who started the tradition that they saw themselves belonging to. For example, Hebrew Bible scholars for over a century have maintained that the book of Isaiah was not composed completely by the famous Isaiah of Jerusalem in the eighth century BCE. Chapters 40–55, for example, were almost certainly written by someone else living a hundred and fifty years later, during the time when the nation of Judah was in captivity in Babylon.

As Meade notes, Isaiah 40–55 was transmitted as part of the book of Isaiah. But, in Meade's view, the author of these chapters was not trying to deceive anyone into thinking he was really Isaiah of Jerusalem, from a century and a half earlier. Meade argues that he was simply claiming to belong to the same prophetic tradition as Isaiah of Jerusalem. So too the final eleven chapters of Isaiah, which were written by yet a third author, living even later. As Meade puts it, by calling these later authors "Isaiah" Jews were not making a claim about the "literary origins" of their writing (i.e., about who originally penned their books), but about their "authoritative tradition" (i.e., about which tradition—Isaiah's—they were continuing on for the new day.)

Meade finds this kind of tradition in other parts of the Hebrew Bible as well and so concludes that, when it comes to the New Testament, authors are doing something very similar. The author of 2 Peter, who was not really Peter, claims to be Peter not because he wants people to think he is Peter. He is not meaning to lie about it. He is indicating which tradition—Peter's—he sees himself belonging to.

A number of scholars have been attracted to this theory, since it can explain how authors could make false claims about themselves without lying about it, and it seems to fit into the ancient Jewish tradition of authorship. But there are very big problems with the theory.

For one thing, most of the evidence doesn't actually work. We're not sure who wrote Isaiah 40–55, other than to say that, first, it was not Isaiah of Jerusalem and, second, it was probably an Israelite living during the Babylonian captivity. We don't know if he himself physically added his own writings to the writings of Isaiah of Jerusalem (e.g., on the same scroll) or if he simply wrote his book using many of the ideas of his predecessor. That is to say, it may be that it was someone else who put the two bits of writing together, so that the author of what is now Isaiah 40–55 wasn't making any authorial claim at all, but was simply writing anonymously. Moreover, nowhere does the author of Isaiah 40–55 ever claim to be Isaiah. This is in stark contrast with, say, the author of 2 Peter, who claims to be Peter, or with the author of Ephesians, who claims to be Paul.

But even more problematic is the fact that writers of the first century, when the New Testament books were being written, did not *know* that Isaiah 40–55 was not written by Isaiah of Jerusalem. Quite the contrary, it was widely assumed that Isaiah wrote all of Isaiah! This notion that later authors were reactualizing the tradition is based on twentieth-century views of authorship of the Hebrew Bible that no one in the ancient world knew about. There is no record of anyone from the ancient world ever acknowledging this view, speaking about this view, reflecting on this view, embracing this view, supporting this view, or promoting this view. No ancient author even *mentions* this view. How would a first-century person such as the author of Colossians have any idea what had happened with the writings of Isaiah five hundred years earlier? He was living in a different country and speaking a different language; he was not a Jew himself; he read Isaiah in Greek rather than Hebrew; and for him all of Isaiah was written by Isaiah.

There is a yet another problem with this view. Even if it were true that the author of 2 Peter understood himself to be continuing the tradition of Peter, would that justify his claim to *be* Peter? What is the logic of claiming actually to be the person whose views you accept? One of the reasons this logic is faulty is that there were lots of Christians representing lots of points of view, many of which were at odds with one another. How would proponents of a tradition have reacted toward others who claimed to be from that *same* tradition, yet had something different to say? Just think of the author of the Pastorals, who claimed to be Paul even though he wasn't, and the author of the *Acts of Paul,* who claimed to be representing Paul's proclamation even though he wasn't. They have just the opposite views of women and their roles in the church. Should we think, then, that early Christians who accepted the view of the Pastorals would find it acceptable for the author of the *Acts of Paul* to put words into Paul's mouth that he didn't speak? Of course not. Would the author of the *Acts of Paul* find it acceptable for the author of the Pastorals actually to claim to be Paul, when he wasn't? Absolutely not. What would each of these authors have called the other? They would have called the other author a liar. And they would have labeled the other author's books *pseuda* (falsehoods, lies) and *notha* (bastards).

PHILOSOPHICAL SCHOOLS

One other reason Meade's explanation of forgery fails is that most of the authors of the New Testament were not part of the Jewish tradition. They were Gentiles. So other scholars have tried to find grounds for legitimizing pseudepigraphal writings in the pagan tradition, where these authors have their roots. Such scholars sometimes claim that it was common for disciples of a philosopher to write treatises and not sign their own name, but the name of their teacher. This, it is alleged, was done as an act of humility, that authors felt that their ideas were not actually theirs, but had been given to them by the leader of their philosophical school. So, to give credit where credit was due, they attached their master's name to their own writings.

New Testament scholars often claim that this can explain why someone claimed to be Paul when writing Colossians, Ephesians, or the pastoral letters. In one of the standard commentaries on Colossians, for example, we read the following: "Pseudonymous documents, especially letters with philosophical content, were set in circulation because disciples of a great man intended to express, by imitation, their adoration of their revered master and to secure or to promote his influence upon a later generation under changed circumstances."[17] A more recent commentator on Colossians and Ephesians states something similar: "Viewing Colossians (or Ephesians) as deutero-Pauline should not be mistakenly understood as meaning that these documents are simply examples of forgery. For example, to write in the name of a philosopher who was one's patron could be seen as a sign of honor bestowed upon that person."[18]

I should point out that, as happens so often, neither of these commentators actually provides any evidence that this was a common practice in philosophical schools. They state it as a fact. And why do they think it's a fact? For most New Testament scholars it is thought to be a fact because, well, so many New Testament scholars have said so! But ask someone who makes this claim what her ancient source of information is or what ancient philosopher actually states that this was a common practice. More often than not you'll be met with a blank stare.

The scholars who do mention ancient evidence for this alleged practice typically point to two major sources.[19] But one of the two says no such thing. This is the third-century Neoplatonic philosopher Porphyry, who is alleged to have said that in the school of the ancient philosopher Pythagoras (who lived eight hundred years earlier) it was a common practice for disciples to write books and sign their master's name to them.[20] This statement by Porphyry is a little hard to track down, because it is not in his surviving Greek writings; it is only in an Arabic translation of one of his works from the thirteenth century.[21]

I doubt if any of the New Testament scholars who refer to this statement of Porphyry's has actually read it, since it is, after all, in Arabic, and most New Testament scholars don't read Arabic. I don't either. But I have a colleague who does, Carl Ernst, an expert in medieval Islam. I asked Professor Ernst to translate the passage for me. As it turns out, Porphyry doesn't say anything about followers of Pythagoras writing books and then signing his name to them. Instead, he says that Pythagoras himself wrote eighty books, two hundred books were written by his followers, and twelve books were "forged" in the name of Pythagoras. The twelve books are condemned for using Pythagoras's name when he didn't write them. The forgers are called "shameless people" who "fabricated" "false books." The two hundred books are not said to have been written by Pythagoras's followers in his name; they were simply books written by Pythagoras's followers.

This, then, is one of the two ancient references sometimes cited by scholars to indicate that the practice of writing in a master's name was "common." I should point out that, in Porphyry's other writings as well as in this passage, he shows a keen interest in knowing which books are authentic and which are forged, and he condemns the forgeries, including the Old Testament book of Daniel, which he thinks could not have been written by an Israelite in the sixth century BCE.

The other reference to a tradition in the philosophical schools does say what scholars have said it says. This one is in the writings of Iamblichus, another Neoplatonic philosopher from about the same time as Porphyry. In his account of Pythagoras's life, Iamblichus says the following: "This also is a beautiful circumstance, that they [i.e., Pythagoras's followers] referred everything to Pythagoras, and called it by his name, and that they did not ascribe to themselves the glory of their own inventions, except very rarely. For there are very few whose works are acknowledged to be their own."[22]

There are lots of problems with taking this one statement as an indication of what "typically" happened in the philosophical schools of antiquity as a model for what the Christian authors did when claiming to be Peter, Paul, James, Thomas, Philip, and others:

1. For this tradition to have made an impact on such a wide array of early Christian authors, it would have had to be widely known. But it wasn't. The tradition is not mentioned by a single author from the time of Pythagoras (sixth century BCE) to the time of Iamblichus (third to fourth century CE). As a result, there is nothing to suggest this view was widely known. Quite the contrary, no one else seems to have known it for eight hundred years.

2. More specifically, Iamblichus was living two hundred years after the writings of 1 and 2 Peter and the Deutero-Paulines.

There is no reference to this tradition existing in the time of the New Testament writings. It could scarcely have been seen as a widely accepted practice at the time.

3. Iamblichus refers to what happened only within one of the many philosophical schools. He makes no claims about a wider tradition in philosophical schools outside of Pythagorean circles.

4. As recent scholars of Pythagoreanism have pointed out, there is reason to think that what Iamblichus says in fact is not even true of the Pythagorean school:[23]

a. First, he was writing eight hundred years after Pythagoras and would have had no way of knowing that what he was saying is true. He may well simply have thought this is how it worked.

b. None of the other philosophers or historians who talk about Pythagoras and his school prior to Iamblichus says any such thing about pseudonymous works written in his name.

c. Iamblichus's comment is completely casual and off the cuff.

d. To cap it all off, when Iamblichus's statement can be checked, it appears to be wrong. The vast majority of the writings of the Pythagorean school were not done in the name of Pythagoras. His followers wrote in their own names.[24]

As a result, the brief and casual comment by Iamblichus (who, it must be remembered, lived more than two hundred years after Paul and Peter) cannot at all be taken as evidence of what happened in the days of Pythagoras and his students (six hundred years before Paul and Peter), let alone what happened commonly in the philosophical schools, let alone what probably happened in early Christianity.[25]

For these reasons, New Testament scholars need to revise their views about philosophical schools and their impact on the forgery practices of early Christians. There is almost nothing to suggest that there was a tradition in these schools to practice pseudepigraphy as an act of humility. I would suggest that scholars have latched onto this idea simply because it gives them a way of talking about what happened in the literary tradition of early Christianity without saying that early Christian authors were guilty of forgery.

The Secretary Hypothesis

THE THREE GROUPS OF scholars I have mentioned all think that under certain conditions pseudepigraphy was an acceptable practice in antiquity. For that reason, in these scholars' opinion, the authors of early Christian writings should not be thought of as lying when they claimed to be someone other than who they were. There is one other school of thought to consider, one that says that in a number of cases what *appears* to be forgery in fact is not. The scholars who argue this are not claiming, on theological grounds, that there could be no such thing as forgery in early Christianity. They are claiming, on historical grounds, that some books that appear to be pseudonymous in fact are not. That is because the real author, who actually was who he claimed to be, used a secretary, and the secretary wrote in a different style from the author himself. Sometimes the real author may have dictated a letter word for word to a secretary. But other times he may have asked his secretary to rework his letter to improve the style. At still other times an author may have simply told a secretary to write a letter for him, so that both the contents and the style of the letter are the secretary's, even if the ultimate "authority" for the letter is the author who is named.

This is a very popular theory; you will find it expressed everywhere in biblical commentaries on the deutero-Pauline and Petrine letters. It explains why 1 Peter seems to have a different writing style from 2 Peter. It explains why the views of the disputed "Pauline" letter of Ephesians seem to differ so radically from the views of the undisputed letter to the Romans. Virtually all of the problems with what I've been calling forgeries can be solved if secretaries were heavily involved in the composition of the early Christian writings. Despite the popularity of this theory, I am going to argue, once again, that it simply does not have credible evidence to back it up.

Whole books have been devoted to the question in recent years. The fullest and most exhaustive is by E. Randolph Richards, called *The Secretary in the Letters of Paul.*[26] Richards looks at all the evidence for secretaries in the ancient world. He diligently peruses the letters of the most famous letter writer of Rome, the statesman and philosopher Cicero. For most of these letters Cicero used secretaries. Richards considers all the other great figures of the empire known to have used secretaries (Brutus, Pompey, and Marcus Aurelius, for example). He looks at every reference to secretaries he can find in the ancient letters that still survive on papyrus, most of which have been discovered in Egypt over the course of the past century. And he considers what early Christian sources themselves have to say about letters and secretaries. It is a full and very useful study.

There is no doubt that the apostle Paul used a secretary on occasion. One of his secretaries tells us that he has written the letter! In Romans 16:22 we read, "I Tertius, the one who wrote this letter, greet you in the Lord." Tertius does not mean to say that he was the "author" of the letter. He was the scribe who wrote what Paul told him to write. Paul also used a scribe for his letter to the Galatians, since at the very end he tells his readers, "See with what large letters I am writing to you with my own hand" (6:11). Commentators are widely agreed that Paul had dictated the letter to a secretary, but here at the end he was writing the final bit himself. He used larger handwriting either because he wasn't as skilled at writing as the secretary, because he had problems with his eyesight and so wrote larger letters, or for some other reason.

Did Paul use a secretary for all of his letters? It is impossible to say. Did the secretaries contribute to the contents of the letter? This is easier to say. Despite what scholars often claim, all of the evidence we have suggests that the answer is no. The same evidence applies to the authors of 1 Peter, 2 Peter, and in fact to all the other early Christian writers.

In his study Richards argues that secretaries were used in four distinct ways for the writing of letters. Most of the time a secretary simply recorded what the author dictated to him, either slowly, syllable by syllable; in some kind of shorthand while the author spoke at natural speed; or something in between. Other times a secretary was asked by an author to correct the grammar and improve the style of what the author either wrote or dictated. On occasion, Richards claims, a secretary was a kind of coauthor who contributed his own thoughts and ideas to a letter. And sometimes, Richards states, a secretary actually composed an entire letter on behalf of the author, so that all the words and thoughts were actually the secretary's, even if the author signed off on what he had written.

If secretaries actually did commonly, or at least occasionally, work in these latter ways, then it would make sense that different letters by the same "author" might read very differently from one another not just in writing style, but in content. So what is the evidence that it worked this way?

There is no doubt about Richards's first category. There is abundant evidence—you can read it all in Richards's study—that authors often dictated letters instead of writing them out themselves. When that happened, the author was really the author. He didn't himself put pen to papyrus, but the thoughts are his thoughts, the words are his words, the grammar is his grammar. No problems there.

It is with the other three categories that we begin to have problems. One very severe problem is the nature of our evidence. Virtually all of it comes from authors who were very, very wealthy and powerful and inordinately well educated. These were the very upper class, the highest tier of the cultured elite: emperors, consuls, and senators. It is a genuine question how relevant that evidence is for people who were of the lower classes, who may have been moderately well educated, which would put them way ahead of most people of course, but far below a Cicero or a Marcus Aurelius. The papyri—that is, the surviving private letters that were written by regular folk instead of the elite of society—do not give us any help in knowing about these other three categories.

Another problem has to do with the nature of the "letters" involved. Most letters in the Greco-Roman world were very short and to the point. They were one page or less. They had very limited content. Most commonly the author would say who he was, indicate to whom he was writing, offer a brief thanks to the gods for the recipient, indicate his information or his request, and then sign off. Bam-bam-bam and done.

The reason this is a "problem" is that the letters of early Christianity that we are concerned about—the letter to the Ephesians, for example, or 1 Peter—are not like that at all. They are lengthy treatises that deal with large and complex issues in the form of a letter. They do have the stylistic features of ancient letters: the names of the author and the recipient, a thanksgiving, the body of the letter, and the closing. But they are so much more extensive than typical letters, for example, in their theological expositions, ethical exhortations, and quotation of and interpretation of Scripture. These New Testament "letters" are really more like essays put in letter form. So evidence that derives from the brief, stereotyped letters typically found in Greek and Roman circles is not necessarily germane to the "letters" of the early Christians.

With these caveats in mind, what can we say about the three other categories that Richards lays out, secretaries who improve an author's style, who coauthor a letter, or who compose a letter? There is some evidence, though it is very limited, that secretaries occasionally were asked to improve the author's style. The evidence is all from the very top echelons of the upper class of ancient Rome, a letter from the military commander Brutus and another from the emperor Marcus Aurelius, for example. It is difficult to know whether this procedure was used widely, or at all, outside of the circles of the ultrarich landed aristocracy.

The evidence of the other types of letters—at least as cited by Richards—is virtually nonexistent, as he himself says. When talking about the possibility that some letters were coauthored by both the author and his secretary, Richards points to one possible example, letters written by Cicero and his secretary Tiro. But Richards then discounts the suggestion that Tiro coauthored the letters with Cicero and shows why the suggestion is probably wrong. Remarkably this is the one and only example that Richards mentions before concluding, "Evidently then . . . secretaries were used as coauthors"! It is hard to see what makes this "evident" when he hasn't cited a single instance of it. Maybe other scholars (or Richards himself) will eventually be able to find some evidence.

There is a similar problem with the idea that secretaries sometimes composed letters themselves for someone else. It is true that illiterate persons sometimes required the services of a scribal secretary to draw up a land deed, marriage certificate, sales receipt, or some other document, and that they occasionally (but rarely) used scribal secretaries to write brief stereotyped letters. Even the upper classes would sometimes instruct a secretary to spin off a quick stereotyped letter for them to someone, as is evidenced on several occasions by Cicero. So far as Richards's evidence goes, it is only Cicero who did this, no one else. But drafting a brief stereotyped letter is completely different from composing a long, detailed, finely argued, carefully reasoned, and nuanced letter like 1 Peter or Ephesians. What evidence is there that essay-letters of that sort were ever handed over to a secretary to be composed? There is absolutely no evidence that I know of.

Richards hasn't seen any evidence of it either. When Cicero asked a secretary to compose a quick stereotyped letter for him and make it look as if it came from him, Cicero, he was doing what no other person is known to have done in antiquity. As Richards himself says: "It is tempting to conclude that an author-initiated request for deception was rare indeed, perhaps singularly restricted to Cicero and to this time in his life" (i.e., when he was old, tired, and unwilling to write a letter himself).[27]

What about other secretaries who may have composed a letter (not even a letter-essay) for another author? Again, according to Richards: "Nowhere was there *any* indication that an ordinary secretary was asked, much less presumed, to compose a letter for the author." On the contrary, "without an explicit reference to the use of a secretary as a composer of a letter, this secretarial method probably should not even be considered a valid option."[28] There is certainly no such explicit reference in the deutero-Pauline or Petrine letters.

I don't know of a single piece of evidence or a single analogy to suggest that Peter or Paul used a secretary who significantly—or insignificantly, for that matter—added to the contents of the letter. That is why it is important to consider not only the style of writing, but also the contents when considering whether Paul did or did not write, say, Ephesians or 1 Timothy, or that Peter did or did not write 1 or 2 Peter. When a person claimed to write a letter, he was owning up to the contents. Sometimes a letter attributed to Paul is at odds with what Paul says elsewhere, as when Ephesians differs from Paul's view of the resurrection of believers as found in his letter to the Romans. Since secretaries did not produce the contents of letters (at least letter-essays of this sort), a secretary could not be responsible for the difference. So Paul is probably in no way responsible for the disputed letter. Other times what one finds in a letter cannot be plausibly explained as coming from the reputed author. Whoever wrote 1 Peter, for example, was a highly educated Greek-speaking Christian who understood how to use Greek rhetorical devices and could cite the Greek Old Testament with flair and nuance. That does not apply to the uneducated, illiterate, Aramaic-speaking fisherman from rural

Galilee, and it does not appear to have been produced by a secretary acting on his behalf.

As I pointed out in Chapter 2, it also helps to think concretely about how the secretary hypothesis might explain how Peter himself could have written 1 Peter. He could not have dictated the letter to a secretary, because he was not trained in Greek compositional and rhetorical techniques. Nor could he have dictated the letter in Aramaic and asked the secretary to translate it into Greek, because the letter contains sophisticated forms of argumentation and presentation that work only in Greek and presupposes knowledge of the Greek Old Testament, not the Hebrew version, which Peter himself would have been familiar with. And it does not seem possible that Peter gave the general gist of what he wanted to say and that a secretary then created the letter for him in his name, since, first, then the secretary rather than Peter would be the real author of the letter, and second, and even more important, we don't seem to have any analogy for a procedure like this from the ancient world.

Historians have to decide what probably happened in the past. Which is more probable—a scenario that does not have any known analogy (Peter asking someone else to write the treatise in his name) or a scenario that has lots and lots of analogies, since it happened all the time? Forgeries happened all the time. Surely that's the best explanation for what is going on here.

The same applies to the letters bearing Paul's name that he did not write, in which the contents, not just the style, differ significantly from the views of Paul himself. These letters were not produced by secretaries. They were produced by later Christian authors claiming to be Paul. As a result, the secretary hypothesis, as promising as it looks at first glance, simply can't explain away the forgeries of the New Testament.

Conclusion

I CAN WRAP UP these first four chapters by making a series of summary statements. There were a large number of literary forgeries in early Christianity, some of which may be found in the New Testament. These really are forgeries, books whose authors claim to be well-known authority figures, even though they were someone else. Some scholars today avoid the term "forgery" and call these writings pseudonymous or pseudepigraphal; technically speaking, these other terms are correct, but they are imprecise. Pseudonymous writings include writings produced under a pen name, and none of the writings we have been considering fall into that category. Pseudepigraphal writings include originally anonymous writings that were later wrongly attributed to well-known figures. The books we are talking about are by authors who lied about their identity in order to deceive their readers into thinking that they were someone they were not. The technical term for this kind of activity is forgery.

Forgery in antiquity was different from forgery today in some important respects, and these differences need to be constantly borne in mind. Most important, in the modern day, forgery connotes an illegal activity that can land a person in jail. In the ancient world there were no laws against such things, and so the practice should not be thought of as illegal. But this difference is not significant enough to require us to use a different term for the practice. "Books" in the ancient world, for example, were quite different from books today. They were written on scrolls and were not mass produced. Still, that doesn't stop anyone from calling them books. Forgeries in the ancient world were different in some ways from forgeries today, but they were still forgeries.

The negative connotations of the term are appropriate to the ancient phenomenon. Ancient authors called such works falsely inscribed writings, lies, and "illegitimate children." Multiple attempts by modern scholars to see the practice in a more positive light simply don't stand up to scrutiny. The most common claims found widely, both among scholars and laypeople, are that this practice was widely accepted in philosophical schools or that the phenomenon can be explained by assuming that an author made use of a secretary who composed the writing himself. Neither explanation has adequate support in the ancient sources.

It is important to recall that ancient writers who mention the practice of forgery consistently condemn it and indicate that it is deceitful, inappropriate, and wrong. If we are to do so as well probably depends on a number of factors. Modern readers who are religiously committed to the teachings of the New Testament may want to excuse the authors who deceived their readers about their identity, on the grounds, for example, that they were lying in order to achieve a greater good. Other readers may be inclined to acknowledge that the authors violated ancient ethical standards and are best described as I have done so here—as forgers.

CHAPTER FIVE

Forgeries in Conflicts with Jews and Pagans

IN THE NEW TESTAMENT, JESUS is reputed to have said, "I did not come to bring peace on earth, but a sword" (Matt. 10:34). Truer words were never spoken. Many Christians in the modern age think of their religion as peace loving, as well it often has been and should be. But anyone with any grasp of history at all knows also just how violent Christians have been over the ages, sponsoring oppression, injustice, wars, crusades, pogroms, inquisitions, holocausts—all in the name of the faith. Maybe all the Christians behind history's hateful acts were acting in bad faith; maybe they were violating the true principles of their own religion; maybe they were out of touch with the peace-loving teachings of the Good Shepherd of the sheep. And no one should deny the amazing good that has been done in the name of Christ, the countless acts of selfless love, the mind-boggling sacrifices made to help those in need. Even so, few religions in the history of the human race have shown a greater penchant for conflict than the religion founded on the teachings of Jesus, who, true to his word, did indeed bring a sword.

Some early Christians realized that the religion would be based on conflict. The author of the New Testament book of Ephesians, allegedly Paul, tells his readers to "put on the full armor of God" (6:10–20). Their struggle was not against mortal flesh, but "against authorities, against the cosmic power of this present darkness, against the spiritual forces of evil in the heavenly places." Against these cosmic enemies Christian believers were to put on the breastplate of righteousness, the shield of faith, the helmet of salvation, and "the sword of the Spirit, which is the word of God." This was not a battle, then, against human enemies, but against the spiritual powers arrayed against God. But it was a battle nonetheless.

It is striking that in his instructions about the Christian "armor" the author of Ephesians also tells his readers, "Fasten the belt of truth around your waist" (6:14). Truth was important for this writer. Early on he refers to the gospel as "the word of truth" (1:13). He later indicates that the "truth is in Jesus" and tells his readers to "speak the truth" to their neighbors (4:24–25). He also claims that the "fruit of the light" is found in "truth" (5:9). How ironic, then, that the author has deceived his readers about his own identity. The book was written pseudonymously in the name of Paul by someone who knew full well that he was not Paul. Falsely claiming to be an impeccable Christian authority, this advocate for truth produced a pseudepigraphon, a "falsely inscribed writing." At least that is what ancient critics would have called it, had they known the author was not Paul. So some Christians went into battle armed not with truth, but with deception. Possibly the author felt justified in lying about his identity. There was, after all, a lot at stake.

Christians entered into conflict not merely with spiritual forces, but also with human ones. Or, perhaps more accurately from the author's point of view, the spiritual forces aligned against Christians manifested themselves in the human sphere, and it was on this level that the battles were actually fought. As historians of early Christianity have long known, Christians in the early centuries of the church were in constant conflict and felt under attack from all sides. They were at odds with Jews, who considered their views to be an aberrant and upstart perversion of the ancestral traditions of Israel. They were at odds with pagan peoples and governments, who considered them a secretive and unauthorized religion that posed a danger to the state. And they were most vehemently and virulently at odds with each other, as different Christian teachers and groups argued that they and they alone had a corner on the truth and other Christian teachers and groups flat-out misunderstood the truths that Christ had proclaimed during his time on earth.

In all these battles, the "full armor of God" included weapons of deceit. Forgery was used by one Christian author or another in order to fend off the attacks of Jews and pagans and to assault the views of other Christians who had alternative, aberrant understandings of the faith. In this chapter I consider the conflicts with outsiders, the Jews and pagans opposed to the Christian faith. In the next chapter I take up the internal conflicts that plagued the Christian church from the beginning.

The Jewish Reaction to Christian Claims

MANY CONSERVATIVE EVANGELICAL CHRISTIANS today cannot understand why Jews do not accept the claim that Jesus is the messiah. For these Christians it all seems so obvious. The Old Testament predicted what the messiah would be like. Jesus did and experienced the things predicted. So of course he is the messiah. The Old Testament said he would be born of a virgin (Isa. 7:14), in Bethlehem (Mic. 5:2); that he would have to flee as a child to Egypt and then come out from there (Hos. 11:1); and that he would be raised in Nazareth, so that he would be called a Nazarene (Isa. 11:1). It predicted that he would minister in Galilee (Isa. 9:1–2) and would be a great healer (53:4). It predicted his triumphal entry into Jerusalem to the acclamations of the crowd (Isa. 62:11; Zech. 9:9), his cleansing of the Temple (Jer. 7:11), and his rejection by the Jewish leaders (Ps. 118:22–23). Most important, it predicted his crucifixion for the sins of others and his glorious resurrection from the dead (Pss. 22; 110; Isa. 53).

Jesus did everything that was predicted. Why don't the Jews see this? It is in their own Scriptures! Can't they read? Are they blind? Are they stupid?

The truth, of course, is that Jews throughout history have been no more illiterate, blind, or stupid than Christians. The typical response of Jews to the Christian claims that Jesus fulfilled prophecy is that the scriptural passages that Christians cite are either not speaking of a future messiah or are not making predictions at all. And one has to admit, just looking at this set of debates from the outside, the Jewish readers have a point. In the passages allegedly predicting the death and resurrection of Jesus, for example, the term "messiah" in fact never does occur. Many Christians are surprised by this claim, but just read Isaiah 53 for yourself and see.

Most ancient Jews rejected the messiahship of Jesus for the simple reason that Jesus was not at all like what most Jews expected a messiah to be. I should stress that a lot of Jews in the ancient world were not sitting on the edge of their seats waiting for a messiah, any more than most Jews today are. But there were groups of highly religious Jews around the time of Jesus who thought that God would send a messiah figure to deliver them from their very serious troubles. All these groups based their expectations on the Hebrew Bible, of course; but there were different expectations of what this messianic savior would be like.[1]

The term "messiah" comes from a Hebrew word that means "anointed one." It was originally, in the Hebrew Bible, used in reference to the king of Israel, a figure like King Saul, King David, or King Solomon. The king was literally "anointed" with oil on his head during his inauguration ceremony, in order to show that God's special favor rested upon him in a unique way (see, e.g., Ps. 2). After a time, when there were no more kings over Israel, some Jews thought that God would send a future king, an anointed one like great King David of old, who, like David, would lead Israel's armies against its enemies and reestablish Israel once again as a sovereign state in the land. This future king, then, was to be the messiah, a completely human being who was a powerful warrior and great ruler of God's people.

Other, more cosmically minded Jews thought that this future savior would be a supernatural figure sent from heaven, a kind of cosmic judge of the earth who would engage the enemy with overpowering force before setting up a kingdom here on earth to be ruled by God's chosen one. Yet other Jews were principally focused on what we might call the "religion" of Israel, as opposed to its political situation. These Jews thought that the future ruler of the people would be a mighty priest who would empower the people of Israel by teaching them the correct interpretation of the Jewish law. He would rule God's people, then, by enforcing the observance of what God had demanded in Scripture.

In short, there were a variety of expectations of what a future "anointed" figure, a messiah, would be like. The one thing these conceptions of the future savior had in common was that they all expected him to be a figure of grandeur and might, empowered by God to overthrow the enemies and to rule the people of God with authority.

The followers of Jesus, on the other hand, claimed that he was the messiah. And who was Jesus? A little known preacher from backwoods Galilee who had offended the ruling authorities and was, as a result, subjected to public humiliation and torture and executed as a low-life criminal on a cross. For most Jews, it would have been hard to imagine anyone *less* like the expected messiah than Jesus of Nazareth.

But that is what Christians claimed, that Jesus was the messiah. The earliest Christians became convinced of this claim, because they believed that Jesus was actually, physically, raised by God from the dead. God had shown that Jesus was not just a lowly criminal or a powerless preacher. God had in fact empowered him to conquer the greatest enemy of all, death itself. Jesus had ascended to heaven and is now seated at the right hand of God, and he is waiting to come back to establish his rule over the earth. According to this early Christian view, the Jewish expectations of the messiah were true. The messiah would overthrow the enemies of God in a show of strength. But before doing that he needed to conquer the bigger enemies, the evil powers of sin and death that were aligned against God and his people. Jesus conquered sin at the cross, and he conquered death at his resurrection. He, then, is the messiah. And he is coming back to finish the job.

For followers of Jesus, therefore, Scripture must have predicted not only the powerful aspects of the messiah's "second" coming, but also the significant events of his "first" coming. So Christians scoured the texts of Scripture to find passages that could feasibly refer to the birth, life, death, and resurrection of Jesus. Christians were certain that these passages (virgin birth in Bethlehem, triumphal entry, death for the sins of others, and so on) referred to Jesus, because Jesus was the messiah and the Scriptures predicted the messiah. Most Jews were not convinced, however, because none of these passages actually speaks about the messiah, the Hebrew Bible never states that the messiah would come twice, and Jesus's life was anything but the glorious life of God's anointed one.

And so there were deep and difficult conflicts from the beginning. In the early stages, Jews far outnumbered Christians and could easily overwhelm them. But Christians continually struck back and kept arguing. And arguing and arguing and arguing. Among other things, many Christian Jews couldn't understand why non-Christian Jews didn't see their point and didn't accept the "fact" that Jesus was the messiah. The proofs were all there, right in the Scriptures themselves! As battle lines became more firmly drawn and both sides dug in and used harsher tactics, Christians began to argue that Jews who rejected Jesus were just as responsible for Jesus's death as the Jewish authorities who had originally called for it. Rejecting Jesus was tantamount to killing him.

And so non-Christian Jews came to be known as people who had killed their own messiah—Christ-killers. They obviously misunderstood their own Scriptures, and they had rejected their own God. As a result, God had rejected them.

It was in this context that a significant amount of literature was produced by both sides, especially by Christians. Some of this literature we still have today. A letter allegedly by Barnabas, companion of the apostle Paul, claims that Jews have always misunderstood their own religion by interpreting the law of Moses literally instead of figuratively, so that the Old Testament is not a Jewish, but a Christian book. There is a writing by the famous second-century Christian martyr Justin, in which he has a debate with a Jewish rabbi and shows him the errors of his interpretations of his own Scriptures. A sermon by Melito, a Christian bishop of the late second century, claims that Jews have not only rejected their messiah, but in killing him, the Son of God, they are guilty of deicide: they have killed God himself. And so it went.

Among the works produced by Christians in this back-and-forth were a number of forgeries, books written in the names of authoritative figures of the past intending to show the brilliant truth of Christianity and the horrendous errors of the Jews. In particular there were a number of forgeries that stressed the true character of Jesus: he was a divine being, not a mere mortal, as acknowledged by the Roman authorities. In these writings it was not the Romans, but the Jewish leaders, or even the Jewish people themselves, who were responsible for Jesus's crucifixion.

Some Resultant Forgeries

THE GOSPEL OF PETER

We have already seen one forgery that was written, at least in part, to set forth this view. The *Gospel of Peter* (discussed in Chapter 2) emphasizes that "none of the Jews" was willing to wash his hands to show that he was innocent of Jesus's blood. In this Gospel it is the Jewish king Herod, not Pilate, who orders Jesus's death. And afterwards the Jewish people show their remorse for killing God's chosen one and acknowledge that now God will surely judge them and bring destruction to their holy city of Jerusalem, a reference to the Roman war that resulted in the burning of the Temple, the leveling of the walls, and the slaughter of the Jewish opposition in 70 CE.

The *Gospel of Peter* is one of the earliest Gospels from after the New Testament period, possibly written around 120 CE or so. Anti-Jewish Gospel forgeries became increasingly popular with time, especially as Christianity grew and was able to assert its power more convincingly.

THE GOSPEL OF NICODEMUS

One of the most intriguing Gospels comes near the end of the time period I am considering in this book, the first four Christian centuries. It is a lengthy account of Jesus's trial, death, and resurrection that falsely claims to be written by none other than Nicodemus, the rabbi well known to Christian readers for his important role in the Gospel of John as a "secret" follower of Jesus (see 3:1–15).[2] The *Gospel of Nicodemus* became an extraordinarily popular and influential book throughout the Middle Ages, as it was widely circulated in the Latin West and was eventually translated and disseminated in nearly all of the languages of western Europe. It was, of course, believed to have been written by Nicodemus himself. But the account was probably composed sometime in the fourth century, three hundred years after Nicodemus's death (assuming he was a historical figure). It may well be based, however, on stories that had been passed down orally for two centuries before being written down.

The Gospel begins by indicating that Nicodemus had originally written the narrative in Hebrew. In fact, the account appears to be an original Greek composition. But by claiming that it appeared first in Hebrew the real author, whoever he was, provided it with an air of authenticity, showing both that the narrative was very old and that it was (supposedly) based on eyewitness testimony.

There is no question that the account is far from historical, as it is rooted in later legends about Jesus's final hours, his death, and his resurrection. The narrative is designed to show that Pilate was completely innocent of Jesus's execution, that the Jewish leaders and people were completely at fault, and that by rejecting Jesus the Jews have rejected God.

The divine character of Jesus is established at the outset of the narrative in one of its most interesting, and amusing, scenes. Before Jesus's trial, the Jewish authorities are speaking with Pilate, insisting that Jesus is guilty of crimes and needs to be condemned. Pilate has his courier bring Jesus into the courtroom. Inside the room are two slaves holding "standards" that have—as Roman standards did—an image of the "divine" Caesar on them. As Jesus enters the room, the standard bearers bow down before him, so that the image of Caesar appears to be doing obeisance in his presence.

The Jewish authorities are incensed and malign the standard bearers, who reply that they had nothing to do with it. The images of Caesar bowed down of their own accord to worship Jesus. Pilate decides to try to get to the bottom of the matter and so tells the Jewish leaders to pick some of their own husky men to hold the standards and to have Jesus go out and enter a second time. The leaders choose twelve muscular Jews, six for each standard, who grasp them with all their might. Jesus reenters the room, and once again the standards bow down before him.

You might think that everyone would get the point, but that would ruin the story. Pilate becomes terrified and tries to get Jesus off the hook, but to no avail. The Jewish authorities declare that Jesus is an evildoer who deserves to die. Repeatedly throughout the course of the trial they accuse Jesus of wrongdoing and insist that he be judged. And just as repeatedly Pilate insists that he is innocent of all charges, expresses puzzlement about why the Jews are so intent on seeing him killed, and urges the Jewish leaders to allow him to release Jesus. But they refuse, wanting him dead. Three times they express their willingness to assume responsibility by speaking the words of Matthew 27:25, "His blood be upon us and our children."

When these words were first written centuries earlier, in Matthew's Gospel, they already expressed anti-Jewish sentiment. By speaking them, the Jewish crowds showed that they were willing not only to incur the guilt for Jesus's death, but also to pass along that guilt to future generations of Jews. Over the centuries the words were used by Christian opponents of Jews to blame the Jews for the death of Jesus and to inflict horrible acts of violence against them in retribution. That heightened form of anti-Judaism is already in evidence here, in the *Gospel of Nicodemus*. The Jewish authorities are shown to be willfully blind to Jesus's true character. Even the emperor worships him (in the standards). And a number of witnesses are called who recount all the miracles he performed as the Son of God.

But to no avail. Jesus is crucified at the instigation of the Jews and their leaders. The rest of the account shows the truth of Jesus's divine character. He is raised from the dead, and the Jewish leaders themselves are given incontrovertible proof of the resurrection through the testimony of reliable witnesses.

Here, then, is a forged account, written some three hundred years after the events it narrates, to show that Jesus's death was undeserved, that the Romans (who were on the side of Christians by the midfourth century) had nothing to do with the crucifixion, that it was completely the Jews' fault, and that by rejecting Jesus the Jews have actually rejected their own God. No wonder an account such as this became so popular throughout western Europe in the Middle Ages, when hatred of the Jews was a constant and disturbing aspect of what it meant to be Christian.

The "Pilate Gospels"

A number of writings from about the time of the *Gospel of Nicodemus* are in one way or another connected with Pontius Pilate and his role in the death of Jesus. Most of these are designed to show that Pilate was not at fault for the death of Jesus and that he felt considerable remorse after the deed was done. In several of these writings we learn that Pilate not only repented of the evil deed, but actually became a believer in Christ. In later Christianity the conversion of

Pilate became part of the accepted lore from the early church. In the Coptic church Pilate was eventually canonized as a Christian saint.

Historically, of course, nothing could be farther from the truth. Pilate continued on as a brutal governor of Judea after the death of Jesus. There is nothing in the historical record to suggest that he even remembered having ordered Jesus's execution, let alone felt regret over it. Still, the reason for his later exoneration and even exaltation in parts of the Christian church is reasonably clear. If Pilate was not responsible for Jesus's death, then who was? The Jews. The legends of Pilate came to be written in a series of documents that may go back to the fourth Christian century or even earlier. A number of them are allegedly written by Pilate himself. All of them, however, are forged.

The Letter of Herod to Pilate

The first document we consider was not said to have been written by Pilate, but to him, by his colleague Herod Antipas, the *Letter of Herod to Pilate*. Historically Pilate is known to have been the Roman governor of Judea, in the southern part of Israel, when Herod Antipas, the son of Herod the Great (the ruler of the land when Jesus was born), was the Jewish ruler of Galilee, in the northern part of the land. Herod Antipas is best known from biblical tradition for having beheaded John the Baptist. In later legends he is said to have regretted what he did very much, as it came back to haunt him.

That is the case in this letter forged in his name, allegedly sent to Pilate.[3] Here Herod indicates that he is sorry to learn that Pilate had Jesus killed, because he, Herod, wanted to see him and to repent for the evil things he had done. God's judgment on sinners, he states, fits their crime. In a bizarre incident that he relates, his own daughter has literally lost her head in a flood that arose while she was playing on the banks of a river. The flood began to sweep her away, when her mother reached out to save her by grabbing her head. But her head was severed, so that the mother was left with just the child's head in her hands. This came, Herod states, as retribution for his having taken the head of John the Baptist.

He himself is suffering, rotting away even before he has died, so that he says, "Already worms are coming from my mouth." Here the pseudonymous author appears to confuse this Herod with the later Herod Agrippa, who according to the New Testament book of Acts was eaten by worms and died (Acts 12). So too the Roman soldier Longinus—the one who allegedly stuck a spear in Jesus's side when he was on the cross—has met a grisly fate. He is condemned to a cave where every night a lion comes and mauls his body until dawn. The next day his body grows back to normal, and the lion then comes again. This will go on until the end of time.

Pilate, however, the recipient of the letter, is portrayed in a positive light, as a representative of the Gentiles. Not they, but the Jews, will face judgment for what they did to Jesus: "Death will soon overtake the priests and the ruling council of the children of Israel, because they unjustly laid hands on the righteous Jesus." It is the Gentiles, then, who will inherit God's kingdom, whereas Herod and the other Jews "will be cast out," because they "did not keep the commandments of the Lord or those of his Son."

The Letter of Pilate to Herod

A second forged letter goes in the opposite direction, from Pilate to Herod.[4] One might expect this letter to be a response to the first, but despite its title, the *Letter of Pilate to Herod*, and the fact that it names some of the same characters (Herod, Pilate, and Longinus, the spear-wielding soldier), they have almost nothing else in common. In fact, this second letter does not refer to the first and stands at odds with it at a key point. Here Longinus, rather than being subject to never ending torment for what he did, is portrayed as a convert who came to believe in Jesus after the resurrection. That, in fact, is the point of this second letter, that when Jesus was raised, not only Longinus, but also Pilate's wife, Procla, and then Pilate himself, all became believers.

According to the narrative of the letter, after Pilate did "a terrible thing" in having Jesus crucified, he hears that he was raised from the dead. Procla and Longinus go to find Jesus in Galilee. There he speaks with them, and they become convinced of his resurrection. When Pilate learns that Jesus has returned to life, he falls to the ground in deep grief. But then Jesus himself appears to him, raises him from the ground, and declares to him, "All generations and nations will bless you." Here Pilate is not only repentant; he is a Christian convert who will be considered fortunate by later adherents of the faith.

The Letter of Pilate to Claudius

We have another letter allegedly from Pilate to a Roman official, but this time it is supposedly directed to the Roman emperor Claudius, written to explain Pilate's role in the death of Jesus, the *Letter of Pilate to Claudius*.[5] It may seem strange for Pilate to be writing to Claudius, in particular, given the fact that it was Tiberius, not Claudius, who was emperor when Pilate condemned Jesus to death (Claudius became emperor a decade later). Possibly this letter was forged so long after the fact that the forger did not have the facts of imperial history from two hundred years earlier straight (do you know who was president of the United States in 1811?).

One of the places the letter is preserved for us is in a fabricated account of the missionary activities of the apostles called the *Acts of Peter and Paul*. In this account we are told that years after Jesus's death, the apostle Peter and the archheretic Simon the Magician, whom we met earlier, appear before the emperor Nero, evidently in the early 60s CE. When the emperor hears about Christ, he asks Peter how he can learn more about him. Peter suggests that he retrieve the letter that Pilate had sent to his predecessor, the emperor Claudius, and to have it read aloud. He does so, and the letter then is quoted in full.

The idea that Pilate may have written a letter to the emperor to explain the death of Jesus was widespread in early Christianity. We have references to some such letter as early as the third century in the writings of the church father Tertullian and in the fourth century in the *Church History* of Eusebius.[6] The letter I am discussing here is probably not the one referred to by these two authors. Possibly this one was composed by a forger who thought that some such letter must once have existed. The themes of the short letter are very similar to ones we have already explored. It is the wicked Jews who are responsible for Jesus's death, and they will be punished by God for it. As "Pilate" states in the letter:

> The Jews, out of envy, have brought vengeance both on themselves and on those who come after them by their terrible acts of judgment. They have been oblivious to the promises given to their ancestors, that God would send them his holy one from heaven . . . through a virgin.

According to the letter Jesus proved that he was the son of God by his many miracles, but the Jewish leaders told lies in order to have him executed. Then they (not the Roman soldiers!) crucified him. When he arose from the dead "the wickedness of the Jews was set aflame," so that they bribed the soldiers to say that Jesus's disciples had stolen the body from the tomb. Pilate has written this letter so that the emperor will know the truth and not be "led to believe the false reports told by the Jews."

The Report of Pontius Pilate

A longer document called the *Report of Pontius Pilate* gives yet another letter of the Roman governor to the emperor, but this time to Tiberius, soon after the death of Jesus.[7] This letter appears to be much closer to what the early third-century Tertullian described when he claimed: "Pilate, who was himself already a Christian with respect to his most innermost conviction, made a report of everything that happened to Christ for Tiberius, the emperor at the time."[8] Again, it is doubtful if the surviving *Report* is the document Tertullian refers to.

Scholars tend to date it to a later period, possibly the fourth century or so. Its chief claims, in any event, are similar to those of the other forgeries we have looked at in this chapter: Jesus was the miracle-working son of God who was wrongly condemned by the Jews to death. Pilate was innocent of the entire proceeding.

The *Report* starts by stressing that Pilate was administering the province of Judea according to "the most gentle directives" of the emperor. Nothing hard-hearted or malicious about this Pilate! But the "entire multitude of the Jews" (not just the Jewish leaders) handed Jesus over to him, "bringing endless charges against him" even though they "were not able to convict him of a single crime."

Pilate goes on to indicate, however, that Jesus had done many miracles, making the blind see, cleansing lepers, raising the dead, healing paralytics, and so on. These were amazing deeds, as Pilate himself confesses: "For my part, I know that the gods we worship have never performed such astounding feats as his." But the Jews are unmoved and threaten a riot, and so Pilate orders him crucified.

At Jesus's death a miraculous darkness covers the earth, and at his resurrection a miraculous brightness appears. At three in the morning the sun begins to shine in full strength, angels are seen in the heavens, there are earthquakes and the splitting of rocks, and great chasms form in the earth. All this spells disaster for the recalcitrant Jews:

> The light did not cease that entire night, O King, my master. And many of the Jews died, being engulfed and swallowed up in the chasms in that night, so that their bodies could no longer be found. I mean to say that those Jews who spoke against Jesus suffered. But one synagogue was left in Jerusalem, since all the synagogues that opposed Jesus were engulfed.

The Handing Over of Pilate

A final example of a "Pilate Gospel" is called the *Handing Over of Pilate*.[9] This is not a letter, but a narrative that reports what happened to Pilate once the emperor Tiberius received his report of what had occurred at Jesus's death and resurrection. The *Handing Over* seems to presuppose the existence of the *Report of Pilate*, but it is stylistically different and has points of disagreement with the earlier text. Scholars tend to think, then, that they were written by different authors.

The *Handing Over* begins by stating that Pilate's letter arrived in Rome and was read to Tiberius Caesar in front of a large crowd, who marveled to learn that the daytime darkness and worldwide earthquake they had experienced came as a result of the crucifixion of the Son of God. Caesar is "filled with anger," and he sends soldiers to arrest Pilate to bring him to Rome. When Pilate arrives, Caesar puts him on trial and upbraids him for executing Jesus: "By daring to do this wicked deed you have destroyed the entire world."

Pilate protests his innocence, however, and insists that "it is the multitude of the Jews who are reckless and guilty." Caesar replies that, even so, Pilate should have known better, since it was obvious from Jesus's miracles that "he was the Christ." As soon as Caesar mentions the name Christ, all of the pagan idols in the senate house, where the trial is being held, fall to the ground and turn to dust. Here, as in the *Gospel of Nicodemus*, the gods of the pagans do humble obeisance before the divinity of Christ and come to naught. In this episode it happens just at the mention of Christ's divine name.

Pilate repeats that Jesus's works showed that he was "greater than all the gods" that they worshiped. But he executed him "because of the anarchy and rebelliousness of the lawless and godless Jews." Caesar and the senate take a vote and decide to destroy the nation of the Jews. They then send in the armies, who destroy the nation and take all the Jewish survivors to sell off as slaves. Pilate himself is condemned to death for his part in the affair.

Before he dies, however, Pilate prays to God and pleads his innocence, once again saying that Jesus's death was because of the "nation of godless Jews." When he finishes his prayer, a voice comes from heaven—the voice of Christ himself—assuring Pilate of his salvation: "All the races and families of the Gentiles will bless you, because under your rule everything spoken about me by the prophets was fulfilled. You yourself will appear as my witness at my second coming." When the executioner chops off Pilate's head, an angel swoops down and takes it, presumably to carry it up to heaven.

The Purpose of the "Pilate Gospels"

The overarching points of these later Pilate Gospels should by now be clear. By exonerating Pilate in the death of Jesus, the accounts make the Jews, not just their leaders, bear all the guilt. The more innocent Pilate is, the more culpable are the Jews. According to some of the legends, Pilate is so innocent that he becomes a devoted believer and follower of Christ. God is therefore angry with the Jews and punishes them for their crime against the Son of God.

These writings were forged in a period that saw heightened animosities between Christians and Jews. Christians realized there would be no rapprochement with the Jews and there was little chance that most Jews would ever come to see the "truth" about Jesus, that he was the messiah of God, not just a lowly crucified criminal. This "truth," then, is what prompted these Christian "false writings." That is to say, a number of Christian authors chose to tell the truth about the divine Christ and about his wicked enemies, the Jews, by forging documents, claiming to be people they weren't. Christian readers of these documents accepted them at face value as real reports from the time, instead of what they were, forgeries from later periods. The authors intended to deceive their readers, and their readers were all too easily deceived.

WRITINGS OF JESUS

We have very few writings from early Christianity that claim to be by Jesus himself, and very few indications that Jesus could in fact write. But there are a few reports of his writing—even though this is not widely known, even among scholars—and a couple of surviving writings that he is (falsely) said to have produced.

Even within the pages of the New Testament there is a record of Jesus writing. This is not a story originally found in the New Testament, however, but a later account that scribes added to the Gospel of John. In fact, it is in one of the best-known stories about Jesus, Jesus and the woman taken in adultery (8:1–11).

In the story the Jewish authorities drag a woman before Jesus and indicate that she has been caught in the act of adultery. According to the law of Moses, they say, she is to be stoned to death. But what does Jesus say? This is an obvious trap. If Jesus says, "Yes, by all means, stone her," he is violating his own teachings on forgiveness and mercy. But if he says, "No, let her go," he is violating the law of Moses. So what is he to do? Jesus, of course, always finds a way out of these traps, and he does so in this case by stooping down and writing on the ground. He then looks up and says, "Let the one without sin among you be the first to cast a stone at her." He then stoops back down and resumes writing. Gradually, ashamed of their own sins, all the Jewish authorities leave, one by one, until there is no one left to condemn the woman.

It is a fascinating account, even if it was not originally part of the New Testament.[10] But what is especially interesting for our discussion here is what Jesus does when he stoops down. He is not said to be drawing or doodling on the ground. He is literally said to be "writing." The Greek term clearly indicates that he is writing words. This is the earliest indication that we have that Jesus was even able to write.[11] One recent study of this passage in fact argues that it was composed years after Jesus's death precisely in order to show that he *could* write.[12]

Several alleged writings of Jesus are mentioned by church fathers. Unfortunately, none of these forgeries survive. The fourth-century *Apostolic Constitutions*, for example, mentions books forged in Jesus's name by the heretics Simon and Cleobius. It is hard to know if such books actually existed or if they were simply said to have existed in order to attack these false teachers for forging them.

The fifth-century theologian Augustine, on the other hand, mentions a letter allegedly written by Jesus that probably did exist.[13] The letter was addressed to the apostles Peter and Paul and endorsed magical practices. Augustine had no difficulty showing that the letter was forged, since Paul was not actually a disciple during Jesus's lifetime, but only after his death. Augustine plausibly argues that the forger had seen paintings of Jesus with Peter and Paul (such as one can still see, for example, in the catacombs of Rome) and made the false inference that Paul was one of Jesus's earthly disciples. On that errant basis the forger made up a letter that Jesus allegedly sent to Paul along with Peter. Regrettably, we no longer have the letter.[14]

A couple of other writings, however, do survive in Jesus's name from the first four centuries. Neither is probably best seen as a forgery, however, since neither seems to be making a serious claim to have been written by the historical Jesus himself. One is found in an account of Jesus's death and resurrection called the *Narrative of Joseph of Arimathea*. According to this highly fictionalized narrative, one of the robbers crucified along with Jesus is pardoned for his sins and promised a place in heaven. From the cross, Jesus writes a letter to the angelic cherubim who are in charge of heaven, instructing them to let this fellow in when he arrives at the gates. This is a terrifically intriguing letter, but it really doesn't seem as though the author intends for his readers to take it seriously as something written by Jesus.[15] But I may be wrong.

Another writing by Jesus is a document discovered in 1945 with a collection of Gnostic texts called the Nag Hammadi library, about which I say more in the next chapter. This document is written in the first person, in the name of Jesus, describing the true nature of his crucifixion and the true way of having salvation through him. It is called the *Second Treatise of the Great Seth* (the first treatise, if it ever existed, no longer survives). Even though Jesus claims to be writing this book, it is the resurrected Jesus writing from heaven. For that reason it is not exactly the same thing as a forgery in the name of the earthly Jesus.

One brief letter that claims to have been written by the earthly

Jesus, however, does survive. The letter was produced by someone who probably wanted to deceive his readers into thinking that it really was by Jesus. If so, it is appropriately called a forgery. This letter is part of a correspondence between Jesus and a certain King Abgar, of the city of Edessa, in Syria. Our first record of this correspondence is in the *Church History* of Eusebius, who claims actually to have uncovered both letters in the Edessan city archives. Eusebius indicates that the letters were written in Syriac, but that he translated them into Greek. He then cites them in full.[16]

The first letter is from the "Ruler Abgar" addressed to "Jesus the Good Savior." Abgar indicates that he has heard all about Jesus's miraculous healings and has concluded that Jesus must either be "God . . . having descended from heaven" or the "Son of God." In either event, Abgar asks that Jesus come to him and heal him of his illness (without stating what it is). He adds that this would be of benefit to Jesus as well, as he has "heard that the Jews are murmuring against and wish to harm" Jesus.

Jesus writes a reply in which he indicates that Abgar is blessed for believing in him sight unseen and comments, "It is written about me that those who see me will not believe me, and that those who do not see me will believe and live" (see Isa. 6:9; Matt. 13:14–17; John 9:39; 12:39–40). In other words, the people among whom Jesus lived and worked ("the Jews" mentioned by Abgar) would not believe and would, therefore, not have life, but death. Jesus goes on to refuse politely Abgar's request to join him in Edessa, as he has to "accomplish everything I was sent here to do" and then "ascend to the One who sent me." Jesus does promise, however, that after his ascension he will send one of his disciples who will heal Abgar and "provide life both to you and to those who are with you."

I assume this final sentence means that the disciple will teach them the gospel, which they will then believe for eternal life. According to later legends Jesus fulfilled his promise to King Abgar. An apostle was dispatched to Edessa, healed the king of his illness, and converted him and the entire city to faith in Christ.

The Abgar correspondence accomplishes an end similar to that of the Pilate Gospels, but in a far more subtle way. Here too Jews are attacked for their opposition to Jesus and are said not be heirs of eternal life because they reject him. This letter too, then, represents antagonism against the Jewish people for their role in the death of Jesus.

As a side note, the correspondence with Abgar appears to have had an interesting afterlife. As it was circulated throughout the early church, scribes changed it in places. Some of our surviving manuscripts of Jesus's letter add a final line that informs King Abgar: "Your city will be blessed, and the enemy will no longer prevail over it." This proved to be a very helpful promise to the citizens of Edessa. In the later fourth century a wealthy Christian woman named Egeria from the western part of the empire (either Spain or France) decided to go on a pilgrimage to visit all the sacred places of the Holy Land. During her journeys she kept a journal in Latin, which we still have today.[17] On her travels, Egeria went to Edessa and saw the letters between Jesus and Abgar, as shown to her by the Christian bishop of the place.

According to the bishop, when the city of Edessa had come under attack by the armies of Persia, the then ruler of the city had taken the letter of Jesus, which promised that the city would not be conquered, and held it up at the city gate. The attacking army was thwarted by the magical power of the letter and retreated, eventually returning home to Persia without harming a soul. Later a copy of the letter was attached to the city gate, and no enemy had tried to attack it since. This, then, was a very useful letter to have on hand, even if it was forged.

Pagan Opposition to Christianity

AS WE TURN FROM considering antagonism toward the Jews by early Christians to opposition occasionally found among pagans, it is important to clear up a few common misconceptions about early

Christianity in the Roman Empire. It is widely thought that from its early days Christianity was an illegal religion, that Christians could not confess their faith openly for fear of governmental persecution, and that as a result they had to go into hiding, for example, in the Roman catacombs. As it turns out, none of that is true. Strictly speaking, Christianity was no more illegal than any other religion. In most times and places, Christians could be quite open about their faith. There was rarely any need to "lie low."

It is true that Christians were sometimes opposed by pagans for being suspicious and possibly scurrilous, just as most "new" religions found opponents in the empire. But there were no imperial decrees leveled against Christianity in its first two hundred years, no declarations that it was illegal, no attempt throughout the empire to stamp it out. It was not until the year 249 CE that any Roman emperor—in this case it was the emperor Decius—instituted an empire-wide persecution of Christians.

Before Decius, persecutions were almost entirely local affairs. More often than not they were the result of mob violence rather than "official" opposition initiated by local authorities. When there was official opposition, it was usually in order to placate the crowds, who did not approve of the Christians in their midst. But what was there not to approve?

For pagans, lots of things. Probably most important, as we have seen, pagans typically worshiped their gods because it was believed that the gods provided people with what they needed and wanted in life: peace, security, prosperity, health, food, drink, rain, crops, children, and everything else that made life both possible and meaningful. The pagan gods were not thought to require much in return. They did not insist that anyone actually "believe" in them, for example; and they did not have complicated "laws" that had to be followed. The gods more or less demanded that they be worshiped in appropriate ways; people were to perform the acceptable and traditional sacrifices that had long been part of their worship and say the prayers that were appropriate to them.

If people worshiped the gods, the gods took care of the people. It was an easy and helpful arrangement. But what happened when the gods were not worshiped, when they were ignored or flouted? Well, then things were not good. The gods could make life very miserable indeed if angered; they could bring war, drought, natural disaster, destruction, death. How, then, would people react if some kind of disaster struck a community? Their natural assumption was to think that one or more of the gods was angry and needed to be placated.

If a group of people in a community rejected the proper worship of the gods, insisted the gods didn't exist, declared that they were evil demons, or simply refused to do the very minimal requirements of public worship, this group would be the most susceptible to blame if disaster hit the community. The Christian church was just such a group. Other religions followed the ancient traditions that had been handed down in worshiping the gods. Even the Jews were widely seen as acceptable, even though they worshiped just their one God. They were known to perform sacrifices on behalf of the emperor's well-being (rather than to him), and this was deemed appropriate. Moreover, their traditions were known to be ancient and venerable, and they did no one any harm, did not behave in socially inappropriate ways, and more or less kept to themselves. The Jews, then, were seen as an exception to the rule that the local and imperial divinities needed to be worshiped.

Christians, on the other hand, were not treated as an exception. Christians for the most part were either Jews who no longer seemed to keep the ancestral Jewish customs (so in what sense were they Jews?) or Gentiles who had abandoned the worship of the gods for the worship of the God of Jesus. Christians flat-out refused to worship the gods that had made the state great and that provided all the necessary and good things of life. If disaster struck a community that housed such Christians, they were the natural scapegoat for retribution. Punish the Christians and return to the gods' good favor. Thus Tertullian's famous lines about Christians being subject to persecution whenever disaster struck a community:

They think the Christians the cause of every public disaster, of every affliction with which the people are visited. If the Tiber rises as high as the city walls, if the Nile does not send its waters up over the fields, if the heavens give no rain, if there is an earthquake, if there is a famine or pestilence, straightway the cry is: Away with the Christians to the lion![18]

Moreover, the Christian refusal to participate in state-sponsored worship was often seen as a kind of political statement that Christians were not concerned for the welfare of the state. This was considered antisocial and dangerous. Other aspects of the Christian religion contributed to this perception. For one thing, Christians worshiped a crucified man, that is, someone who had been condemned by the state. Wasn't that a kind of political statement, that Christians were more or less thumbing their noses at the judgment of the state? And even apart from that, wasn't it a matter of sheer lunacy to abandon the tried and true religion of the state in order to worship a crucified criminal?

Another problem was that, unlike Judaism, Christianity was such a new phenomenon. People in the ancient world loved nothing more than antiquity, and there was nothing that could authenticate a religion or a philosophy more than a claim to having ancient roots. The old was venerable; the new was suspect. And what was Christianity? It was the worship of a man who lived quite recently, in "modern" times. How could it possibly be true?

Not only was this new religion seen as dangerous and false; it was also seen as corrupt and perverted. Christians did not hold open meetings that everyone could attend. There were no church buildings that opened up on Sunday morning for anyone interested in learning about the new faith. Churches for the first two hundred years almost always met in private homes, and the meetings themselves were private. Only Christians attended. The religion was thought by others, therefore, to be secretive. And not only that, there were also rumors about what happened at these meetings.

For one thing, since the majority of Christians were from the lower, working classes, the weekly meetings as a rule took place either before the work day began, before dawn, or after it was over, after sundown, that is, when it was dark. These nocturnal meetings were rumored to be held among people who were "brothers" and "sisters" and who were known to "love one another" and to "greet one another with a kiss." And they held periodic "love feasts" in which they celebrated the love of their god for them and their love for each other. If you wanted to start a rumor mill going about the early Christians, how much better could it get? Christians, whose meetings were not public, were thought to be engaged in licentious and incestuous activities, brothers and sisters gorging themselves, probably getting drunk, and holding love feasts in the dark.

Worse than that, it was reported that at these love feasts Christians ate the flesh of the Son of God and drank his blood. Eating the flesh and drinking the blood of a child? In addition to incest, Christians were thought to be committing infanticide and cannibalism, killing babies and then eating them.

These charges may all sound extremely far-fetched, but they were commonly leveled against Christians by their pagan enemies. In one early Christian source called the *Octavius*, written by the third-century author Minucius Felix, we read of a pagan who expresses his disgust at what happens at the Christian nighttime services. This view, according to Minucius Felix, derives from the famous pagan scholar Fronto, the tutor of the emperor Marcus Aurelius:

> On a special day they [i.e., the Christians] gather for a feast with all their children, sisters, mothers—all sexes and all ages. There, flushed with the banquet after such feasting and drinking, they begin to burn with incestuous passions. They provoke a dog tied to the lampstand to leap and bound towards a scrap of food which they have tossed outside the reach of his chain. By this means the light is overturned and extinguished, and with it common knowledge of their actions; in the shameless

dark with unspeakable lust they copulate in random unions, all equally being guilty of incest, some by deed, but everyone by complicity.[19]

But these weekly activities pale in comparison with their periodic sacred meals, celebrated with the new converts to the faith:

The notoriety of the stories told of the initiation of new recruits is matched by their ghastly horror. A young baby is covered over with flour, the object being to deceive the unwary. It is then served before the person to be admitted into their rites. The recruit is urged to inflict blows onto it—they appear to be harmless because of the covering of flour. Thus the baby is killed with sounds that remain unseen and concealed. It is the blood of this infant—I shudder to mention it—it is this blood that they lick with thirsty lips; these are the limbs they distribute eagerly; this is the victim by which they seal their covenant; it is by complicity in this crime that they are pledged to mutual silence; these are their rites, more foul than all sacrileges combined.[20]

These were the kinds of charges that Christians had to defend themselves against. If local mobs believed such things, it is no wonder that they opposed Christians, sometimes with violence.

And if the masses were against the people who participated in the new religion, what choice did local officials have but to oppose them as well? Local persecutions of Christians were designed less to punish them for their crimes than to get them to renounce their religion and return to the true fold. That is why, in virtually all the early accounts of the Christian martyrs, the judges ruling in the cases brought against Christians plead with them to recant their faith.[21] These authorities' goal was not to hurt the Christians, but to convince them to stop being Christian. Christians were seen as a threat to both the political health of the empire, to the extent that the gods could become upset and exact vengeance, and the fabric of society, through their grossly immoral behavior.

Christians of course defended themselves against all such charges, and did so in a number of ways. Starting in the second half of the second century, intellectual pagans started occasionally converting to this new faith. These were a new breed of Christian: literate, highly educated, trained in rhetorical skills, able to make sustained philosophical arguments and to write them down, and willing to take a public stand defending the faith. These intellectual defenders of the faith are normally called "apologists." As we have seen, "apology" in this context is not an attempt to say you're sorry; it comes from the Greek work *apologia*, which means "a reasoned defense." Among the more famous Christian apologists of the second and third centuries were Justin Martyr of Rome, Athenagoras of Athens, Tertullian of Carthage, and Origen of Alexandria.

These authors insisted to anyone who would listen that Christians were not opposed to the state, but were in fact fully supportive of the state. The state survived and thrived not because of offerings made to dead idols, but because of prayers made to the living God, who had power and sovereignty over all. The worship of a crucified man was not a statement of opposition to the state; quite the contrary, the state representatives—Pontius Pilate, for example—had emphatically declared Jesus not guilty. Jesus's death was a miscarriage of justice perpetrated by the recalcitrant Jews, who had rejected their own messiah and therefore their own God. God had, as a result, rejected them in favor of his faithful people, the Christians. Rather than being a "new" religion, therefore, Christianity was quite ancient. It was in fact the true expression of ancient Judaism, a religion older than anything in either pagan philosophy or myth.

The best of the pagan philosophers, according to some of the apologists, shared views made sharper by the Christian message of the one true God, who had become manifest in his son Jesus. Jesus himself had taught an exceedingly high set of morals, and his followers were far more ethical than anyone else. Of course they did not murder infants; they did not even allow abortion. Of course they did not commit cannibalism; they were completely circumspect in what they ate and did not indulge in gluttony or drunkenness. Of course they did not commit incest; their love for one another was chaste. In fact, many of them practiced lifelong chastity, even if married. Of course they did not support fornication or adultery; for them, not only was it wrong to have sex with someone other than your spouse; it was a sin even to want to do so.

For the apologists, in short, Christianity was an ancient, philosophically respectable, and highly moral religion that stood over against the false religions of both pagans and Jews. Eventually this message caught on, as more and more pagans converted to the faith. Ultimately, once Christianity became the religion of the empire, the apologists' view would be accepted as obvious and commonsensical. Before that, though, Christians had to fight for their religious beliefs and practices. And one of the ways they fought was through their literary endeavors, which included the production of forgeries.

Some Resultant Forgeries

SEVERAL FORGERIES ALREADY SEEN

A number of the forgeries we have already considered functioned as well in the apologetic defense of the faith against pagan assaults. Here I need to stress a point I have not yet made. It would be a mistake to think that an author must have produced a forgery for one and only one purpose. This isn't the case for other books, and it is certainly not the case for forgeries either.

This book that I'm writing now—what is its purpose? In fact, there are multiple purposes. I want to inform my readers about an important ancient literary phenomenon. I want to correct mistakes that other scholars have made in discussing that phenomenon. I want readers to think more deeply about the role of lies and deception in the history of the Christian religion. I want to show the irony in the fact that lies and deception have historically been used to establish the "truth." I want my readers to see that there may be forgeries in the New Testament. I want to tell interesting stories about intriguing and relatively unknown writings from antiquity. I want to entertain my readers. In fact, I want to accomplish lots of things. Hardly any writing has just one purpose. So too forgeries. As a rule they were multifunctional.

Take, for example, the group of writings that I have called the "Pilate Gospels." These serve to show that the Jews were the ones responsible for the death of Jesus. They do so by emphasizing, quite strenuously, that the Roman governor Pontius Pilate declared Jesus to be innocent of all charges. That emphasis functions as a kind of Christian anti-Judaism, allowing Christian readers to conclude that Jews were wicked Christ-killers. But it also functions to help Christians defend themselves against attacks leveled at them by pagans. In response to pagans who insisted that Jesus was a convicted criminal opposed by the Roman state, Christians could argue that it wasn't true, that the appointed governor of Judea found Jesus innocent and crucified him only because the maleficent Jews forced him to do so. Jesus was no criminal, and neither are his followers.

Or consider the letters between the apostle Paul and the Roman philosopher Seneca. On one level these letters satisfied Christian curiosity. How could the most significant theologian of the young faith not have been known to the other great minds of his day? These letters showed that in fact Paul was known and respected by the greatest thinker of them all, the incomparable Seneca. But more than satisfying curiosity, these letters fulfilled an apologetic role in showing that, far from being a backwater religion of lower-class peasants, Christianity from the outset was a highly respectable philosophical tradition. How highly respected was it? The greatest Roman philosopher of the first century revered the apostle Paul and praised his uncanny insights.

In a different way some of the earliest Christian letters—the New Testament ones allegedly by Peter and Paul—may well have served to try to ward off attacks from pagan antagonists. Take 1 Peter as an example. Here is a letter in which a pseudonymous author, claiming to be Simon Peter, comforts Christians of Asia Minor who are undergoing suffering. But the letter is not only meant to provide comfort; it is also meant to provide a defense against precisely the accusations leveled against the Christians that created the conditions for suffering.

For example, Christians are thought to be opposed to the government, and so the author urges his readers: "Be submissive to every human institution for the Lord's sake, whether to the emperor as the one who is supreme or to overseers who have been sent by him for the punishment of those who do wrong and praise of those who do right. For this is the will of God: that by doing good you silence the ignorance of foolish people" (2:13–15). Pagans also charge Christians with living flagrantly immoral lives, and so the author urges: "Abstain from the passions of the flesh that wage war against your soul; maintain good behavior in front of the Gentiles, so that if they slander you as evildoers they may observe your good works and glorify God" (4:11–12). Pagans claim that Christians are socially disruptive, and so the author tells slaves to be submissive to their masters, wives to be submissive to their husbands, husbands to treat their wives considerately, and all to behave well: "Do not return evil for evil or verbal abuse for verbal abuse, but give a blessing instead" (3:8). Since these admonitions allegedly come from Peter himself—the most important leader of the early church—they take on special importance as representing the very core of the Christian message, from the very beginning.

There was a very different function for one other forgery we have already looked at, the *Gospel of Nicodemus*. In antiquity this book was sometimes called the *Acts of Pilate*, since its first half records an account of Jesus's death from the perspective of the Roman governor himself, Pontius Pilate. This account is, of course, very sympathetic toward both Pilate and Jesus. Jesus is innocent of the charges brought against him, and Pilate proclaims his innocence repeatedly, acknowledging the divine character of Jesus's miracles and life and finally ordering his execution only after being forced to by Jesus's Jewish opponents.

We may be able to isolate a more precise reason for the writing of this book. According to Eusebius, in the year 311, an anti-Christian pagan book was forged called the *Acts of Pilate*. This writing portrayed Jesus in an extremely negative way, indicating that he fully deserved everything he got, as seen through the eyes of Pontius Pilate. So impressed with this book was the Roman emperor Maximin Daia that he had it posted in public places throughout the empire and decreed that it should be used in schools for training children to read.[22]

This pagan *Acts of Pilate*, then, was an enormously popular and widespread book; unfortunately it no longer survives. Is it an accident that some years later an *alternative* version of the *Acts of Pilate* appeared, one in which Jesus is portrayed as innocent, not guilty, and in which Pilate is shown to support Jesus and declare him divine, rather than oppose him and declare him worthy of death? In the opinion of a number of scholars, the *Acts of Pilate* that we now have (also known as the *Gospel of Nicodemus*) was produced precisely in order to counter the pagan *Acts of Pilate*, as a way of setting the record straight.

THE SIBYLLINE ORACLES

In ancient Rome it was believed that there had been, in remote antiquity, a prophetess who was known as the Sibyl. She was extraordinarily long-lived; according to the poet Ovid she lived a thousand years.[23] According to venerable tradition, the Sibyl had written extensive poems that were prophetic in nature, designed not only to tell the future, but also to tell rulers of Rome what to do in times of crisis. The various writings attributed to the Sibyl were collected over the years and stored in one of the great sacred spaces in Rome, the Temple of Jupiter Capitolinus. A group of priests, eventually named "The Fifteen," were appointed to preserve and interpret these writings as the need arose and as they were directed by the Roman senate. Some records indicate that the Sibylline oracles, as they were called, were consulted some fifty times between 500 and 100 BCE, in times of plague, famine, or prodigy (i.e., when some highly unusual supernatural event seemed to occur), in order to learn what the prophetess had said concerning what should be done about it.[24]

A great tragedy occurred in 83 BCE when the Temple of Jupiter was burned, and the books of the oracles with it. The senate directed that other copies of the oracles should be collected from various places, especially the city of Erythrea, and an attempt was made to reconstitute the original writings. Eventually these too came to be destroyed. Today we know of only two brief sayings that probably belonged to this second group of Sibylline oracles, and none from the first.

The tradition that there had once lived a pagan prophetess who could reliably foretell the future was so strong that the temptation to create oracles, or prophecies, in her name proved irresistible to later peoples, especially to Jews, and after them Christians. As I have already pointed out, Jews were widely accepted throughout the empire. Even so, they occasionally had to fight for their right to coexist with pagans and to defend their religion against pagan attacks. By forging oracles in the name of the Sibyl, Jews were able to claim that their religion was very ancient, as attested by this most ancient of prophetesses, and compatible with the best of the pagan religions.

A number of forged Jewish Sibylline oracles were brought together into a collection, which was later taken over by unknown Christian authors.[25] These writers modified a number of the oracles by inserting their own Christian "prophecies" into them; they also added some entirely new oracles to the collection. This Christianized version of the *Sibylline Oracles* was handed down through the centuries, and we still have twelve books of them today.

The Jewish and Christian writings forged in the name of the Sibyl were written over a span of some seven hundred years and were finally assembled by a Byzantine Christian scholar sometime in the sixth century CE. Because of problems in how the books were copied over the centuries, the twelve books are numbered somewhat out of sequence, as books 1–8 and 11–14. Some of these are Jewish; some of them are Jewish books that have had extensive Christian insertions made into them (e.g., books 1–2 and 8); and others are exclusively Christian (book 6 and probably 7). The Christian portions of the oracles forged in the name of the Sibyl predict the coming of Christ and attack Jews for failing to believe in this one who was to come.

Just to give an example of how these apologetic forgeries work, consider the first book, which is largely Jewish until the final section, which contains a Christian insertion. The book begins with the Sibyl's statement: "Beginning from the first generation of articular men down to the last, I will prophesy all in turn, such things as were before, as are, and as will come upon the world."[26] Here, then, is a reliable ancient pagan prophetess who will tell the future. After narrating the creation of the world and then all the generations of the human race, the Sibyl continues, in the Christian insertion, to indicate the following:

> Then indeed the son of the great God will come, incarnate, likened to mortal men on earth. . . . He will show eternal life to chosen men. He will cure the sick and all who are blemished, as many as put faith in him. The blind will see, and the lame will walk. The deaf will hear; those who cannot speak will speak.

But, she says, "Israel, with abominable lips and poisonous spittings will give this man blows." She goes on to describe Christ's death and resurrection, and the eventual destruction of "the Hebrews" for the evil deed they performed against Christ.

One of the more powerful passages in the surviving Sibylline oracles is the very short book 6, which represents a hymn to Christ: "I speak from my heart of the great famous son of the Immortal, to whom the most High, his begetter, gave a throne to possess before he was born." It goes on to talk about his glorious coming into the world, his rejection, and the consequences for Israel, for whom evil afflictions are in store:

For with your hostile mind you did not perceive your god when he came before mortal eyes. But you crowned him with a crown from the thornbush and you mixed terrible gall for insult and drink. That will cause great afflictions for you.

Possibly the most intriguing passage in the *Sibylline Oracles* comes in the Christian insertion in book 8, where a long section of prophecies forms an acrostic. If you take the first letter of each of these lines and put them together in sequence, they spell out the Greek words "Jesus Christ, Son of God, Savior, Cross." This kind of acrostic is meant to have symbolic, hidden meaning. Among other things it shows that there was considerable forethought that went into the composition of the poem, made all the remarkable by the fact that it was allegedly constructed by a pagan prophetess living centuries before the birth of Jesus.

The Christian Sibylline oracles were well known in antiquity. As early as Justin Martyr in the middle of the second century they are referred to as predicting the truths of Christianity.[27] As you might imagine, pagans intent on attacking Christians knew full well that these oracular "predictions" of the coming of Christ, his activities on earth, his rejection by the Jews, and his vindication were not original to an ancient Sibyl, but had been inserted into these writings or created whole cloth by Christian authors.[28] This is one instance in which unknown forgers among the Christians were rightly suspected. They were also, of course, roundly condemned, as almost always happened with forgers in antiquity.

Conclusion

CHRISTIANS OF THE FIRST three centuries often felt themselves under attack for their faith, and for good reason. They *were* under attack. From the early years of the church, non-Christian Jews rejected the Christian message that Jesus was the Jewish messiah sent in fulfillment of the Jewish Scriptures, and this led not only to serious debate over the proper interpretation of Scripture but also to serious animosity. The animosity heightened as Christian Jews felt that their non-Christian Jewish opponents refused to listen to reason and were obviously being either willful or blind. As Christianity grew in numbers and power, the tensions increased. Eventually, of course, Christianity would get the upper hand, and once that happened, it became an unfair fight. The entire ugly history of Christian anti-Judaism was the result.

While Christians were fighting their Jewish neighbors on the one hand, they were having to ward off the attacks of pagans on the other. Far more than official persecution, it was local opposition to Christians among their former families, friends, and neighbors—and eventually mobs—that caused Christians the most problems in the early centuries before the Roman emperors came to be active sponsors of empire-wide persecutions in the mid-third century. Many pagans viewed Christians as politically dangerous, socially disruptive, and flagrantly immoral. Christians had to defend themselves against these charges by showing they were obedient members of the state, socially coherent and conservative, and the most moral beings on the planet.

The two prongs of the Christian counterattack were, as we have seen, closely related. By attacking Jews for rejecting their own messiah, Christians were able simultaneously to declare the innocence of Jesus and his followers to governmental officials and other interested pagan observers. By claiming to be the true representatives of the ancient Jewish religion, Christians not only attempted to displace the Jews, but also to provide a sense of antiquity for their own religious claims; they were as old as Moses, who was older by far than any pagan lawgivers or philosophers. By painting the Jews as immoral haters of God, Christians were able to pass themselves off as superior moral beings of no threat to the social order.

Into this maelstrom of attack and counterattack, some Christian authors introduced the weapons of literary forgery. The ultimate goal of the church was to establish itself as true and, of course, to show that all other religions were, as a consequence, false. So once more we have one of the great ironies of the early Christian religion: some of its leading spokespersons appear to have had no qualms about lying in order to promote the faith, to practice deception in order to establish the truth.

CHAPTER SIX

Forgeries in Conflicts with False Teachers

I'VE ALWAYS ENJOYED A GOOD, reasoned debate on a controversial issue. In high school I was on the debate team and loved it. My debate colleagues and I were good at it already as sixteen-year-olds, able to take either side of a hot topic and argue for it, then turn around and argue the opposing side in the next debate. I still do public debates around the country today, almost always with evangelical Christian scholars, on topics of importance, especially to evangelical Christians. "Can Historians Prove That Jesus Was Raised from the Dead?" (I always argue that, no, no one can *prove* it.) "Are the Gospel Accounts of Jesus Reliable?" (No, not completely.) "Does the Bible Provide an Adequate Answer to Why There Is Suffering?" (No, not really.) And so on.

I also think debates can be useful pedagogically in the classroom; they help undergraduate students learn how to mount arguments, assess evidence, and see the strengths of a position they personally reject. So I have my students debate controversial topics in my course on the New Testament. "Did Paul and Jesus Represent Fundamentally Different Religions?" "Were the Apostle Paul's Views of Women Oppressive?" "Does the New Testament Condemn Modern Practices of Homosexuality?"

Sometimes in setting up these debates I find out in advance which side students want to take (affirmative or negative) and then assign them to the *opposite* side, forcing them to argue for a position they personally reject. It's a great exercise. Politicians should try it sometime, to see that their opponents may actually have something important and persuasive to say.

In my many years of formal debate and in my many more years of informal discussion, I've come to realize something very significant. We tend to get in the hottest arguments about topics that we really care about and with people we are closest to. Only rarely do we get intense and bothered about something that doesn't matter to us. And our most heated arguments are almost always with friends and loved ones rather than absolute strangers.

Debates Among Early Christians

THE SAME WAS TRUE with the arguments carried out by the early Christians. As we saw in the previous chapter, Christians were in conflict with Jews and pagans over the validity of their religion. These debates were sometimes heated. They were, after all, about issues that mattered deeply to Christians. But the hottest early Christian debates were with other Christians, as they argued over the right things to believe and the right ways to live. These internal Christian debates were often filled with vitriol and hatred. Christians called one another nasty names, said ugly things about one another, and pulled out all stops to make their Christian opponents look reprehensible and stupid, denying, in many instances, that the opponents even had the right to call themselves Christian. Anyone perceived as a false teacher was subject to verbal lashing; outsiders to the faith—pagans and Jews—were treated with kid gloves by comparison.

Christian arguments with false teachers in their midst happened a lot, as far back as we have records. Our earliest Christian author was Paul, and in virtually every one of his letters it is clear that he had opponents on all sides. Many Christian readers over the years have failed to see the significance of Paul's constant attacks on false teachers. One thing that these attacks show, beyond dispute, is that virtually everywhere Paul went, even within his own churches, he and his views were under steady assault by Christians who thought and believed differently. It is easy to miss this rather obvious historical fact, because the writings of Paul's opponents have not survived the ravages of time, whereas his writings became part of the New Testament. But if we could transport ourselves back to the 50s CE, we would find that everywhere Paul went, he confronted Christian teachers who thought he preached a false gospel. This was true even in the churches that he himself founded. And these opponents were not the same in every place; different locations produced different opponents, with different views.

Just as key examples, in the churches of Galatia, Paul's Christian opponents claimed that he had perverted the true gospel message of Jesus and his apostles when he insisted that Gentiles did not have to be circumcised and become Jewish to be followers of Jesus. Nonsense, replied his opponents. Jesus was a Jew, his followers were Jews, he taught the Jewish law, he was the Jewish messiah sent from the Jewish God to the Jewish people—following Jesus of course meant being Jewish. This view lost out in the ensuing debates, but it certainly had extensive and avid supporters in its day.

In the church of Corinth Paul's opponents insisted that he was a weak and pathetic speaker who showed no evidence of being empowered by God. They, on the other hand, had superior divine gifts demonstrating the supremacy of their message that true believers had already been raised with Christ to experience the power and joy of the heavenly existence in the here and now.

In the city of Rome Paul was maligned by Christian leaders who claimed he was not a true apostle. These Christians attacked Paul both for thinking that Gentiles were superior to Jews in the church and for advocating a gospel that led to an immoral lifestyle.

And so it goes—at every turn Paul had opponents. We should not write these opponents off as fringe minority groups of no importance.

They were everywhere, and Paul saw them as dangerous. His views eventually won out, but in his own day the differences of opinion were widespread and highly threatening. And Paul was not the only apostle under fire. In every early Christian community believers attacked other believers for their false beliefs.

This was a problem for a religion that claimed to stand for "the" truth. If the followers of Jesus represented the single, unified truth of God, why was it that the Christian church was not single and unified? In fact, it was anything but that, not just in the days of Paul, but throughout the entire first four centuries. Just in the second and third centuries, for example, we know of powerful and influential Christian teachers like Marcion who maintained that there is not just one God, but two Gods. Some Gnostics said there were 30 divine beings, or 365. These Christians claimed that they were right, and that everyone else was wrong. Had one of these other groups won the debates, the world would be a very different place today.

In the second and third centuries some Christians said that Jesus was the most righteous man who had ever lived and was chosen by God to be his messiah. But he was not at all divine. A human being can't be divine. Other Christians, again like Marcion, insisted that Christ was completely divine and not at all human. Still other Christians, including the Gnostics whom I've already mentioned, maintained that Jesus Christ was two beings: a man Jesus and a divine Christ who came into Jesus to empower him for his ministry and who then left him prior to his death, since the Christ cannot suffer. Yet other Christians said that Jesus was God the Father himself come to earth.

At this same time there were Christians who denied that God had created the world. Or had called Israel to be his people. Or had authored the Jewish Scriptures. There were other Christians who insisted that the Jewish Scriptures were sacred, but were not to be interpreted literally. Yet other Christians said that they had to be interpreted literally and followed literally, as do some even today.

Early Christians were nothing if not radically diverse. Yet all of these Christian groups claimed not only to be right, but also to be uniquely right—their view, and their view alone, represented the one and only divine truth. As a corollary, they each claimed that their view of the truth was the view taught by Jesus himself and through him to the apostles. And all of these groups had books to prove it, books allegedly written by apostles that supported their points of view.

Christians today may wonder why these various groups didn't simply read their New Testaments to see that their views were wrong. The answer, of course, is that there was no New Testament. The New Testament emerged out of these conflicts, as one of the Christian groups won the arguments and decided which books would be included in Scripture. Other books representing other points of view and also attributed to the apostles of Jesus were not only left out of Scripture; they were destroyed and forgotten. As a result, today, when we think of early Christianity, we tend to think of it only as it has come down to us in the writings of the victorious party. Only slowly, in modern times, have ancient books come to light that support alternative views, as they have turned up in archaeological digs and by pure serendipity, for example, in the sands of Egypt.

What were Christian teachers to do when they were convinced that their particular understanding of Jesus and of the faith was true, but they didn't have any apostolic writings to back it up? One thing they sometimes did—or, arguably, often did—was to invent apostolic writings. Nothing generated more literary forgeries in the names of the apostles than the internal conflicts among competing Christian groups. These forgeries established apostolic authority for a group's own views and attacked the views of other groups. Many of the forgeries that we have already considered do so at great length, and there are others that are yet to be considered here.

Forgeries Directed Against Unknown Opponents

WHEN READING EARLY CHRISTIAN attacks on false teachers, it is often difficult to know what exactly the opponents believed. That is because in most instances we don't have any of the opponents' own writings, and so we have to reconstruct their views from what their enemies say about them. That often doesn't give one much to go on. Try to imagine reconstructing one presidential candidate's (real) views from what the other candidate says in order to attack him. This kind of reconstruction is much easier to do today, when we have mass media and extensive reporting on both sides of any issue, so that it is harder to flat-out lie about the other person's view. Politicians today, as a rule, have to be relatively sneaky. In the ancient world there was virtually nothing to stop flagrant distortion and misrepresentation. How would anyone know, without a newspaper or magazine article stating the opponents' real views?

In other instances the arguments against opponents are made for readers who have the opponents right there among them, so that both the writer and the readers know perfectly well what the opponents' views are. As a consequence, the writer feels no need to spell them out. That is fine for ancient readers who know what the author is talking about. But for those of us living two thousand years later it can be very frustrating. We get only hints at the character of the false teaching and have to do our best to stitch it together from what little we're told.

In yet other instances an author may attack false views that he himself has made up simply as a foil for his own thoughts. This is especially the case with forged writings in which the author pretends to be living in an earlier age. The false teachings attacked are not necessarily views that anyone held. They are simply an alternative perspective that the author maligns in order to set out the "truth" of his point of view.

We have to contend with all such cases when dealing with the forged writings of early Christianity, including those of the New Testament. Several writings attack false teachings, but it is well nigh impossible to say what the opponents actually believed, if in fact they really existed at all.

COLOSSIANS

This is the case with the letter to the Colossians, written in Paul's name but almost certainly pseudonymous, as we saw in Chapter 3. The author, whoever he was, urges his readers not to be led astray by false teaching: "See that no one makes you prey through philosophy and empty deceit according to human tradition, according to the elemental spirits of the cosmos and not according to Christ" (2:8). He goes on to charge his readers with what they should and should not believe and with what religious practices they should and should not engage in. But whom is he arguing against?

This is a classic case of scholars having almost no way to know. Not that that has stopped anyone from trying. One scholar writing in 1973 pointed out that there were forty-four different scholarly opinions about what the false teachers under attack stood for.[1] In a five-year stretch in the early 1990s there were four major books written on the subject by expert scholars; they each represented a different view.[2] My view is that we'll never know for sure.

What we can say is that the author portrays these false teachers, whether they really existed or not, as urging their Christian readers in the worship of angels, basing their views on divine visions they had had. They also allegedly urged their followers to lead an ascetic lifestyle, avoiding certain foods and drinks, and observing, probably, Jewish Sabbaths and festivals (thus 2:16–18, 21–23). The author, claiming to be Paul, is opposed to all this. He thinks Christ alone is to be worshiped, for in Christ (not in angels) can be found the complete embodiment of the divine. Moreover, those who are "in Christ" have already experienced the benefits of the resurrection; there is no need for them to engage in ascetic practices.

Why would an author claim to be Paul in order to attack these unknown opponents? Evidently because doing so allowed the author to malign people he disagreed with while setting out his own point of view, even though his view is, in fact, different from Paul's, as we saw in Chapter 3.

JUDE

Consider next the New Testament book of Jude. This short book is even more obviously directed against false teachers in the Christian community. After greeting his readers, the author explains the reason for his letter:

> Beloved, ... I found it necessary to write to you in order to exhort you to struggle for the faith that was delivered to the saints once and for all. For some people have secretly snuck in who were written about long ago as being subject to this condemnation. They are unholy people who corrupt the grace of our God, changing it into licentiousness, denying our Lord Jesus Christ. (vv. 3–4)

Here the opponents are described in rather nasty terms, but the terms get nastier as you progress through the letter. One point worth emphasizing is that even though these opponents have come into the Christian community (as members), they deny Christ. This should not be taken to mean that they deny being Christian. Quite the contrary, they are portrayed as Christian teachers. By saying that they deny Christ the author is claiming that they aren't really Christians, because what they teach is false. It is not too hard to imagine that they would say the same thing about him. But his writing became Scripture. Their writings, if they ever existed, were forever lost.

In any event, throughout this book the author has nothing good to say about the opponents. They defile the flesh (whatever that means), reject authority, and revile the holy angels. They are irrational animals, they carouse together, and they are "waterless clouds" and "fruitless trees, twice dead, uprooted." They are ungodly and do ungodly deeds; they are "grumblers, fault-finders, following their own passions, who boast with loud mouths" (vv. 8–16).

Here again it is hard to say if the author is attacking a real, historical group. He certainly is filled with vitriol for his enemies, but it is impossible to put together a coherent picture of what these people actually taught, based on the rapid-fire name-calling that the author engages in. Possibly the original readers of the book knew exactly whom he was referring to and what they taught. Or possibly the author is simply using an imaginary set of enemies to set up a foil for his own teaching about the true nature of Christian faith, which was "once and for all handed over to the saints" (v. 3). In either event, in his attempt to attack falsehood, the author himself has apparently committed deception. He claims to be Jude (v. 1), and by this claim he seems to be saying that he is the brother of Jesus.

Five persons are named Jude (or Judas—same Greek word) in the New Testament, the most infamous of whom, of course, is Judas Iscariot. One of the others is Jude, the son of Mary and Joseph the carpenter, one of the four brothers of Jesus mentioned in Mark 6:4. The author of this short letter is almost certainly claiming to be that particular Jude, because he identifies himself as "Jude, the brother of James." Since most ancient people did not have last names, an author with a common name would typically identify himself (so that you would know *which* Jude he was) by mentioning a known relative, almost always his father. But here the author names not his father, but his brother, James. This must mean that James is the member of the family who is particularly well known.

And what James in the early church was especially well known? The most famous James was the head of the first church, the church in Jerusalem. This James was the brother of Jesus, mentioned throughout the New Testament, for example, by the apostle Paul on several occasions (see Gal. 1:19). If this Jude is identifying himself as the brother of *that* James, then he is, by implication, obviously the brother of Jesus.

But it is almost certain that the historical Jude did not write this book. Its author is living during a later period in the history of the church, when the churches are already well established, and when false teachers have infiltrated them and need to be rooted out. In fact, the author speaks of "remembering the predictions of the apostles"

(v. 17) as if they, the apostles, lived a long time before. In contrast to them, he is living in "the last days" that they predicted (v. 18). This is someone living after the apostolic age.

There is another reason for being relatively certain that Jude did not write the book (referred to earlier, in Chapter 2). Like the lower-class Galilean peasant Peter, the lower-class Galilean peasant Jude could almost certainly not write. Let alone write in Greek. Let alone compose a rhetorically effective letter evidencing detailed knowledge of ancient Jewish texts in Greek. This is an author claiming to be Jude in order to get Christians to read his book and to stand opposed to false teachers who hold a different view of the faith.

Forgeries in Opposition to Paul

PAUL WAS A LIGHTNING ROD for controversy not only during his own lifetime, but also afterward. Some Christians saw him as the greatest authority of the early church, whose vision of Christ on the road to Damascus authorized him to proclaim the true understanding of the gospel. Others saw him as an outsider to the apostolic band, an interloper who transformed the original message of Jesus and his apostles into a different religion far removed from the truth.

We have already seen that supporters of Paul forged letters in his name. These pseudonymous authors obviously felt that Paul's authority could prove persuasive in the context of the various controversies and struggles the Christian community was encountering. So we have a range of Pauline writings that he did not in fact write: Ephesians, Colossians, 2 Thessalonians, 1 Timothy, 2 Timothy, Titus, *3 Corinthians*, letters to Seneca, and no doubt numerous other letters that have not survived from the early church.

But Paul's detractors also produced forgeries. In these cases, the pseudonymous writings countered Paul's teachings, or at least teachings that were thought to be Paul's teachings, whether they actually represented the views of the historical Paul or not. These forgeries were not, of course, written in Paul's name, but in the names of other authorities of high repute, who cast aspersions either directly or indirectly on the so-called apostle to the Gentiles.

THE NONCANONICAL *EPISTLE OF PETER*

One of these we have already considered in Chapter 2, the *Epistle of Peter*, which appears as a kind of introduction to the *Pseudo-Clementine Writings*. This letter presupposes what was widely assumed in the ancient church and is still assumed by many scholars and laypeople today: Peter and Paul did not see eye to eye on the true gospel message.

The historical Paul himself indicates in his authentic writings that he and Peter were sometimes at odds. This is nowhere clearer than in Paul's letter to the Galatians, where he indicates that Peter chose not to share meals with Gentile (formerly pagan) Christians in the city of Antioch when Jewish Christians arrived in town (see 2:11–14). Presumably Peter thought these visitors would be offended by his decision not to keep kosher. Peter's withdrawal from Gentiles (to keep kosher) may have been simply an attempt not to make waves among Jewish believers who thought it was important for Jews to maintain their Jewish identity even after becoming followers of Jesus. For Paul, on the other hand, Peter's withdrawal was an affront to the gospel. This gospel, in his view, proclaimed that Jew and Gentile were equal before God in Christ and that there was no need for followers of Jesus to follow the law, including kosher food laws.

Paul confronted Peter in public and called him a hypocrite for eating with the Gentiles when no Jewish brothers were present, but refusing to do so when they arrived. It is very unfortunate indeed that we don't know how Peter replied or who, in the general opinion, got the better of the argument. All we know is Paul's side, as he reports it in the letter to the Galatians. But it is clear that he and Peter were sometimes at odds, and it is not at all clear that they ever reconciled over the issue.

This tension between Peter and Paul over the keeping of the law, as we have seen, is very much at issue in the noncanonical *Epistle of Peter*, where the author, claiming to be Peter, but actually writing long after his death, attacks a person whom he calls his "enemy." This enemy has preached a "lawless gospel to the Gentiles," that is, a gospel that says one is made right with God apart from the law. This personal enemy of Peter has falsely claimed that he, Peter, agrees with his false understanding of the faith. "Peter," however, does not agree with it and attacks his enemy for claiming that he does.

This, then, is a thinly veiled attack on Paul written by a Jewish Christian who thought that it was proper, and even necessary, for Jews who believed in Jesus to continue observing the Jewish law. Failing to do so meant a breech in true religion. Paul, for this author, is not an apostolic authority. He is a false preacher.

THE *PSEUDO-CLEMENTINE WRITINGS*

A similar teaching is found in the *Pseudo-Clementine Writings* themselves.[3] If you will recall, these are a set of long narratives allegedly written by Clement, the fourth bishop of Rome (i.e., the pope), in which he describes his travels, his meeting with the apostle Peter, and his conversion to become a follower of Jesus. Most of the books narrate his subsequent adventures while participating with Peter on his missionary journeys. In particular these accounts relate how Peter engaged in conflicts and miracle contests with Simon the Magician, who claimed to be the true representative of God, but who, according to Peter, was a false teacher. In some passages of these books it is clear that Simon is understood to be someone else—Peter's real-life enemy, the apostle Paul.

Nowhere is this more clear than in several passages in the *Pseudo-Clementine Writings* known as the *Homilies*.[4] In one passage Peter elaborates God's way of dealing with the world from the very beginning. Peter points out that there have often been pairs of people who appear in sacred history. The first to appear is always the inferior of the two. So, for example, the first children born to Adam and Eve were the wicked Cain (first) and the righteous Abel (second). So too the father of the Jews, Abraham, had two children: the firstborn, Ishmael, who was not to inherit the promises, and then Isaac, who was. Isaac then had two sons, Esau, the profane, and Jacob, the pious. And on and on through history.

This pattern applies to the Christian mission field, argues "Peter." The first missionary to the Gentiles was "Simon" (i.e., Paul); he was necessarily inferior. The second, the superior, was Peter himself, who claims, "I have come after him [Simon/Paul] and have come in upon him as light upon darkness, as knowledge upon ignorance, as healing upon disease" (2.17). Not a very affirming portrayal of Paul! Peter has followed in Paul's missionary path, straightening out everything that Paul had gotten wrong.

A second passage is even more condemning. As is well known, Paul was often said to have been commissioned to be an apostle by Christ in the vision he had on the road to Damascus (see Acts 9). Paul was not one of the original followers of Jesus. On the contrary, he started out as a persecutor of the Christian church. But then Christ appeared to him and converted him, telling him to become his missionary to the Gentiles. Paul himself, the historical Paul, took this commissioning with the utmost seriousness and claimed in books such as Galatians that, since he received his gospel message directly from Jesus, he was beholden to no one. Anyone who preached a message contrary to his message was advocating falsehood rather than truth (Gal. 1:6–9). He, Paul, had the truth from Christ himself. And among other things, this truth was that Gentiles were not to adopt the Jewish law in order to find salvation in Christ (thus Gal. 2:15–16).

The author of the *Pseudo-Clementines* heartily disagrees and portrays Peter himself as mocking Paul for his claims to have direct access to the teachings of Jesus, based on a single brief vision. In *Homily* 17 Peter says to "Simon" (i.e., Paul):

You alleged that . . . you knew more satisfactorily the doctrines of Jesus than I do because you heard His words through an apparition. . . . But he who trusts to apparition or vision and dream is insecure. For he does not know to whom he is trusting. For it is possible either that he may be an evil demon or a deceptive spirit, pretending in his speeches to be what he is not.

Visions cannot be trusted, because you have no way of knowing, really, what you are seeing. So if Paul's authority is rooted exclusively in a vision, it is no authority at all.

Peter continues with an argument that would seem hard to refute:

Can anyone be rendered fit for instruction through apparitions? And if you will say, "It is possible," then I ask, "Why did our teacher abide and discourse a whole year to those who were awake?" And how are we to believe your word, when you tell us that He appeared to you? And how did He appear to you, when you entertain opinions contrary to His teaching? But if you were seen and taught by Him, and became His apostle for a single hour, proclaim His utterances, interpret His saying, love His apostles, contend not with me who accompanied Him. For in direct opposition to me, who am a firm rock, the foundation of the Church, you now stand.

Paul may have had a brief vision of Jesus. But Peter was with him for months—a year!—not asleep and dreaming, but awake, listening to his every word. And Jesus himself declared that it was Peter, not Paul, who was the "Rock" on whom the church would be built. Paul is a late interloper whose authority rests on entirely dubious grounds. It is the teachings of Peter that are to be followed, not those of Paul.

Whether or not this is the view of the historical Peter is something we will probably never know. But it is certainly the view of Peter set forth in the forged writings known as the *Pseudo-Clementines*.

JAMES

In the New Testament itself we find a book that appears to attack Paul's teachings, or at least a later misinterpretation of Paul's teachings. This is a letter that claims to be written by someone named James. In the early church it was widely assumed that this James was the brother of Jesus.

James was known throughout the history of the early church to have been firmly committed to his Jewish roots and heritage, even as a follower of Jesus.[5] According to the New Testament he was not a disciple of Jesus during his lifetime (see John 7:5), but he was one of the first to see the resurrected Jesus after his death (1 Cor. 15:7), and because of that, presumably, he came to believe in him. No doubt it was his filial connection that elevated him to a position of authority in the church.

The apostle Paul, who personally knew James (Gal. 1:19), indicates that he was committed to keeping the Jewish law and appears to have insisted that the other Jewish followers of Jesus do so as well (2:12). He was well known for his great piety; one early source indicates that he prayed so often and at such length that his knees became as calloused as a camel's. The best historical records indicate that he died around 62 CE, after heading the Jerusalem church for thirty years.

James was a very common name among Jews in first-century Palestine, and among Christians as well. A number of people named James are in the New Testament. Matthew 10:3–4 indicates that two of Jesus's twelve disciples had the name. To differentiate the two Jameses, normally they are given additional identity markers, such as "James the son of Zebedee" or "James the son of Alphaeus." The author of the book of James, however, does not identify himself further, suggesting he expected his readers to know which James he was. There seems to be little doubt, then, that he is claiming to be the most famous James of all, Jesus's brother. This view is corroborated by the fact that he writes his letter to the "twelve tribes in the Dispersion," a reference to the twelve tribes of Israel who are scattered throughout the Roman world. James, the chief Jewish Christian, is writing to the dispersed Jewish Christians.

The book contains a number of ethical admonitions that urge

readers to live in ways appropriate for the followers of Jesus. They are to have faith and not to doubt; to endure trials, be slow to anger, watch their tongues, control their desires and not to show partiality, be jealous or ambitious, seek wealth, or show favoritism to the wealthy, and so on. Many of these admonitions seem to reflect the teachings of Jesus himself, for example, from the Sermon on the Mount (Matt. 5–7).

The author is particularly concerned with one issue, however, an issue that reflects a bone of contention with other Christians. Some Christians are evidently saying that to be right with God, all you need is faith; for them, doing "good works" is irrelevant to salvation, so long as you believe. James thinks this is precisely wrong, that if you do not do good deeds, then you obviously don't have faith:

> What use is it, my brothers, if a person says he has faith but has no works? Is faith able to save him? If a brother or sister is naked and has no daily food, and one of you says to them, "Go in peace; keep warm and be filled," without giving them what their bodies need, what use is that? So also faith, if it does not have works, is dead, being by itself. (2:14–17)

The author goes on to argue that having faith apart from works cannot bring salvation and in fact is worthless. This is shown above all by the example of Abraham, father of the Jews, who was saved by what he did, not just by what he believed:

> But someone will say, "You have faith and I have works." Show me your faith apart from works and I will show you my faith by my works. You believe that God is one? You do well: even the demons believe, and they shudder. But do you wish to know, O shallow man, that faith apart from works is barren? Wasn't Abraham our father justified by works when he offered Isaac his son on the altar? You see that faith was working with his works and faith was completed by the works. And the Scripture was

fulfilled which says, "And Abraham believed God, and it was counted to him as righteousness." And he was called a friend of God. You see that a person is justified by works, and not by faith alone. (2:18–24)

Here, then, is a sharp invective against anyone who maintains that it is faith alone that can put a person into a right standing before God (in James's words, that can "justify" a person). His evidence is Abraham, and the Scripture he quotes in support is Genesis 15:6: "And Abraham believed God, and it was counted to him as righteousness."

One of the reasons this passage is significant is that it sounds almost like a parody of something that Paul himself wrote, earlier, in his letter to the Galatians, when he was trying to convince his Gentile readers that they did not have to do the works of the law in order to be justified (be made right with God), but that faith in Christ alone was all that was needed. What is most striking is that Paul tries to demonstrate his case by referring specifically to Abraham and by quoting Genesis 15:6. Here is what Paul writes:

> We know that a person is not justified by the works of the law but through faith in Jesus Christ; so we ourselves have believed in Christ Jesus, so that we might be justified by faith in Christ and not by works of the law, because no one will be justified by works of the law. . . . Thus Abraham "believed God and it was counted to him as righteousness." You see therefore that those who have faith are the children of Abraham. (Gal. 2:16; 3:6–7)

For centuries scholars of the New Testament have maintained that the book of James is responding to the teaching of Galatians. Paul taught that it was faith in Christ that put people into a right relationship with God, independently of whether or not they did the works of the law. James insisted that works were needed, that faith alone could not bring justification. The two authors use the same language ("justify," "faith," "works"), they appeal to the same Old Testament figure, Abraham, and they both cite the same verse, Genesis 15:6. Since Martin Luther at the beginning of the Reformation, some interpreters have insisted that James is contradicting Paul. Luther's conclusion was that James had gotten it precisely wrong.

More recent scholars, however, have called this reading of James into question. In large measure that is because, even though the letter uses the same terms as Paul, James demonstrably means something different by these terms. When Paul uses the term "faith," as we saw in an earlier context, he means something relational by it; faith in Christ means trusting that Christ's death and resurrection can restore a person to a right standing before God. This, for Paul, comes "apart from the works of the law," meaning that one does not have to do the works prescribed by the Jewish law in order to trust Christ. One does not need to observe the Sabbath, keep kosher food laws, be circumcised if male, and so on.

James means something different, however, by both "faith" and "works." For him, faith does not have the relational meaning of "trusting someone." It refers to intellectual assent to a proposition: "Even the demons believe [God is one], and they shudder" (2:19). In other words, even demons know that there is only one real God, but it doesn't do them any good. This decidedly does not mean that the demons trust God; they simply have the intellectual knowledge of his existence. Faith—intellectual assent to the propositions of the Christian religion—will not save anyone, according to James. But would Paul disagree with *that*? Probably not.

Even more striking, when James speaks of "works," he is not referring to actions required by the Jewish law: Sabbath observance, kosher food requirements, and so on. He is clearly talking about good deeds: feeding the hungry, clothing the naked (the two examples he gives), and so on. For James, an intellectual assent to Christianity that does not manifest itself in how one lives is of no use. It can't save a soul.

And so the book of James may seem to be contradicting Paul, but it is not really contradicting him. What is one to make of that? Actually it is not too difficult to see what happened historically. In Chapter 3 we saw that there were later authors, such as the author of Ephesians, who claimed to be Paul, but who transformed his teaching that the works of the Jewish law could not bring salvation into a teaching that said "good works" could not save (see Eph. 2:8–9; see also Titus 3:5). For an author like the pseudonymous writer of Ephesians, doing good deeds does not contribute to making a person right with God. James therefore is reacting not to what Paul said but to what later Christians misunderstood Paul as saying.

These later Pauline Christians interpreted Paul's argument that it was faith, not works, that justified to mean that it doesn't matter what you do or how you live. It matters only what you believe. Paul's teaching on "works of the law" was taken to be a general principle about "good deeds." And Paul's teaching about "trust in Christ" was altered into a teaching about "what to believe." For these later Christians, then, what mattered was your belief, not your life. They thought this teaching came from Paul, and so they too appealed to Abraham, the father of all believers, and to Genesis 15:6, which indicated that Abraham was justified by his faith, not his works. James reacted against that by arguing the opposite: you can't have true faith without it being reflected in how you live your life. "Faith without works is dead."

This, then, was another controversy over the teachings of Paul as they came to be reinterpreted in his churches after his day. James does not name Paul explicitly, but it is perfectly clear that his teachings are what he has in mind, at least as they were being interpreted in his day. But was he really James, or was he someone else claiming to be James?

There are excellent reasons for thinking that this letter was not written by the brother of Jesus, but was forged in his name. For one thing, the teaching being opposed must have arisen later than the writings of Paul. That is to say, it is a later development of Pauline thinking in a later Pauline community. The teaching is indeed similar to the teaching found in Ephesians, written after Paul's lifetime in his name. But it goes even farther than Ephesians, since the author of

Ephesians would never have said that it didn't matter how you lived so long as you have faith. Just the opposite in fact! (See Eph. 2:10.) Whoever is writing the book of James is presupposing an even later situation found among Paul's churches. But since the historical James was probably martyred in 62 CE, two decades or so before Ephesians was written, the book could not very well have been written by him.

Moreover, the one thing we know best about James of Jerusalem is that he was concerned that Jewish followers of Jesus continue to keep the requirements of Jewish law. But this concern is completely and noticeably missing in this letter. This author, claiming to be James, is concerned with people doing "good deeds"; he is not at all concerned with keeping kosher, observing the Sabbath and Jewish festivals, or circumcision. His concerns are not those of James of Jerusalem.

The real clincher, though, is one we have seen before in relation to both Peter and Jude. This author has written a very fluent and rhetorically effective composition in Greek. He is intimately familiar with the Greek version of the Old Testament. The historical James, on the other hand, was an Aramaic-speaking peasant from Galilee who almost certainly never learned to read. Or if he did learn to read, it was to read Hebrew. If he ever learned Greek, it would have been as a second language in order to speak it, haltingly no doubt. He never would have gone to school. He never would have become proficient in Greek. He never would have learned how to write, even in his native language, let alone a second tongue. He never would have studied the Greek Old Testament. He never would have taken Greek composition classes. He never would have become skilled in Greek rhetoric.

This book was not written by an illiterate Aramaic-speaking Jew. Whoever wrote it claimed to be James, because that would best accomplish his objective: to stress that followers of Jesus need to manifest their faith in their lives, doing good deeds that show forth their faith, since without works faith is dead.

Forgeries in Support of Paul

JUST AS THERE WERE forgers who wanted to emphasize that Paul stood at odds with the Jerusalem disciples Peter and James and that Paul, therefore, misinterpreted the Christian message, there were others who took Paul's side and wanted to argue that he was in perfect harmony with the teachings of Peter and James, and that all three, therefore, were on the side of truth. This is at least one of the over-arching points of two of the books we already considered in Chapter 2, 1 and 2 Peter, as well as a book that scholars have as a rule been loath to label a forgery, even though that is what it appears to be—the New Testament book of Acts.

1 PETER

We have seen a number of reasons for thinking that, whoever wrote 1 Peter, it was not actually Peter. There are, however, additional reasons, two of which relate to my claim, here, that the book was written to show that Peter and Paul were completely simpatico. The first has to do with the audience of the letter. The one thing we know about the historical Peter's missionary activities is that he went to the Jews in order to try to convert them to believe in Christ. When Paul met with the "Jerusalem apostles" (Peter, James, and John), they agreed that just as Peter was in charge of the mission to the Jews, Paul would go to the Gentiles (Gal. 2:6–9). What is striking about 1 Peter is that it is written to Gentiles, not Jews (2:10; 4:3–4). But that's Paul's area, not Peter's. Moreover, the geographical destination of the letter is Paul's. The letter is directed to Christians living in five regions of Asia Minor, a place where Paul had started churches. Nothing con-nects the historical Peter with these places.

These features of the letter seem less odd when seen in the total context of what the letter is trying to accomplish. Not only is it pro-viding comfort to those who are suffering for their faith; in doing so it is trying to make Peter sound like Paul, the missionary to the Gentiles in Asia Minor. Why would it want to do that? Surely it is for reasons we have seen: there were other Christians who maintained, even in the churches of Asia Minor, that Peter and Paul were at each other's throats and represented different understandings of the gospel. Not for the author of 1 Peter. He writes a letter in the name of Peter that sounds very much like a letter of Paul.

The two people that the pseudonymous author names in the letter, Silvanus and Mark (5:12–13), are otherwise known as companions of Paul (see, e.g., 1 Thess. 1:1; Philem. 24). The use of Scripture in the letter is very similar to the way Paul uses Scripture; Hosea 2:25 is quoted in 2:10, for example, to show that Gentiles are now the people of God, just as Paul uses the same verse in Romans 9:25. The moral exhortations of the letter sound like Paul's; for example, Christians are to be "subject to every human institution," as in Romans 13:1–7. And most important, the theology espoused in the letter is the theology of Paul. Just as isolated examples, which could be multiplied many times over: it is faith that leads to salvation (1:9); the end of all things is at hand (4:7); and the death of Christ brings salvation from sins (2:24; 3:18). These may all sound like things every Christian could well say. But when you look at the actual wording of the passages, you would be hard pressed at times to say that this isn't straight from Paul: "He himself bore our sins in his body on the tree, that we might die to sin and live to righteousness" (2:24); "For Christ also died for sins once for all, the righteous for the unrighteous, that he might bring us to God" (3:18).

It is not convincing to mount a counterargument by saying this letter contains some differences from Paul's own letters as well. One can argue that about all of Paul's undisputed letters; each one has distinctive things to say. The point is that this letter forged in the name of Peter appears to go out of its way to embrace views attested otherwise for Paul. Here we have a forger who wants to insist that the two great apostles of the church were completely on the same page in their understanding of the gospel, in the face of other Christians who argued that they were at odds with one another.

2 Peter

Something similar can be said of 2 Peter. In this case the author goes even farther out of his way to insist that he is Peter, as he not only names himself "Simeon Peter" in 1:1, but stresses that he was personally present with Jesus on the mount at the transfiguration: "We were eyewitnesses of his majesty . . . for we were with him on the holy mountain" (2:16–19). This really is Peter! And he really likes Paul! In fact, he more than likes Paul—he thinks Paul's letters are Scripture.

As we have seen, 2 Peter stresses that even though a long time has passed since Jesus declared that the end of all things would be "soon," everything is in fact going according to plan. Soon in God's calendar is not the same as soon in ours, for "with the Lord one day is as a thousand years and a thousand years as one day" (2:8). God has in fact put off the time of the end in order to provide more time for more people to be saved: "Consider the patience of our Lord as salvation." This, claims the author, is taught by "our beloved brother Paul," who, we are told, "wrote to you according to the wisdom that was given to him, speaking about these thing in all his letters, in which there are matters hard to understand, which the unlearned and unstable twist to their own destruction, as they do with the rest of the Scriptures" (3:15–16).

There are several important points here. Paul is Peter's "beloved brother." They agree on all essential points. Other Christians have misinterpreted ("twisted") Paul's letters. They do this as well with the "other" Scriptures. Among other things, this means that "Peter" considers the letters of Paul to be Scripture. For this author, then, if anyone interprets Paul's letters to mean that he and Peter disagree, they have flat-out misinterpreted the letters. Paul's letters speak the truth, and Peter agrees with them.

Except, of course, that the person who wrote this letter was not actually Peter, but someone later claiming to be Peter. One of the ultimate goals of this pseudonymous writer is perfectly clear: he very much wanted his readers to think that the apostle to the Jews and the apostle to the Gentiles had no differences of opinion.

THE ACTS OF THE APOSTLES

The Acts of the Apostles is the earliest surviving account we have of the spread of Christianity in the years immediately after the death of Jesus. It is a historical narrative that tries to explain how Christianity moved geographically from its beginnings in the city of Jerusalem, throughout Judea, into Samaria, and then into other parts of the Roman Empire, until it finally reached the city of Rome itself. But Acts is concerned not only with the geographical spread of the religion, but also with what you might call its "ethnic" spread. The author is particularly interested in the question of how the Jewish religion of Jesus and his followers became a religion adopted by Gentiles, non-Jews. Given the author's interest in the conversion of former pagans to the new faith, it is no surprise that the ultimate hero of the story is Paul, known in the early church as the apostle to the Gentiles par excellence.

Paul in this narrative does not start out as a follower of Jesus, however. Quite the contrary. As the budding Christian church grows by fits and starts in its early months through the preaching of such empowered apostles as Peter, who is the main character of the book's first twelve chapters, it also incurs the hatred of Jews who refuse to convert and see the newfound religion as blasphemous and dangerous. Eventually the chief opponent of the new faith is Saul of Tarsus, a highly religious Jew who is authorized to hunt down and imprison anyone who professes faith in Christ.

But then in one of the greatest turn-arounds in early Christian history—or in all of history, some would argue—the great persecutor of the faith becomes its most powerful preacher. En route to persecute Christians in the city of Damascus Paul has a vision of the resurrected Jesus and comes to believe that the faith he had once opposed is true (Acts 9). After meeting with those who were apostles before him—Peter and others—Paul devotes himself as zealously to propagating the new faith as he had once devoted himself to oppressing it. Paul travels throughout the Mediterranean regions of Asia Minor, Macedonia, and Achaia (modern Turkey and Greece), visiting major urban areas, preaching the gospel, converting mainly Gentiles, and starting churches.

Early in his missionary work a major point of contention arises among the leaders of the church, however. Don't the Gentiles who are coming to believe in Jesus need to convert to Judaism, if they are to be followers of the Jewish messiah? Don't they need to be circumcised and to keep the Jewish law? Some of the Christian leaders think that the answer is yes; others think the answer is no. Peter himself, in this story, firmly thinks no. In no small measure this is because, even before Paul's missionary journeys, God has revealed to Peter, personally, in a vision, that Gentiles are to be accepted into the faith without becoming Jews (Acts 10–11). Peter in fact is the first to convert a Gentile.

And so when a church conference is called to decide the matter in Acts 15, halfway through the narrative, there are some outside, unnamed spokespersons for the view that Gentile converts should be required to keep the law. But the main insiders—not just Paul, but also Peter and James, head of the Jerusalem church—are completely on the other side and stand shoulder to shoulder in insisting that the salvation of Christ has gone to the Gentiles, who do not have to accept the Jewish law in order to be saved.

Newly authorized by this unified decision, Paul goes back to the mission field and establishes more churches, before running into trouble with the Jewish authorities during a visit to Jerusalem. Most of the final third of the book of Acts deals with Paul's imprisonment and trials as he attempts to defend himself, insisting that he has not been doing anything contrary to the Jewish law. He, instead, has always supported the law in preaching that Jesus himself is the Jewish messiah who has been raised from the dead (even though he thinks Gentiles are not required to keep the law). Paul eventually appeals to present his case before the Roman emperor, as he is entitled to do as a Roman citizen. The book ends with his journey to Rome and his house arrest there, where he is shown preaching to all who will hear while waiting for his trial.

As should be clear from this summary, one of the overarching themes of Acts is that Peter, the hero of the first third of the book, and Paul, the hero of the rest, were completely aligned in every respect. They agreed on the practical question of whether Gentiles should be required to keep the Jewish law; they agreed on the need and approach to the mission to convert Gentiles; they agreed on every theological issue. To this extent the book of Acts lines up very nicely with the two other books of the New Testament we have already considered, 1 and 2 Peter, and against a number of books from outside the New Testament, such as the *Epistle of Peter* and the Pseudo-Clementine *Homilies*. One could also argue that it stands at odds with what Paul himself had to say in the book of Galatians, where Peter is not treated in a friendly way.

As it turns out, there are many other differences between what the book of Acts says about Paul and what Paul says about himself in his letters. I won't go into all the gory details here, as they are more fully discussed in other places that are easily accessible.[6] Just with respect to Galatians, though, I might point out that, whereas Acts is quite clear that Peter realized, even before Paul did, that it was a good and right thing to share meals with Gentiles who did not keep kosher, in Galatians 2 this is precisely what Peter refuses to do when Jewish "brothers" show up in town. One could argue that Paul was right, that Peter was simply being hypocritical. But there is nothing in Galatians to suggest that Peter actually saw it this way or that he thought Paul was right about the matter. The historical Peter may have thought that sharing meals with Gentiles when Jews were around was wrong. If so, then the historical Peter thought differently from the way the Peter of the book of Acts thought.

There are other differences between Acts and Galatians that are even harder to reconcile. Here I'll mention just two. In Galatians

Paul tries to convince his Gentile readers that it would be an enormous mistake if they were to become circumcised and begin following the Jewish law. He wants to insist that his understanding of this matter came directly from God, in the revelation he had of Christ that turned him into a follower. He did not—he emphatically and decidedly did not—get this message from those who were apostles before him, Peter, James, and the others. In fact, he stresses, after the vision of Christ that converted him, he did not even go to Jerusalem to talk with the apostles. He went away into Arabia, then back to Damascus, and did not go to Jerusalem for another three years (1:15–19). This makes the story of Paul's conversion in the book of Acts very interesting. Here we are told that Paul is blinded by his vision of Jesus on the road to Damascus; he then enters the city and regains his sight. And what's the very first thing he does when he leaves town? He makes a beeline straight to Jerusalem to see the apostles (Acts 9:1–26). Well, which is it? Did he stay away from Jerusalem, as Paul himself says, or did he go there first thing, as Acts says?

Moreover, whom does he see there? Paul insists in Galatians 1:18–19 that in his fifteen-day visit he saw only two people, Peter and James, the brother of Jesus. Paul is emphatic on this point, which he stresses by swearing an oath: "What I am writing to you, before God, I am not lying!" (1:19–20). It's not clear why he wants to stress the point so strongly. Is it because he doesn't want anyone to think that his message was passed along to him by the original disciples of Jesus, most of whom he never met? In any event, what is clear is the contrast with Acts. There, when Paul arrives in Jerusalem directly after being converted, he meets with apostles and spends some time among them—not just with Peter and James, but apparently with all of them (9:26–30).

These differences between what Acts says about Paul and what Paul says about himself can be multiplied time and again, especially if we were to turn to Pauline letters other than Galatians. One reason the differences matter is that Paul wants to distance himself from the apostles to claim that his message came directly from Christ, not from those who were apostles before him. The book of Acts, on the other hand, wants to insist that Paul conferred with the other apostles before he started taking his message out into the mission field. Moreover, for Paul the other apostles gave him no message that Christ had not already revealed to him. If the others, even Peter and James, disagreed with him, then they were disagreeing not with him, but with God, who had revealed himself to Paul through Christ. For Acts, on the other hand, there is no possibility of Paul and the others disagreeing. God informed them all equally of the truth of the gospel, and they all preach the gospel. It is the same message, the same theology, the same practical conclusions: they are all on the same page, up and down the line.

The other reason the differences between Paul and Acts matter is because Acts claims to be written by someone who was a companion of Paul. But given the numerous discrepancies between Paul's letters and the book of Acts, that looks highly unlikely. The author of Acts never names himself, and to that extent he is writing anonymously. But church tradition, starting about a century after the book was written, attributed the book to someone named Luke. And why Luke?

The reasoning is a bit complicated, but it goes like this. The first important point to make is that the Gospel of Luke and the book of Acts, both of them anonymous, were written by the same author. This is shown by their similar theological views, their shared vocabulary and writing style, and such clear indications as the opening verses of the two books, both of which are dedicated to someone named Theophilus. The second book actually indicates that it is the second of two books written to this person. Almost certainly, then, the author of Acts is the author of Luke. Acts is the second volume of a two-volume work.

But why think it was written by someone named Luke? Even though the Gospel of Luke gives no hint as to its author, there are clues that surely must be intentional in the book of Acts. In four passages of Acts the author stops speaking in the third person about what "they" (Paul and his companions) were doing and starts speaking about what "we" were doing (16:10–17; 20:5–16; 21:1–18; 27:1–28:16). This is someone who is claiming to have been with Paul as a traveling companion during his missionary journeys. But he doesn't say who he is.[7]

Readers over the centuries have thought, however, that his identity could be inferred. This author is someone who is especially concerned with the Gentile mission of the early church and who is particularly invested in showing that Gentiles do not have to become Jews in order to be Christian. It is sensible to conclude that this person was probably himself a Gentile. So now we are narrowing the matter down a bit; the author is allegedly a Gentile traveling companion of Paul. Do we know of any such persons?

In the letter to the Colossians we learn of three persons who were Gentile companions of Paul: Epaphras, Demas, and Luke the physician (Col. 4:12–14). Of these three, it seems unlikely that Demas could be the author, since we learn elsewhere that Demas "abandoned" Paul (2 Tim. 2:10). Epaphras appears to have been known as the founder of the church in Colossae (Col. 1:5–7), a church that is never mentioned in Acts. That would be odd, if its founder were the author. This leaves then one candidate, Luke the Gentile physician. So we have the age-old assumption that the book of Acts was written by Luke, a traveling companion of Paul. This assumption is found already in the late second-century church father Irenaeus. Irenaeus was writing a century after the book of Acts was produced. He is nonetheless the first surviving Christian author to make extensive reference to the book, and he indicates, based on his knowledge of the "we" passages, that "Luke was inseparable from Paul, and was his fellow-laborer in the gospel, as he himself clearly evinces."[8]

Despite this ancient tradition, the problems with identifying Luke as the author of the book are rife. For one thing, the idea that Luke was a Gentile companion of Paul comes from Colossians, a book that appears to have been forged in Paul's name after his death. To be sure, there is also a Luke named in Paul's authentic letter of Philemon (v. 24), but nothing is said there about his being a Gentile. He is simply mentioned in a list of five other people. An even bigger problem presents itself in the fact that there are so many discrepancies between what Acts says about Paul with what Paul says about himself.

I've mentioned only three of these discrepancies. There are many others.[9] They involve just about every aspect of the historical Paul. Paul's theology and preaching differ between Acts and the letters; other differences are in Paul's attitude toward pagans, his relationship to the Jewish law, his missionary strategy, and his itinerary. At just about every point where it is possible to check what Acts says about Paul with what Paul says about himself in his authentic letters, there are discrepancies. The conclusion is hard to escape that Acts was probably not written by one of Paul's traveling companions.

But why would the author then speak in the first person on four occasions? Anyone reading this book so far should have no trouble figuring out why. The author is making a claim about himself. He is not naming himself. He is simply claiming to be a traveling companion of Paul's and therefore unusually well suited to give a "true" account of Paul's message and mission. But he almost certainly was not a companion of Paul's. On the one hand, he was writing long after Paul and his companions were dead. Scholars usually date Acts to around 85 CE or so, over two decades after Paul's death. On the other hand, he seems to be far too poorly informed about Paul's theology and missionary activities to have been someone with firsthand knowledge. If the author is claiming to be someone he is not, what kind of work is he writing? A book written with a false authorial claim is a forgery. Obviously the authorial claim in this case is not as bold-faced as in, say, 1 Timothy or *3 Corinthians*, whose authors directly say they are Paul. But the claim of Acts is clear nonetheless; the author indicates that he was a participant in and eyewitness to Paul's mission, even though he was not.

It should not be objected that if the author wanted his readers to be convinced he was a companion of Paul, he would have been a lot more explicit about his identity, that is, he necessarily would have named himself or been more emphatic in his self-identification as a cotraveler with Paul. This kind of objection about what an author "would have" done is never very persuasive. For modern readers to tell ancient authors what they should have done in order to be more convincing is actually a bit amusing. Why should the author of Acts have done anything other than what he did? How could he possibly have been any more successful at deceiving his readers? He was spectacularly successful doing it the way he did. Readers for eighteen hundred years accepted without question that the author was none other than Luke, the traveling companion of Paul. By inserting just a small handful of first-person pronouns into his account the author succeeded in producing a forgery that continues to deceive readers down to the present day.

The reason for the forgery, in any event, is clear, or at least one of the many reasons is. This author wants his readers to think he is Paul's companion and therefore has firsthand knowledge of Paul's mission. Paul, in this account, agrees with the apostles before him, especially Peter and James, on every point of theological and practical importance. The earliest church was in firm and essential harmony. Peter and Paul were not at odds, as other authors were claiming. Together they declared that salvation has gone to the Gentiles, who do not have to be Jews in order to be Christians.

Gnostic and Anti-Gnostic Forgeries

EARLY CHRISTIAN GNOSTICISM

The most intense and vitriolic conflicts of the second and third centuries involved a variety of Christian groups that scholars have called "Gnostic." Gnostic Christianity was a remarkably complex phenomenon, but for our purposes here I need give simply a broad and basic overview.[10]

As I mentioned in Chapter 3, the term "Gnostic" comes from the

Greek word *gnosis*, which means "knowledge." A wide range of early Christian groups claimed that salvation did not come from faith in the death and resurrection of Jesus, but from acquiring the secret knowledge, *gnosis*, that Christ taught. This knowledge was actually self-knowledge, knowledge of who you really were, deep inside, where you came from, how you got here, and how you can return. Gnostics maintained that some of us are not just flesh-and-blood human beings. We have a spark of divinity within us that originated in the heavenly realm, but that has fallen into the material world and become trapped inside our mortal bodies. The goal of Gnostic religions was to teach the secret knowledge needed to free this element of the divine, so that it can return to its heavenly home. In the Christian forms of Gnosticism (there were non-Christian forms as well), it is Christ who comes from the heavenly realm above to provide us with this secret knowledge.

There were a large number of Gnostic groups with a mind-boggling array of different teachings and beliefs. Many of these groups described the fall of the divine sparks through complicated and confusing mythological tales that tried to explain how both the divine realm above and this material world below came into existence. Even though the myths of the various groups differed from one another significantly, many of them shared similar features.

In many of these myths the originating point of all that is was a divine being who was completely spirit; there was nothing material about him/it. This divine being generated other divinities who were manifestations of his various characteristics: silence, intellect, truth, word, life, and so on. Some of these divine beings generated yet other divine beings, until there was a populated realm of the divine. But one of these beings—in some texts it is Sophia, the Greek word for "Wisdom"—fell from the divine realm and generated other beings who were not fully divine, since they came into existence outside of the realm of the divine. One of these other beings ignorantly thought that it was the superior God and, with the help of the others, captured its mother and created the material world as a place to imprison her, inside human bodies. This ignorant creator God is the God of the Old Testament, the God of the Jews.

So the material world we live in is not a good place; it is a place of imprisonment. The God of the Jews is not the ultimate divinity, but is inferior, ignorant, and possibly even malicious. The goal of salvation is not to be put into a right relationship with the creator God, but to escape his clutches. Salvation does not come when this fallen creation is returned to its original pristine state (a return to the Garden of Eden); it comes by escaping this material world. The end of time will not bring a salvation of the flesh; it will bring a deliverance *from* the flesh. This salvation comes when the sparks trapped within our bodies learn the secrets of how they came to be here and the knowledge of how they can escape.

Since in the Christian Gnostic systems it is Christ who comes from the divine realm to deliver this secret knowledge, he obviously could not be a part of this material world itself. He was not a fleshly being. So we have the two forms of docetic thought that I mentioned in Chapter 2. Some Gnostics maintained that Jesus only appeared to be human (like Marcion, who was not a Gnostic). Others claimed that the divine Christ entered into the man Jesus at his baptism and then left him before he died, since the Christ could not suffer. In either way of understanding Christ, he was not a real, flesh-and-blood, suffering, and dying human who was returned to the flesh at his resurrection. Like the other sparks of the divine, he escaped the flesh and the material world, which houses it, in order to return to his heavenly home.

Because Gnostics who taught such views denigrated the material world and the God who created it, they were seen as a serious threat by other Christians who maintained that there was only one God, not an entire realm of divinities; that God had made the world and that it was good, not inferior or evil; that he had formed human flesh and would redeem human flesh; and that salvation came in the body, not separate from the body. Moreover, Christian opponents of Gnosticism maintained that Christ himself was a real flesh-and-blood human being whose real suffering and death brought salvation and whose resurrection was a resurrection in the flesh, in which he now lives and will live forevermore.

These alternative anti-Gnostic views were taught by such prominent Christian authors as the second-century Irenaeus and the third-century Tertullian, authors whose writings have been known and widely read for many centuries. The Gnostics ended up losing these debates, and their own works were by and large destroyed. It is only in modern times that Gnostic writings have been discovered, most notably in a remarkable but completely serendipitous uncovering of an entire library of Gnostic texts in 1945 near the Egyptian town of Nag Hammadi.[11]

This so-called Nag Hammadi library contains forty-six different documents, a few of which are in duplicate. Some of them detail the mythological views of this or that Gnostic group, others are mystical reflections on the nature of reality or of the human's place in it, others are secret revelations that Jesus delivers to his disciples after his "resurrection," and still others are collections of Jesus's earthly teachings. Some of these writings were produced in the names of the apostles. They are, in other words, Gnostic forgeries.

GNOSTIC FORGERIES

We knew about Gnostic forgeries for a long time before we actually had any of them. The fourth-century heresy hunter Epiphanius, for example, in a book that attacks eighty different groups of "heretics," talks about one particularly nefarious Gnostic group that he calls the Phibionites. In his attack on this group Epiphanius reports that they used a whole range of pseudonymous writings, including a *Gospel of Eve*, the *Lesser Questions of Mary* (*Magdalene*), the *Greater Questions of Mary*, the *Books of Seth*, the *Apocalypses of Adam*, the *Birth of Mary*, and the *Gospel of Philip*.[12] The *Gospel of Philip* was discovered at Nag Hammadi, although it is impossible to know whether it is the same book that Epiphanius was referring to. We also have a writing called the *Birth of Mary*, but there is nothing Gnostic about it, and so it too may be a different book. None of the other books survives.[13]

But plenty of other Gnostic forgeries do. Among the Nag Hammadi writings that set forth Gnostic views in the names of the apostles is a *Secret Book of John* (i.e., the son of Zebedee), which lays out in graphic detail one version of the Gnostic myth, and an *Apocalypse of Paul*, which describes a mystical ascent of the apostle through the heavens, narrated in the first person. There are two apocalypses of James and the aforementioned *Gospel of Philip*. And most famously of all there is the *Gospel of Thomas*, a collection of 114 sayings of Jesus allegedly recorded by Judas Didymus Thomas, who was reputed in some regions of the early church to have been the twin brother of Jesus.[14]

Rather than discuss all the Gnostic forgeries here, I will consider just two, which are particularly interesting, because they not only attest a Gnostic point of view, but also argue against the view that eventually became "orthodox," that is, the view represented by such authors as Irenaeus, Tertullian, and Epiphanius, which was eventually accepted as "true" over against the teachings of "false gnosis."

The Coptic Apocalypse of Peter

We have already seen one *Apocalypse of Peter* in Chapter 2. At Nag Hammadi a second one was discovered, a secret revelation given to Simon Peter.[15] The one we already examined emphasized strongly the bodily nature of the afterlife, where people are blissfully rewarded or horrifically punished, physically, for how they lived in this life. The *Coptic Apocalypse of Peter* takes a radically different view, arguing that those who believe in the importance of the flesh, whether Christ's own flesh or the fleshly life of humans, have completely misunderstood and corrupted the truth.

This book is also written in the first person, allegedly by Jesus's disciple Peter. It begins with a discussion between Christ and Peter on the day of Jesus's death, after which it narrates what "really" happened at the crucifixion. This is one of the more bizarre descriptions of Christ's death that you will ever read. In the opening dialogue Christ strongly emphasizes the need for proper "knowledge" for salvation and condemns Christians who lack this knowledge, saying that "they are blind and have no leader" (72.12–13). The non-Gnostic leaders of the Christian churches who praise Christ are blaspheming him and are themselves both blind and deaf (73.13–14). This is especially the case, because they "hold on to the name of a dead man"; that is, they think that it is the crucified Jesus who matters for salvation. But how wrong they are! "They do not understand" (76.28–35). These "bishops and deacons" are dried up and barren channels who provide no life-giving water.

After Christ's attack on those who value material existence and who think that his death brings salvation comes the narrative of the crucifixion. While Peter and Christ are talking, Peter sees Jesus, down below the hill where they are standing, "apparently" seized by his enemies and crucified. But above the cross he sees another image of Christ, this one laughing at the entire proceeding. Considerably confused, Peter asks the Christ standing next to him what he is seeing. Christ replies that the one above the cross is the "living Jesus," and the one on the cross "is the substitute," that is, the stand-in for the real Jesus, who cannot be crucified because he is not really a flesh-and-blood human being. The body being crucified is "the abode of demons, the stony vessel in which they live, the man of Elohim" (the name of the Old Testament God). The one above the cross is laughing at the ignorance of those crucifying him, because they are blind and think that they can kill the Christ. But they can't. He is a spirit, beyond suffering.

This, then, is a Gnostic evaluation of the world and Christ's place in it. Christ's death is not what matters. Salvation comes by accepting his true teaching, which denigrates the material world and the human flesh. His flesh did not matter, and neither does the flesh of his followers. This view is presented through an impeccable authority, a firsthand account by Peter himself, or at least by a writing forged in his name.

The Book of Thomas the Contender

An even more direct attack on the flesh is found in another Gnostic writing known as the *Book of Thomas the Contender*, also found at Nag Hammadi.[16] This book too is pseudepigraphal; it is said to be a revelation to Thomas, Jesus's twin brother, but written down by "Matthaias." Scholars typically take this figure to be Matthew, author of the First Gospel.

In this book Christ gives a revelation just before he ascends to heaven. The goal of the revelation is to emphasize the importance of self-knowledge: "Those who have not known themselves have known nothing, but those who have known themselves already have acquired knowledge about the depth of the All" (138.16–18). Knowing oneself means knowing that the real you is not the "you" of your body. It is the spirit, which is separate from the flesh.

Christ points out that the human body is like that of all the animals, as it comes into being through intercourse. Moreover, it survives by eating other creatures and changing. But anything that changes will eventually dissipate and exist no more. So too with humans: "The vessel of their flesh will pass away" (141.6–7). The one who hopes to have salvation in the flesh is therefore to be pitied: "Woe to you who hope in the flesh and in the prison that will perish."

Since the body is not to be redeemed, the desires of the body are not to be indulged. One of the overarching points of the book is that fleshly lusts entrap a soul in the body, and anyone who succumbs to the fires of desire will be punished in the fires of the afterlife. So the author exhorts his readers to seek for the salvation that comes by escaping the body: "Watch and pray that you may not remain in the flesh, but that you may leave the bondage of the bitterness of this life. . . . When you leave the pains and the passions of the body, you will receive rest from the Good One. You will reign with the King, you united with him and he with you, from now on and forever" (145.9–14).

This is not really a revelation to Thomas written down by Matthias, however. It is another Gnostic forgery, produced in order to oppose the teachings of other Christians that fleshly existence matters.

ANTI-GNOSTIC FORGERIES

Gnostics were not, of course, the only ones who used forgeries to promote their views. The "orthodox" Christians who opposed them responded in kind by publishing forgeries of their own.

3 Corinthians

We have already seen one forgery that could well have served an anti-Gnostic purpose, *3 Corinthians*. Earlier I talked about *3 Corinthians* being directed against Marcion, who, like the Gnostics, devalued the life of the flesh. It is hard to know exactly whom the pseudonymous author has in mind when he affirms the flesh of Christ and the salvation of the flesh. Possibly he is attacking all groups that held to contrary views. But at least his own view is not hard to discern. His overarching emphasis is that Christ came into this world that he might "save *all flesh* by *his own flesh* and that he might raise us *in the flesh* from the dead as he has presented himself to us as our example."

For this author, Jesus was really born of Mary. This was in fulfillment of what the prophets of the Old Testament had declared. These prophets were spokespersons of the one true God, who had created the world and who was the "almighty," not some kind of lower, inferior divinity. Precisely in "his own body, Jesus Christ saved all flesh," and it will be in the flesh that his followers will experience ultimate salvation at the resurrection. Here, then, in *3 Corinthians*, forgeries of the heretics are countered by a forgery of the orthodox, a letter claiming to be written by Paul, but in fact written by an author living much later.

Epistula Apostolorum

As a second and final example of an orthodox forgery I can mention a second-century book known as the *Epistula Apostolorum*, the "Epistle of the Apostles."[17] This is a letter allegedly written after the resurrection by the twelve apostles, who name themselves and write in the first person, in opposition to the "false apostles" Simon and Cerinthus. Simon we have met before as the archheretic of the second century, maligned, for example, in the *Acts of Peter* and the *Pseudo-Clementines*. Here he is accompanied by another notorious heretic, Cerinthus. Both are attacked for being filled with "deceit." This charge is thick with irony, of course, in a writing that is forged in order to make its readers believe the apostles were really writing it.

The letter presents a revelation that Jesus gives to the apostles after his resurrection, much as the *Book of Thomas the Contender* and other Gnostic writings give the "secret teachings" of Christ after the resurrection. But here the emphasis is completely anti-Gnostic. Few documents stress as heavily as this one the importance of the flesh. Jesus is said to have had a real crucifixion and a real physical resurrection, as noted by the apostle Andrew, for example, who saw Jesus's footprints on the ground after he had been raised: "A ghost, a demon leaves no print in the ground," he insists (chap. 11). The apostles stress: "We felt him, that he had truly risen in the flesh."

Christ himself says, "I . . . put on your flesh, in which I was born and died and was buried and rose again" (chap. 19); and he indicates that "the flesh of every one will rise with his soul alive and his spirit" (chap. 24). Anyone who teaches anything different (the authors of the *Book of Thomas the Contender* and the *Coptic Apocalypse of Peter*!) will suffer eternal punishment, involving real, physical pain (chap. 29).

It is interesting that this book explicitly claims to be written against those who "deliberately say what is not true" (chap. 50). This is a book that deliberately claims to be written by apostles who had been dead for a century.

Conclusion

ONE OF THE MOST fascinating features of early Christianity is that so many different Christian teachers and Christian groups were saying so many contrary things. It is not just that they said different things. They often said just the opposite things. There is only one God. No, there are many gods. The material world is the good creation of a good God. No, it comes from a cosmic disaster in the divine realm. Jesus came in the flesh. No, he was totally removed from the flesh. Eternal life comes through the redemption of the flesh. No, it comes through escaping the flesh. Paul taught these things. No, Paul taught those other things. Paul was the true apostle. No, Paul misunderstood the message of Jesus. Peter and Paul agreed on every theological point. No, they were completely at odds with one another. Peter taught that Christians were not to follow the Jewish law. No, he taught that the Jewish law continued to be in force. And on and on and on, world without end.

Not only did those on every side in all of these debates think that they were right and that their opponents were wrong; they also maintained in all sincerity and honesty that their views were the ones taught by Jesus and his apostles. What is more, they all, apparently, produced books to prove it, books that claimed to be written by apostles and supported their own points of view. What is perhaps most interesting of all, the vast majority of these apostolic books were in fact forged. Christians intent on establishing what was right to believe did so by telling lies, in an attempt to deceive their readers into agreeing that they were the ones who spoke the truth.

Chapter Seven

False Attributions, Fabrications, and Falsifications: Phenomena Related to Forgery

THROUGHOUT THIS BOOK I HAVE focused on "literary" forgery, a deception in which the author of a literary text claims to be someone else. We all know of other, nonliterary kinds of forgeries as well: forgeries of documents (fake wills, marriage certificates, driver's licenses; other forms of identification), works of art, money, and so on. In all of these cases the forger intends to deceive and mislead people for his or her own purposes.

There are many other ways to deceive people, of course. Sometimes deception comes from hiding the truth, for example, by distorting or not telling the whole truth, as our president did for months during the Monica Lewinsky fiasco; or by removing evidence that can reveal the truth, as when another, earlier president, or one of his lackeys, erased crucial portions of the Watergate tapes. Sometimes deception comes from doctoring the truth, as happened when the American and British people, and possibly their elected officials, were fed misinformation about the threat to the United States posed by Iraq's stockpiling of weapons of mass destruction. Sometimes deception comes when people make excessive claims about themselves or their work, as when James Frey stated that his book *Million Little Pieces* was autobiographical, when in fact it was fictional, arousing the ire not only of millions of potential readers, but also of the great Oprah herself. And sometimes deception occurs when someone claims as his or her own work the work of another, for example, in instances of plagiarism, which are reaching epidemic proportions on college campuses around the country thanks to that boon and bane of modern human existence, the Internet.

All of these alternate forms of deception were available in antiquity as well, of course (well, apart from the Internet). To round out my study of forgery, I would like to consider some of them in this chapter, restricting myself specifically to literary forms of misinformation. The first is not necessarily a form of deception; it is the other kind of pseudepigraphy that I mentioned at the outset of my discussion. Whereas some pseudepigrapha—writings under a "false name"—are forgeries, others involve "false attributions"; in this case someone other than the author claims that an anonymous writing was written by a well-known person, when in fact it was not. Sometimes, to be sure, that can be a form of deception (though not by the author). Other times it is just a well-intentioned mistake.

False Attributions

IT WAS A LOT more common to write a book anonymously in antiquity than it is today. Just within the pages of the New Testament, nine of the books—fully one-third of the writings—were produced by authors who did not reveal their names. When church fathers were deciding which books to include in Scripture, however, it was necessary to "know" who wrote these books, since only writings with clear apostolic connections could be considered authoritative Scripture. So, for example, four early Gospels that were all anonymous began to be circulated under the names of Matthew, Mark, Luke, and John about a century after they were written. The book of Acts was known to have been written by the author of the Third Gospel, so it too was assigned to Luke. The anonymous book of Hebrews was assigned to Paul, even though numbers of early Christian scholars realized that Paul did not write it, as scholars today agree. And three short anonymous writings with some similarities to the Fourth Gospel were assigned to the same author, and so were called 1, 2, and 3 John. None of these books claims to be written by the author to whom they were ultimately assigned. But since the real authors made no claims for themselves, the books are not forgeries. They are simply false attributions—assuming, for the moment, that the names attached to them are not those of the people who actually wrote them.

MISATTRIBUTIONS BY MISTAKE

Often in early Christianity anonymous writings were assigned to certain authors for fairly neutral reasons—readers simply wanted to know who wrote them. Just to give a simple example, in the third and fourth centuries there was a book in circulation called *Against All Heresies*. The book, which we still have today, gives a description of thirty-two individuals or groups who held beliefs that the anonymous author considered false. One of the great heresiologists—that is, heresy hunters—of the early Christian centuries was Tertullian, from the early third century. Some readers of *Against All Heresies* came to think that even though the book was anonymous, it must have been written by him. So scribes who copied the book identified Tertullian as the author, and the book was added to the collection of Tertullian's writings, even though it never claims to be written by him.

Modern scholars are convinced on stylistic grounds that Tertullian did not write the book. Who then did? We do know of a book with this title written by the church writer Victorinus of Pettau, who was active around the year 270 CE, half a century after Tertullian. Some scholars have thought that this is the book we have.[1] Others have argued that it was written by an unknown author seventy years earlier, in Greek rather than in Tertullian's Latin, so that the book we now have is a translation into Latin of an originally anonymous work. The reality is that we will never know for sure. The readers and scribes in the ancient world who thought that Tertullian wrote it were almost certainly wrong, but there may not have been any ulterior motive in their assigning it to him. They may simply have made a mistake.

ATTRIBUTIONS MADE TO INCREASE THE AUTHORITY OF A WRITING

In other instances the attribution of a writing to an author may have been made in order to add greater weight to its significance. For example, one of the earliest Christian writings from outside the New Testament is a letter sent from the church of Rome to the Christians of Corinth, urging them to reinstate a group of church elders who had been unceremoniously removed from office. Traditionally the book has been known as *1 Clement*. This is a long letter—sixty-five chapters in modern editions—that uses numerous scriptural and rhetorical arguments to make its point, which is that leaders of the church have divine authority and are not to be replaced at the whim or on the vote of a local congregation. Anyone who acts against the leadership of the church is doing so out of profane jealousy. The church of Corinth is to restore its leaders to their rightful place.

Even though the letter claims to be written by the "church" that is in Rome, obviously someone wrote it, not hundreds of people serving on a letter-writing committee. Eventually the letter came to be attributed to a figure we have met before in our study, Clement of Rome, allegedly the fourth bishop of Rome, who had been appointed to that office by none other than Simon Peter, Jesus's great disciple and apostle of the church. Once the name of Clement was associated with the letter, it obviously took on greater force and persuasive power. This is not simply a lengthy exhortation written by a group of unknown and unnamed individuals. It is a book written by one of the great authorities of the early Christian church. Largely as a result of this attribution, the letter enjoyed great success in the early church.

Some Christians thought that it should be included among the writings of the New Testament.[2]

MISATTRIBUTIONS OF THE GOSPELS

Yet other anonymous writings were, of course, later deemed to be part of the Christian Scriptures. That never happened, however, unless it was known, or at least claimed, that the books had been written with apostolic authority. This is the case of the four New Testament Gospels, all of which were originally anonymous and then later connected with the names of apostles and apostolic companions.

It is always interesting to ask why an author chose to remain anonymous, and this is never more so than with the Gospels of the New Testament. In some instances an ancient author did not need to name himself, because his readers knew perfectly well who he was and did not need to be told. That is almost certainly the case with the letters of 2 and 3 John. These are private letters sent from someone who calls himself "the elder" to a church in another location. It is safe to assume that the recipients of the letters knew who he was.

Some have thought the Gospels were like that—written by leading persons in particular congregations who did not need to identify themselves, because everyone knew who they were. But then as the books were copied and circulated, names were still not attached to them. As a result the identities of the authors were soon lost. Then later readers, rightly or wrongly, associated the books with two of the disciples (Matthew and John) and with two companions of the apostles (Mark the companion of Peter and Luke the companion of Paul).

Another option is that the authors did not name themselves because they thought their narratives assumed greater authority if told anonymously. If the Gospel stories about Jesus are claimed by a particular author, then in some sense they seem to lose their universal appeal and applicability; they are seen as one person's version of the story, rather than "the" version of the story.

There is one reason in particular for thinking that this is what the Gospel writers had in mind. It involves the way these narratives are written. In all four Gospels, the story of Jesus is presented as a continuation of the history of the people of God as narrated in the Jewish Bible. The portions of the Old Testament that relate the history of Israel after the death of Moses are found in the books of Joshua, Judges, 1 and 2 Samuel, and 1 and 2 Kings. All of these books are written anonymously. These books take the story of God's people from their conquest of the promised land (Joshua) to their ups and downs under charismatic rulers called judges (the book of Judges) and then under a series of kings (1 Samuel–2 Kings). This biblical history includes a promise to the first truly great king, David, that he would always have a descendant on the throne ruling Israel (2 Sam. 7:14). But the history concludes with disaster, when the Babylonian armies wipe out the nation and remove the king from power (end of 2 Kings).

Many Jews expected that in the future God would fulfill his promise to David and bring a new anointed one, a new "messiah," to rule his people Israel. The Gospels are written to show that in fact this new messiah is none other than Jesus (see Mark 1:1; John 20:30–31). To be sure, Jesus was different from the kind of messiah that other Jews were expecting.[3] Rather than coming as a great king, like David, he came as a prophet speaking of the *future* kingdom of God. He himself would bring this kingdom not by being installed as king in Jerusalem, but by dying on the cross to bring salvation. This was a salvation not from the enemies of Israel, the Romans, but from the ultimate enemies of God, the powers of sin and death. Jesus conquered these alien powers at his death and resurrection, and he is returning soon as king of the earth.

This is the message of the Gospels, and it is portrayed in these books as continuous with the anonymously written history of Israel as laid out in the Old Testament Scriptures. This can be seen, for example, in our earliest Gospel, Mark, which begins by quoting an Old Testament series of prophecies anticipating the coming of the messiah and then introducing Jesus as the one to whom these prophecies pointed. It can be seen in the Gospels of Matthew and Luke, which portray the birth of Jesus as a fulfillment of the predictions of Scripture, using imagery and language heavily dependent on Old Testament narratives to give their opening stories a "biblical" feel. It can even be seen in the Gospel of John, which begins with a powerful poem about Christ's coming into the world here at the end of time in terms highly reminiscent of the stories of the creation in the book of Genesis (Genesis: "In the beginning, God created the heavens and the earth"; John: "In the beginning was the Word, and the Word was with God, and the Word was God").

The Gospel authors, each in his own way, seem to be portraying the story of Jesus as a continuation of the story of the people of God, Israel. He is the fulfillment of all that was anticipated by the authors and prophets of the Old Testament. So it makes sense for these Gospel writers to remain anonymous, as the writers of biblical history were almost always anonymous.

The anonymity of the Gospel writers was respected for decades. When the Gospels of the New Testament are alluded to and quoted by authors of the early second century, they are never entitled, never named. Even Justin Martyr, writing around 150–60 CE, quotes verses from the Gospels, but does not indicate what the Gospels were named. For Justin, these books are simply known, collectively, as the "Memoirs of the Apostles." It was about a century after the Gospels had been originally put in circulation that they were definitively named Matthew, Mark, Luke, and John. This comes, for the first time, in the writings of the church father and heresiologist Irenaeus, around 180–85 CE.

Irenaeus wrote a five-volume work, typically known today as *Against Heresies*, directed against the false teachings rampant among Christians in his day. At one point in these writings he insists that "heretics" (i.e., false teachers) have gone astray either because they use Gospels that are not really Gospels or because they use only one or another of the four that are legitimately Gospels. Some heretical groups used only Matthew, some only Mark, and so on. For

Irenaeus, just as the gospel of Christ has been spread by the four winds of heaven over the four corners of the earth, so there must be four and only four Gospels, and they are Matthew, Mark, Luke, and John.[4]

Modern readers may not find this kind of logic very compelling, but it is not difficult to see why orthodox writers like Irenaeus wanted to stress the point. Lots of Gospels were in circulation. Christians who wanted to appeal to the authority of the Gospels had to know which ones were legitimate. For Irenaeus and his fellow orthodox Christians, legitimate Gospels could only be those that had apostolic authority behind them. The authority of a Gospel resided in the person of its author. The author therefore had to be authoritative, either an apostle himself or a close companion of an apostle who could relate the stories of the Gospel under his authority. In the year 155, when Justin was writing, it may still have been perfectly acceptable to quote the Gospels without attributing them to particular authors. But soon there were so many other Gospels in circulation that the books being widely cited by orthodox Christians needed to be given apostolic credentials. So they began to be known as Matthew, Mark, Luke, and John.

Why were these names chosen by the end of the second century? For some decades there had been rumors floating around that two important figures of the early church had written accounts of Jesus's teachings and activities. We find these rumors already in the writings of the church father Papias, around 120–30 CE, nearly half a century before Irenaeus. Papias claimed, on the basis of good authority,[5] that the disciple Matthew had written down the sayings of Jesus in the Hebrew language and that others had provided translations of them, presumably into Greek. He also said that Peter's companion Mark had rearranged the preaching of Peter about Jesus into sensible order and created a book out of it.[6]

There is nothing to indicate that when Papias is referring to Matthew and Mark, he is referring to the Gospels that were later called Matthew and Mark. In fact, everything he says about these two books contradicts what we know about (our) Matthew and Mark:

Matthew is not a collection of Jesus's sayings, but of his deeds and experiences as well; it was not written in Hebrew, but in Greek; and it was not written—as Papias supposes—independently of Mark, but was based on our Gospel of Mark. As for Mark, there is nothing about our Mark that would make you think it was Peter's version of the story, any more than it is the version of any other character in the account (e.g., John the son of Zebedee). In fact, there is nothing to suggest that Mark was based on the teachings of any one person at all, let alone Peter. Instead, it derives from the oral traditions about Jesus that "Mark" had heard after they had been in circulation for some decades.

Eventually, though, it came to be seen as necessary to assign authors' names to the four Gospels that were being most widely used in orthodox circles, to differentiate them from the "false" Gospels used by heretics. The process is not hard to detect for the First and Fourth Gospels. Since it was thought that Matthew had written a Gospel (thus Papias), one of the Gospels was called by his name, the one thought to be most Jewish in its orientation, since Matthew was, after all, a Jew. The Fourth Gospel was thought to belong to a mysterious figure referred to in that book as "the Beloved Disciple" (see, e.g., John 20:20–24), who would have to have been one of Jesus's closest followers. The three closest to Jesus, in our early traditions, were Peter, James, and John. Peter was already explicitly named in the Fourth Gospel, and so he could not be the Beloved Disciple; James was known to have been martyred early in the history of the church and so would not have been the author. That left John, the son of Zebedee. So he was assigned the authorship of the Fourth Gospel.

Some scholars have argued that it would not make sense to assign the Second and Third Gospels to Mark and Luke unless the books were actually written by people named Mark and Luke, since they were not earthly disciples of Jesus and were rather obscure figures in the early church. I've never found these arguments very persuasive. For one thing, just because figures may seem relatively obscure to us today doesn't mean that they were obscure in Christian circles in the early centuries. Moreover, it should never be forgotten that there are lots and lots of books assigned to people about whom we know very little, to Philip, for example, Thomas, and Nicodemus. Furthermore, Mark was far from obscure; he was at one time Paul's companion and was thought to be Peter's right-hand man, so that what he wrote could be trusted to be Peter's version of the Gospel. This connection is made not only in Papias, but eventually in the writings of Tertullian, who states explicitly: "That which Mark published may be affirmed to be Peter's, whose interpreter Mark was."[7]

With respect to the Third Gospel, it should be remembered that its author also wrote the book of Acts, and there he implicitly claims to have been a companion of Paul's. Because Acts stresses that Christianity succeeded principally among Gentiles, the author himself may have been a Gentile. Since there was thought to be a Gentile named Luke among Paul's companions, he was assigned the Third Gospel.

The authority of the Gospels was then secure: two of them were allegedly written by eyewitnesses to the events they narrate (Matthew and John), and the other two other were written from the perspectives of the two greatest apostles, Peter (the Gospel of Mark) and Paul (the Gospel of Luke). It does not appear, however, that any of these books was written by an eyewitness to the life of Jesus or by companions of his two great apostles.[8] For my purposes here it is enough to reemphasize that the books do not claim to be written by these people and early on they were not assumed to be written by these people. The authors of these books never speak in the first person (the First Gospel never says, "One day, Jesus and I went to Jerusalem . . ."). They never claim to be personally connected with any of the events they narrate or the persons about whom they tell their stories. The books are thoroughly, ineluctably, and invariably anonymous. At the same time, later Christians had very good reasons to assign the books to people who had not written them.

As a result, the authors of these books are not themselves making false authorial claims. Later readers are making these claims about them. They are therefore not forgeries, but false attributions.

OTHER FALSE ATTRIBUTIONS

Very much the same can be said about the remaining anonymous books of the New Testament. Scholars are highly unified in thinking that Paul did not write the book of Hebrews, even though it was included in the canon of the New Testament by church fathers who thought that it was.[9] The letters 1, 2, and 3 John sound in many ways like the Gospel of John, but they are strikingly different as well, especially in the historical context they presuppose. They were probably not written by the same author, who was not John the son of Zebedee in any event, but by a later Christian living in the same community, which had begun to experience a different range of problems from those presupposed in the Fourth Gospel. Later Christian writers who accepted the books as sacred authorities needed to assign them to an apostle, however, and so it made sense to claim that they, like the Fourth Gospel, had been written by John the son of Zebedee.

Assigning anonymous books to known authorities did not stop with the writings of the New Testament. Just to give one additional example, I might mention one of the most interesting books not to make it into the canon of Scripture. For centuries there were Christians who thought the book should be included. I think we can all be glad that it was not. This book provides one of the most vitriolic attacks on Jews and Judaism from early Christianity. Had it been included in Scripture, Jewish-Christian relations may well have turned out even worse, if that can be imagined, than they did. This book was originally written anonymously, but it later came to be attributed to one of Paul's closest companions and co-workers and so is known as the *Epistle of Barnabas*.[10]

This book is somewhat like a letter in that its author addresses a group of readers, but it is really more like an extended essay. The point of the book is to show the superiority of Christianity to the Jewish religion. The author makes this point by maligning Judaism as a religion that is and always has been false, all the way back to the time of Moses himself. That is because, according to this author, the ancient Israelites broke the covenant that God made with them at the very beginning, when Moses was given the Ten Commandments. When Moses descended from Mount Sinai with commandments in hand, he saw that the people had already committed idolatry. In anger he threw the two tablets of the law down, smashing them into bits. According to the author of *Barnabas*, this represented the breaking of the covenant (4.7–8; 14.1–4). And God never did renew the covenant with the Jews. They were lost from that day on.

The Jews, of course, were given more laws by Moses, including a new set of the Ten Commandments. But since they had alienated themselves from God, they never understood these laws and made the fatal mistake of assuming that God meant them to be taken literally instead of figuratively. As a result the Jews had always misinterpreted their own laws. When God orders the Jews not to eat swine, for example, he does not literally mean for them to avoid pork. He means that people should not behave like swine, grunting loudly when hungry, but being silent when full. People should turn to God with their prayers not only when they are in need, but also when things are good (10.1–3).

So too when God commands that the day of the Sabbath be observed, he does not mean that everyone should be lazy one day of the week. The seventh "day" needs to be understood symbolically, bearing in mind that "with the Lord a day is as a thousand years and a thousand years as a day." The Sabbath commandment means that the Sabbath day, the millennium, should be looked forward to and anticipated by God's people. The creation will last for six days—six thousand years—after which there will be a thousand-year period on earth in which God and his people will rule supreme. Jews misunderstood this message and foolishly assumed that God meant for them not to work on Saturdays (15.1–9).

Barnabas goes through a number of the laws of the Old Testament to show that God never intended them to be followed literally, but to be understood figuratively. Since Jews never understood the point, they never were the true people of God. It is the followers of Jesus who have the true interpretation of Scripture. As a result, Jews are not God's people; Christians are. And the Old Testament is not a Jewish book, but a Christian one.

This "letter" was originally published anonymously, possibly because the first readers knew full well who had written it. It could not have been written by one of Paul's closest co-workers and companions, Barnabas, because it did not appear until many years after his death—it is usually dated to 130–35 CE. But why was it eventually attributed to him? No one knows for sure, but I think a good case can be made that some readers of the book wanted to make a particular point by the attribution, a point related to the arguments going on in Christianity in the second century, some fifty years or so after the book was written.

In the later second century one of the biggest threats facing "orthodox" Christianity was the worldwide church established by Marcion and his followers. If you'll remember, Marcion had claimed Paul's authority for his view that there were two Gods, the inferior wrathful God of the Old Testament and the superior loving God of Jesus. Paul was thought to be the true representative of Jesus's message, the one who understood that salvation comes apart from the Jewish law. Marcion took Paul's differentiation between the gospel of Christ and the law of the Jews to an extreme, so that there was in fact no connection between them. Christ represented a different God. The Old Testament God, the God of the Jews, the creation, and the law, was to be escaped by Christians, not worshiped by them.

Marcion therefore rejected the Old Testament entirely, claiming that it had nothing to do with the gospel of Jesus. The *Epistle of Barnabas* takes a different perspective. In fact, one could argue that it takes precisely the opposite perspective. Here, rather than having nothing to do with Christianity and the message of Jesus, the Old Testament has everything to do with them. It is the Christian book par excellence, because it proclaims the gospel of Christ—figuratively.

Why then assign the book to Paul's closest companion? Because by doing so the book becomes the perspective of the real Paul, as opposed to the Paul of Marcion, who allegedly had nothing to do with the Old Testament and its laws. Now Paul, by association through Barnabas, proclaims the true message. The Old Testament in fact is Scripture. It is truth from God. It is a proclamation of the gospel of Christ. It is a fully Christian book.

By assigning this popular tractate to Barnabas, then, opponents of Marcion were able to claim Paul for their view and to show that the apostle stood for an understanding of Christianity that was very much at odds with the views set forth by the chief heretic of the second century, who had claimed Paul as his own.

Fabrications

As I'VE INDICATED, a false attribution is not necessarily a deception; it may simply have been a mistake or someone's "best guess" about the author of an anonymous work. My hunch is that most writers who claimed that a particular, famous person was the author of this or that writing probably believed it was true, whether or not they knew it to be true. The same thing decidedly cannot be said about forgers. Whoever wrote 1 Timothy knew full well that he wasn't really the apostle Paul. He made that part up.

Other kinds of literature are "made up" as well. As with false attributions, however, it is not always clear that the person who writes this literature knows that it is made up. He may think that what he says is accurate. When this involves historical narratives, he may think that what he says is historically factual, even if his account is in fact legendary. But at some point, someone ultimately, always, comes up with a legendary account. Of course it is always possible that even in such cases the author who comes up with the story may think it really happened. And sometimes stories just seem to appear out of nowhere. But in many cases, surely the person who makes up the story knows what he is doing.

We have seen a number of made-up stories already in books that were forged. Whoever forged the *Gospel of Peter* wrote the account of Jesus emerging from the tomb so tall that his head reached above the skies, with a walking, talking cross emerging behind him. This is not a historical narrative; it is fiction. I would call it a "fabrication," that is, a "made-up story that tries to pass itself off as historical."

In many instances, fabrications are disseminated by anonymous authors who are not forgers. This was the case, for example, with the accounts found in the *Acts of Peter,* which tells stories of Peter's miracle-working contests with Simon the Magician, in which he performs such astounding feats as raising a smoked tuna from the dead. These "historical" narratives are in fact fabrications. Whoever first came up with them—whether the author of the text or someone who told the story orally before the author heard it—was telling something that he possibly (likely? probably?) knew was not historically accurate. So too with the *Acts of Paul* (or the *Acts of Paul and Thecla*), where Paul is said to have preached a distinctive gospel of salvation that said a person is made right with God not through Jesus's death and resurrection, but by living a chaste life, avoiding all sexual activity.

As with ancient myths (as mentioned in Chapter 2), it is often difficult to know whether readers of such stories took them as historical accounts, or simply as entertaining narratives, or as something else. But in many instances it is clear that some readers understood such stories to be "false" tales, since they were so vociferously opposed in some circles. One need think only of Serapion's reaction to the *Gospel of Peter* (see Chapter 2) or Tertullian's harsh words about the *Acts of Paul* (Chapter 3). In both cases the contents of the story were seen as objectionable and the account was charged with having been falsely fabricated in order to promote false understandings of the faith.

This shows that for some ancient readers, at least, such historical fabrications were not thought of simply as innocuous fictions, but either as false tales, in that they did not convey the "truth," or as false histories, in that that they narrated events that did not actually happen. In either case, in the views of their opponents they were harmful fabrications. Whether harmful or not, numerous fabrications circulated in the early church about Jesus and those connected with him: his family, his disciples, and his other acquaintances. We have scores of such stories from the first four centuries of the church.

THE PROTO-GOSPEL OF JAMES

One of the most historically influential set of such tales comes in a book called the *Proto-Gospel of James*.[11] The *Proto-Gospel* was enormously popular among Christians throughout the Middle Ages—even more popular than many books of the Bible. It had a significant impact on the Christian imagination and on Christian art.[12] Readers have called it a proto-Gospel, because it mainly narrates events that transpired prior to the accounts of Jesus's birth and life found in the New Testament Gospels. The book largely concerns Jesus's mother, Mary, her birth and early life, her conception and giving birth to Jesus. I have said it is forged, because it falsely claims to have been written by Jesus's half brother James, who in this account is the son of Joseph from a previous marriage. There are debates about when the book was first written, but since it appears to know the Gospels of Matthew and Luke from the end of the first century and appears to be referred to by the theologian Origen at the beginning of the third century, it is often dated sometime in the mid to late second century.

One of the chief questions driving this narrative concerns Mary's suitability for her role as the mother of the Son of God. Surely Jesus's mother was no ordinary person! And in this story, Mary is anything but ordinary. Her own birth is miraculous. Her mother, Anna, is barren, but miraculously conceives as a result of her prayers and the prayers of her husband, the wealthy aristocratic Jew Joiachim. As a young child Mary is inordinately special. Devoted to God from birth, she is taken by her parents to the holy Jewish Temple as a three-year-old and is raised there by the priests, who do not need even to feed her, since she receives her daily food from the hand of an angel.

When she is about to reach puberty, Mary can no longer remain in the Temple, presumably because menstruation was thought to bring ritual impurity. So the priests gather to decide how to find her a husband. Instructed by God, they have all the unmarried men of Israel come together, each of them bringing a wooden rod. The high priest gathers all the rods and takes them into the sanctuary. The next day he redistributes them to each man, and a great sign appears. A dove emerges from Joseph's rod, flies around, and lands on Joseph's head. He is thus the one chosen to take the young Mary as wife.

But Joseph is highly reluctant, since he is an old man who already has grown sons, and surely he will become a laughingstock among his fellow Israelites if he marries such a young girl. The high priest convinces Joseph that he has no choice, and so he takes Mary in marriage.

The stories about Mary and Joseph continue, often amplifying the accounts found in the New Testament Gospels of Matthew and Luke (the only two New Testament Gospels that speak about the birth of Jesus), sometimes giving completely new stories. None is as odd or memorable as the account of what happens immediately after Mary gives birth to Jesus outside of Bethlehem. Joseph is said to have gone off to find a midwife who can assist at the birth. He finds one, but they arrive too late. Coming to the cave where Mary had been left, they see a bright light and then an infant appearing out of nowhere. The midwife is immediately convinced that this has been a miraculous birth and runs off to find a companion, Salome, who refuses to believe that a virgin has given birth. She comes to the cave and decides to give Mary a postpartum inspection to see if her hymen has remained intact. It has indeed, to no surprise to readers. But Salome's hand begins to burn as if it has caught fire. This is her punishment for refusing to believe in the power of God at the birth of Jesus. When she prays to God and asks for forgiveness, she is told to pick up the child. When she does so, her hand is healed.

Numerous other tales of the miraculous are found in the account, all of them, of course, originating in the pious imaginations of later storytellers or the author of the account rather than in historical events. These are not accurate accounts of events that actually transpired, but later stories put in the guise of historical narrative. Were they read as historical accounts or simply as entertaining narratives? A case can be made that they were read both ways. Some Christians based serious theological claims on them, such as the doctrine of the "perpetual virginity of Mary," that is, the view that Mary remained a virgin even after giving birth to Jesus. Such Christians certainly thought these accounts were "true," and surely many (most?) of them believed the events that they narrate really happened.

THE GOSPEL OF PSEUDO-MATTHEW

The same can be said of the stories found in the *Gospel of Pseudo-Matthew*. It is called this because it was thought in the Middle Ages to have been written by Matthew himself. Originally, however, the book was a heavily reworked version of the *Proto-Gospel*. It too claimed to have been written by Jesus's half brother James.[13]

Among the more interesting accounts of this narrative are the miracles Jesus performs when the Holy Family flees to Egypt after his birth. We learn, for example, that en route they stop to rest outside a cave. To the terror of Joseph and Mary, out of the cave come a troop of dragons. The two-year-old Jesus, however, is not the least bit afraid. He waddles and stands before the fearsome beasts. When they see who he is, they bow down in worship before him. The author tells us that this fulfilled the predictions of Scripture: "Then was fulfilled what was spoken by the prophet in the Psalms, who said, 'Praise the Lord from the earth, O dragons and all the places of the abyss,'" a reference to the Greek version of Psalm 148:7.

Later on their journey, the family stops to rest under a palm tree, and Jesus's mother, Mary, looks wistfully at the fruit in the high, upper branches, wishing there were a way to get some to eat. Joseph upbraids her, since there is obviously no way to climb the tree. But the young Jesus intervenes and orders the tree to bend down to give its precious fruit to his mother. And it does so. Mary eats to her heart's content, and Jesus blesses the tree for its obedience, telling it that as a reward one of its branches will be carried to heaven and planted in paradise. Straightaway an angel descends and removes a branch to take it to its new heavenly home.

Once the family arrives in Egypt they have no place to stay, and so they go for shelter into a pagan temple. Inside this temple are 365 idols representing the gods who are to be worshiped, one for each day of the year. But when Jesus enters, the idols all fall over on their faces in obeisance to the true divinity in their midst. Once the local ruler learns what has happened, he comes himself and worships the child, telling all his friends and his entire army that now the Lord of all the gods has come into their midst.

THE INFANCY GOSPEL OF THOMAS

At roughly the time the *Proto-Gospel of James* was starting to circulate, another fabricated account of Jesus appeared, today known as the *Infancy Gospel of Thomas*.[14] Driving this narrative is a question that has been asked by numerous Christian throughout the ages: If Jesus was the miracle-working Son of God as an adult, what was he like as a child? The *Infancy Gospel* contains stories about Jesus between the ages of five and twelve.

The account begins with Jesus as a five-year-old playing by a stream near his home in Nazareth. The young Jesus gathers some of the water of the stream into a pool and orders it to become pure. And it does so, by his word alone. Jesus then stoops down and forms twelve birds out of the mud. A Jewish man who is walking by becomes upset, because it is the Sabbath and Jesus has violated the law by "working." The man heads off to tell Joseph what his son has done, and Joseph rushes to the stream to upbraid the boy for breaking the Sabbath. In response, Jesus claps his hands and cries out to the birds to come to life and fly away, and they do so. Here Jesus is shown to be above the law and to be the lord of life. Beyond that, he has gotten off the hook with his father by destroying, in effect, any incriminating evidence. Mud birds? What birds?

Another child who is playing beside Jesus takes a branch and scatters the water he has carefully gathered together. This angers the young Jesus, who tells the boy, "You unrighteous, irreverent idiot! What did the pools of water do to harm you? See, now you also will be withered like a tree, and you will never bear leaves or root or fruit." The child immediately withers on the spot.

In the next story Jesus is said to be walking through his village when another child runs up to him and accidentally bumps him on the shoulder. Jesus is irritated and says to the boy, "You'll go no farther on *your* way." And the child falls down dead. The parents of the boy carry him off with some harsh words for Joseph: "Since you have such a child, you cannot live with us in the village. Or teach him to bless and not to curse—for he is killing our children!"

Eventually Joseph decides that Jesus needs to receive an education, and on three occasions he sends him off to teachers who try to instruct him, but to no effect. In one instance the teacher tries to teach Jesus the alphabet, in Greek, and practices reciting with him. But Jesus will not respond, until finally he says to the teacher, "If you are really a teacher and know the letters well, tell me the power of the Alpha [i.e., the first letter of the alphabet], and I will tell you the power of the Beta [the second letter]." The teacher gets angry and smacks Jesus upside the head. Big mistake. Jesus curses him, and he dies on the spot. Joseph takes Jesus back home with instructions to Mary: "Do not let him out the door; for those who anger him die."

Eventually, however, Jesus starts using his power not to harm, but to help: raising children from the dead, curing his brother James of a deadly snakebite, and proving to be remarkably handy with his miraculous skills around his father's carpenter shop. The account ends with Jesus as a twelve-year-old in the Temple in Jerusalem, showing his intelligence and spiritual superiority in his discussions with the teachers of the law, a story otherwise known from the Gospel of Luke.

It is hard to know what to make of these stories of Jesus the wunderkind.[15] Some modern readers have thought that they portray Jesus in a very negative light indeed. But it is not clear that early Christian readers would have seen them that way. The stories may have been designed simply as good Christian entertainment. Or they may have been serious attempts to show how the miracle-working Son of God was active and filled with divine power even in the early years, long before his public ministry.

FABRICATIONS WITHIN THE CANON

It should not be thought that Christians started fabricating stories about Jesus only after the New Testament was completed. In fact, there can be little doubt that some accounts were manufactured in the early years of the Christian movement. Some of these fabrications made their way into the New Testament.

We could go to great lengths to talk about New Testament narratives that purport to present historical events, but are in fact invented stories. Such narratives can be found among the stories about Jesus's birth, life, teachings, death, and resurrection as well as in stories about his followers, such as Peter and Paul, after his death in the book of Acts.

With regard to the stories of Jesus's birth, one does not need to wait for the later Gospels, mentioned above, to begin seeing the fabricated accounts; they are already there in the familiar versions of Matthew and Luke. There never was a census under Caesar Augustus that compelled Joseph and Mary to go to Bethlehem just before Jesus was born; there never was a star that mysteriously guided wise men from the East to Jesus; Herod the Great never did slaughter all the baby boys in Bethlehem; Jesus and his family never did spend several years in Egypt. These may sound like bold and provocative statements, but scholars have known the reasons and evidence behind them for many years. Since I devote considerable attention to them—and to other fabricated accounts of the Gospels—in another recent book, however, I will not go into the details here.[16]

It is almost impossible to say whether the people who made up and passed along these stories were comparable to forgers, who knew full well that they were engaged in a kind of deception, or whether they, instead, were like those who falsely attributed anonymous books to known authors without knowing they were wrong. My guess is that most of the people who told these stories genuinely believed they happened. Even so, we should not say that these storytellers were not involved in deception. They may not have meant to deceive others (or they may have!), but they certainly did deceive others. In fact, they deceived others spectacularly well. For many, many centuries it was simply assumed that the narratives about Jesus and the apostles—narratives both within and outside the New Testament—described events that actually happened. Most readers still read the canonical accounts that way. But many of these stories are not historical narratives. They are, instead, fabricated accounts, whether made up intentionally in order to prove a point or simply brought into being, somehow, when Christians passed along "information" about Jesus and those connected to him.

Falsifications

IN ADDITION TO FORGERY, false attribution, and fabrication, there is another kind of deceptive literary activity that can be called "falsification." This occurs whenever someone copies an author's text by hand, but alters it in some way, omitting something, adding something, or just changing the wording. If someone were to copy Paul's first letter to the Corinthians and add a few extra verses that he thought up himself, then the next person to read that manuscript would naturally assume that Paul himself had written the inserted words. That is very similar to what happens with forgery: someone writes his own words, but attributes them to someone else. In this case, however, rather than composing an entire document in someone else's name, a copyist has written a portion of a document and included it in the other person's book.

The practice of altering texts in the process of copying them happened all the time in antiquity.[17] In a world without electronic means of publication, photocopy machines, or even carbon paper, it was well-nigh impossible to ensure that any copy of a text would be 100 percent accurate, without changes of any kind. This is true for all books copied in the ancient world. That is why, when great kings wanted to start significant libraries in their cities, they were sometimes willing to pay sizable amounts of money for "originals" of the great classics. You could never be sure if copies would be completely true to the original.

All of the early Christian writings were, necessarily, susceptible to the vicissitudes of copying. We don't have any original copies of any books of the New Testament or of any other early Christian book. What we have are copies that have been made from copies of the copies of the copies. In most instances our earliest complete copies are from centuries after the originals.

Just about every copyist made mistakes in copying. As a result, if you were to copy a copy of an original, in most instances you would copy not just the words of the original, but also the mistakes your predecessor made in copying the original. And whoever came after you and copied your copy would reproduce both your mistakes and the mistakes of your predecessor as well as introduce some mistakes of her own. And so it goes, year after year, century after century. The only time mistakes are removed is when a copyist realizes that a predecessor had copied something incorrectly and then tries to correct the mistake. The problem is that there is no way to know whether the copyist corrects the mistake correctly or not. He may also correct it incorrectly, that is, change it to something that is different from both the copy he is copying and from the original that was first copied. The possibilities are endless.

We do not need to speculate that Christian scribes altered the texts they copied. You can take any book of early Christianity and compare the surviving copies, whether it is a book from the New Testament, say, one of the Gospels or Paul's letters, or a book from outside the New Testament, say, the *Infancy Gospel of Thomas* or the *Epistle of Barnabas*. The copies will all differ, often in lots of minor insignificant ways and sometimes in big ways.

In the vast majority of the cases, the changes that copyists made were simply an accident: the slip of a pen, the misspelling of a word, the accidental omission of a word or a line. Sometimes, though, scribes changed their texts because they wanted to do so, either because they thought their scribal predecessors made a mistake that needed to be corrected or because they wanted to add something to the text (or take away something or change something). As I've indicated, this kind of falsification is close to forgery; it is one author passing off his own words as the words of a respected authority.

I have talked about these kinds of changes in a couple of my earlier books and don't want to belabor the point here. Instead, I simply give a few examples of the kind of thing I mean from the pages of the New Testament. In Chapter 5 I talked about the famous story found in later manuscripts of the Gospel of John about the woman who was caught in the act of adultery and brought to Jesus for judgment. This is the account in which Jesus delivers one of his most famous sayings: "Let the one without sin among you be the first to cast a stone at her." The story, however, is not found in the oldest manuscripts of the Gospel of John. Moreover, the writing style (in the Greek) is significantly different from the writing style of the rest of the Gospel. In addition, the story breaks the flow of the narrative of John 7–8, where it is found. In other words, if you take the story out of John, the context makes much better sense, as the story immediately before the account flows better directly into the story immediately after it. For these and numerous other reasons there is virtually no debate among New Testament scholars that this story, as wonderful, powerful, and influential as it is, was not originally part of the New Testament. It was added by a scribe.

In this instance we are dealing with both a falsification of the text (making it say something different from what it originally said) and a fabrication (since it is a story that has been made up). There are many other instances of this kind of thing in the surviving manuscripts of the New Testament. Another famous example occurs at the end of the Gospel of Mark. It is sometimes said by people who have not read the concerning chapter of Mark's Gospel closely enough that it "lacks a resurrection narrative." Strictly speaking, that is not true. In Mark's Gospel Jesus is certainly raised from the dead. The women go to the tomb three days after he was buried in order to give his body a proper burial, but the body is not there. Instead, there is a man in the tomb who informs them that Jesus has been raised from the dead. Mark, therefore, believes that Jesus was physically raised from the dead, and he tells his readers as much. But what is most astonishing is what happens next.

The man at the tomb instructs the women to go to the disciples and tell them that Jesus will go before them to Galilee and that they are to meet him there. But instead of telling the disciples, "the women fled from the tomb . . . and they did not say anything to anyone, for they were afraid" (16:8). And that's where the Gospel ends. There is definitely a resurrection of Jesus here. But the disciples never learn of it, and there is no account of Jesus's meeting with any of them.

This ending is brilliant. It brings readers up short and makes them say, "*What???* How could the women not tell anyone? How could no one learn of Jesus's resurrection? How could Jesus not appear to anyone afterwards? That's *it*? That's the end? How could that be the end?"

Scribes felt the same way. And, different scribes added different endings to the Gospel. The ending that became the most popular throughout the Middle Ages was found in the manuscripts used by the translators of the King James Version in 1611, so that it became widely familiar to English Bible readers. In an additional twelve verses the women (or at least Mary Magdalene) do go tell the disciples, who do then see Jesus and become convinced he has been raised. It is in these verses that we find the famous words of Jesus that those who believe in him will be able to speak in foreign tongues, pick up serpents, and drink poison without suffering any harm.

But Jesus never said these words, and Mark never claimed he did. They were added to Mark by a later scribe and then recopied over the years.[18] This is a fabricated story that has been put into the Bible by a copyist who falsified the text.

There are hundreds of significant changes in the manuscripts of the New Testament, but let me here just mention one other. In the previous examples one could argue that the falsifications were not exactly the same as forgeries, since both John from the first example and Mark from the second were written anonymously. Technically speaking, the scribes who changed the texts were not saying their words came from the pen of a known authority figure. I would dispute that claim, I think, because by the time scribes made these changes, it was widely thought that the Fourth Gospel was in fact by John and the Second by Mark. But there is no ambiguity about my final example, since it involves one of the undisputed letters of Paul.

One of the most hurtful passages for the cause of women who want to be active in the Christian church occurs in 1 Corinthians 14:34–35. Here Paul is recorded as saying:

> Let the women in the churches keep silent. For it is not permitted for them to speak; instead let them be submissive, just as the law itself says. If they wish to learn anything, let them ask their own husbands at home. For it is shameful for a woman to speak in church.

Women are to be silent and submissive to their husbands. They are not to speak at all in church. This obviously makes it impossible for a woman to utter a prophecy in church, pray publicly and openly in church, or teach in church. Women are not allowed even to ask a question in church.

These verses are very much like what one reads in one of the Pauline letters that is *not* authentic, 1 Timothy, which, as we saw in Chapter 3, also indicates that women are to be subject to men and not to exercise any authority over them (2:11–15). But just as 1 Timothy is forged, so too has this passage in 1 Corinthians been falsified. These verses in chapter 14 were not written by Paul. Someone added them to the passage later, after the letter had been placed in circulation.

Scholars have adduced many reasons for this view. For one thing, the verses seem to intrude in the passage in which they are found. Immediately before these verses Paul is talking about prophecy in the church; immediately afterwards he is talking about prophecy. But this passage on women interrupts the flow of the argument. Take them out, and it flows much better.

Even more, it is hard to believe that Paul would tell women that they could not speak in church here in 1 Corinthians 14, when just three chapters earlier he indicated that they could indeed do so. In 1 Corinthians 11 Paul urges women who pray and prophesy in church to do so only with veils on their heads. If they were allowed to speak in chapter 11, how could they be told not to speak in chapter 14? It makes better sense that those scholars are right who think that the verses were not originally part of the text of 1 Corinthians. Someone has falsified the book by adding the verses to it, making the passage say what these copyists wanted it to say rather than allowing Paul to say what he meant to say.[19]

Plagiarism

PLAGIARISM INVOLVES TAKING SOMEONE else's writing and passing it off as your own. As I indicated at the outset of this chapter, it has become an increasingly serious problem on college campuses. Techniques of plagiarism have improved through the use of the Internet, and it is oh so easy to find lots of things written about lots of topics—if not complete essays of approximately the same length as your required term paper, at least chunks of writing that are easily copied into a paper at a critical point. Luckily, methods of detection of plagiarism have improved with advances in technology, as many professors now use sophisticated software designed to identify it. The penalties for being caught can be harsh. At my university, anyone detected and convicted of plagiarism is dismissed from school. Not for a day or two, but permanently.

It is sometimes claimed by scholars that plagiarism is a modern phenomenon without ancient corollary. Some years ago, for example, there appeared an influential and popular book called *The Five Gospels*, put out by a team of scholars from the Jesus Seminar. This book represented the results of the labor of many years, in which scholars worked to decide which of the sayings in the Gospels of Matthew, Mark, Luke, John, and Thomas actually go back to the historical Jesus. Sayings that Jesus really said, in the opinion of these scholars, were printed in red; sayings that were relatively close to something he said were printed in pink; sayings that were not really like something he said were in gray; sayings that he absolutely did not say were in black.

Most of the sayings in the Gospels were in gray and black. This incensed a lot of people. A number of scholars who were not involved in the project, however, were more concerned by *which* sayings were in black. In my opinion, the members of the Jesus Seminar typically got precisely wrong what Jesus actually said.

Apart from that, the volume contains at least one statement that scholars would call a "howler," a mistake so outrageous that the scholars who produced it should have known better. This is in the Introduction to the book, where it states: "The concept of plagiarism was unknown in the ancient world."[20]

I don't know how anyone who has actually gone to the trouble of reading the ancient sources could say such a thing. It is flat-out wrong. Ancient authors knew all about plagiarism, and they condemned it as a deceptive practice. For starters, consider the words of Vitruvius, a famous Roman architect and engineer of the first century BCE, in book 7 of his ten-volume work on architecture: "We are . . . bound to censure those, who, borrowing from others, publish as their own that of which they are not the authors."[21] Or take the comments of Polybius, one of the great historians of the ancient Greek world, writing a hundred years earlier, who reports that historians near his own time who have stolen the writings of ancient historians and passed them off as their own have behaved in a "most shameful" manner. Those who do so engage in "a most disgraceful proceeding."[22]

Some authors were incensed when their own works were plagiarized. On several occasions the witty Roman poet Martial upbraided others for stealing his writings and copying them out under their own name, as if they had composed them: "You mistake, you greedy thief of my works, who think you can become a poet at no more than the cost of a transcript and a cheap papyrus roll. Applause is not acquired for six or ten sesterces."[23]

In a number of places the historian of philosophy Diogenes Laertius speaks of philosophers and literary authors who tried to pass off the works of others as their own, "stealing" them and publishing them as if they themselves had written them. This was true, he indicates, of a disciple of Socrates named Aeschines, who took several of Socrates's dialogues from his widow and claimed that they were his own compositions. It was also true of Heraclides, whom we met in Chapter 1, who "stole" an essay from another scholar about the ancient Homer and Hesiod and published it as his own. And it was true of the philosopher Empedocles, who was excluded from attending the lectures of the famous sixth-century BCE Pythagoras, because he was "convicted at that time of stealing his discourses."[24]

Like forgery, plagiarism is deceptive, because it intends to lead readers astray. But in another sense plagiarism can be seen as the flip side of forgery. Forgers write their own words and claim they are the words of another; plagiarists take the words of another and claim they are their own.

It is an interesting question whether ancient scholars would have accused some of the early Christian writers of plagiarism. The issues tend to be complicated by the fact that possible instances of plagiarism involve borrowed texts that are anonymous; moreover, the plagiarists themselves often do not actually identify themselves by name, but are either anonymous or claim to be someone else. Can a forger plagiarize? Maybe so.

If so, what are we to say of the book of 2 Peter? Scholars have long recognized that chapter 2 and the beginning of chapter 3 sound very much like the book of Jude, in its vitriolic attack on false and highly immoral persons who have infiltrated the Christian church. Very close similarities exist between Jude 4–13, 16–18 and 2 Peter 2:1–18; 3:1–3. There are not many extensive exact verbal repetitions, but they share many of the same ideas, thoughts, and often words. If a modern student simply rewrote a text by changing many of the words but keeping all the ideas, without acknowledging her source, she could well be considered to have plagiarized. But perhaps the issue is not so clear-cut in this case.

What, then, about the Gospels? Scholars since the nineteenth century have argued that the reason Matthew, Mark, and Luke are so much alike—telling many of the same stories, usually in the same sequence, often in precisely the same words—is that they used the same sources. In fact, it is everywhere recognized today that one of them was a source for the other two. Almost all scholars think that Mark was used by Matthew and Luke. Some scholars continue to hold to the view that Matthew was the source for Mark and Luke, but that is very much a minority position. In either case, we have one document that is taken over by others, frequently verbatim. It is true that none of the authors names himself. To that extent the later authors are not, strictly speaking, plagiarizing, in that they are not publishing someone else's work under their own name. But they are taking over someone else's work and publishing it as their own. Ancient scholars who spoke about this phenomenon would have called this "stealing." In modern parlance it is perhaps best to call it a kind of plagiarism.

There are other instances of the phenomenon from outside the New Testament. I mentioned earlier in this chapter, for example, that the *Gospel of Pseudo-Matthew* takes over the narrative of the *Proto-Gospel of James*, publishing it in an edited form (sometimes heavily edited, but in other places hardly edited at all), without acknowledging where the story came from. This is comparable in many ways to what the authors of the New Testament Gospels of Matthew and Luke did with Mark. Another book I mentioned in Chapter 1, the *Apostolic Constitutions*, is even more flagrant, taking over virtually whole-sale three documents from earlier times, the *Didache*, from around the year 100, the *Apostolic Tradition*, from the late second century, and the *Didascalia*, from the third, combining them together into one large document, and publishing it as if it had been information handed down directly from the apostles. But it was not; it was taken over—stolen, to use the ancient parlance—from earlier writings of the Christian tradition.

Conclusion

WHAT CAN WE SAY in conclusion about the forms of deception we have considered in this chapter? False attributions, fabrications, falsifications, plagiarism—they all, indeed, involve deceptive practices. Readers who read books that had been wrongly ascribed to apostles or their companions, or that contained stories that were made up, or that presented texts that had been altered by scribes, or that contained passages or entire accounts that were "stolen" from the writings of earlier authors without acknowledgment—readers of all such materials were deceived in one way or another. Some were deceived into thinking that what they read was really composed by the people claimed as their authors; others were misled to think that the historical events that were narrated were actual historical occurrences. In every case they were wrong. They had been deceived. Just as people continue to be deceived, when they think, for example, that the tax collector Matthew wrote the First Gospel, that Paul told women that they had to be silent in church, or that the author of 2 Peter came up with the ideas and phrases found in his second chapter himself.

One key aspect of forgery, however, does not appear to be involved in every instance of these other forms of deception. Forgery almost always involves a flat-out lie. Forgers claim to be someone else, knowing full well their own real identity. That is not always the case with the comparable phenomena I have been discussing here. Sometimes anonymous works were simply attributed to people who were thought to have written them, and it was all a mistake. Sometimes, possibly, stories were innocently fabricated, just as historically inaccurate stories are made up all the time, without any intention to deceive. Sometimes scribes altered the texts they were copying by accident without meaning to do so.

But other instances probably involved a good deal of intentionality. A theologian who wanted to convince his opponents that his views were those of the apostles may well have claimed that the Fourth Gospel was written by John, without knowing if that was true or not. A storyteller who made up an account about Jesus in order to prove a point may well have known that he was passing off a fiction as a historical event. A scribe who wanted a text to say something other than what it did may well have changed the text for just that reason. In some cases it is hard to imagine how else the resultant deception could have come about. Whoever added the final twelve verses of Mark did not do so by a mere slip of the pen.

In sum, there were numerous ways to lie in and through literature in antiquity, and some Christians took advantage of the full panoply in their efforts to promote their view of the faith. It may seem odd to modern readers, or even counterintuitive, that a religion that built its reputation on possessing the truth had members who attempted to disseminate their understanding of the truth through deceptive means. But it is precisely what happened. The use of deception to promote the truth may well be considered one of the most unsettling ironies of the early Christian tradition.

CHAPTER EIGHT

Forgeries, Lies, Deceptions, and the Writings of the New Testament

WHEN I GIVE PUBLIC TALKS about the books that did not make it into the New Testament, people often ask me about apocryphal tales they have heard. What do we know about the "lost years" of Jesus, that gap of time between when he was twelve and thirty? Is it true that he went to India to study with the Brahmins? Was Jesus an Essene? Don't we have a death warrant from Pontius Pilate ordering Jesus's execution? And so on.

Very few of the apocryphal stories that people hear today come from the ancient forgeries I have been examining in this book. Instead, they come from modern forgeries that claim to represent historical facts kept from the public by scholars or "the Vatican." The real facts, however, are that these mysterious accounts have uniformly been exposed as fabrications perpetrated by well-meaning or mischievous writers of the nineteenth and twentieth centuries. Their exposure, however, has done little to stop laypeople from believing them.

Modern Forgeries, Lies, and Deceptions

I DISCUSS FOUR MODERN forgeries here, just to give you a taste of the kinds of things that have been widely read. All four, and many others, are discussed and demolished in two interesting books by bona fide scholars of Christian antiquity, Edgar Goodspeed, a prominent American New Testament scholar of the mid-twentieth century, and Per Beskow, a Swedish scholar of early Christianity writing in the 1970s.[1]

THE UNKNOWN LIFE OF JESUS CHRIST

One of the most widely disseminated modern forgeries is called *The Unknown Life of Jesus Christ*.[2] From this account we learn that Jesus went to India during his formative teen years, the "lost years" before his public ministry, and there learned the secrets of the East. The book made a big splash when it appeared in English in 1926; but as it turns out, it had already been exposed as a fraud more than thirty years earlier. The reading public, it is safe to say, has a short attention span.

The book was first published in France in 1894 as *La vie inconnue de Jésus Christ*, by a Russian war correspondent named Nicolas Notovitch. Almost immediately it was widely disseminated and translated. In one year it appeared in eight editions in French, with translations into German, Spanish, and Italian. One edition was published in the United Kingdom, and three separate editions in the United States.

The book consisted of 244 paragraphs arranged in fourteen chapters. Notovitch starts the book by explaining how he "discovered" it. In 1887, he was allegedly traveling in India and Kashmir, where he heard from lamas of Tibet stories about a prophet named Issa, the Arabic form (roughly) of the name Jesus. His further travels took him to the district of Ladak, on the border between India and Tibet, to the famous Tibetan Buddhist monastery of Hemis. While there he heard additional stories and was told that written records of the life of Issa still survived.

Notovitch left the monastery without learning anything further. But after a couple of days he had a bad accident, falling off his horse and breaking his leg. He was carried back to the monastery to recuperate and, while there, came to be on friendly terms with the abbot. When Notovitch inquired about the stories of Issa, the abbot agreed to give him the full account. He produced two thick volumes, written in Tibetan, and began to read them out loud to Notovitch, in the presence of a translator who explained what the texts said, while Notovitch took notes.

The Unknown Life of Jesus Christ is the published edition of the careful notes that Notovitch allegedly took. When Jesus was thirteen, according to the account, he joined a caravan of merchants to go to India to study their sacred laws. He spent six years with the Brahmins, learning their holy books, the Vedas. But Jesus was completely disenchanted with the Indian caste system and openly began to condemn it. This raised the ire of the Brahmins, who decided to put him to death.

Jesus fled to join a community of Buddhists, from whom he learned Pali, the language of Theraveda Buddhism, and mastered the Buddhist texts. He next visited Persia and preached to the Zoroastrians. Finally, as a twenty-nine-year-old, armed with all the sacred knowledge of the East, he returned to Palestine and began his public ministry. The narrative concludes by summarizing his words and deeds and giving a brief account of his death. The story of his life was then allegedly taken by Jewish merchants back to India, where those who had known Issa as a young man realized that it was the same person. They then wrote down the full account.

Although the narrative of *The Unknown Life of Jesus Christ* may sound like a rather second-rate novel, it was published as a historically factual account and was widely believed as providing the key to the questions that Christians had long asked about the lost years of Jesus. What was he doing then? And how had he acquired such extensive and compelling religious knowledge before beginning his public ministry?

It was not long, however, before scholars interested in historical fact began to question the account and to expose it as a complex hoax. The tale was taken on by no less eminent an authority than Max Müller, the greatest European scholar of Indian culture of the late nineteenth century, who showed that the tale of the "discovery" of the book and the stories it told were filled with insurmountable implausibilities. If this great book was a favorite at the monastery of Hemis, why is it not found in either of the comprehensive catalogues of Tibetan literature? How is it that the Jewish merchants who went to India with tales of Jesus happened to meet up with precisely the Brahmins who knew Issa as a young man—out of the millions of people in India? And how did Issa's former associates in India realize, exactly, that the crucified man was their former student?

In 1894 an English woman who had read the *Unknown Life* visited Hemis monastery. She made inquiries and learned that no Russian had ever been there, no one had been nursed back to health after breaking his leg, and they had no books describing the life of Issa. The next year a scholar, J. Archibald Douglas, went and interviewed the abbot himself, who informed him that there had been no European with a broken leg in the monastery during his fifteen years in charge of the community. Moreover, he had been a lama for forty-two years and was well acquainted with Buddhist literature. Not only did he never read aloud a book about Issa to a European or to anyone else; he was certain that no such book as *The Unknown Life* existed in Tibet.

Additional internal implausibilities and inaccuracies of the story are exposed by both Goodspeed and Beskow. Today there is not a single recognized scholar on the planet who has any doubts about the matter. The entire story was invented by Notovitch, who earned a good deal of money and a substantial amount of notoriety for his hoax.

THE CRUCIFIXION OF JESUS, BY AN EYE-WITNESS

An equally interesting modern apocryphon, *The Crucifixion of Jesus, by an Eye-Witness*, deals not with the beginning of Jesus's adult life, before his ministry, but with its ending and aftermath.[3] The account comes in the form of a letter written, in Latin, seven years after Jesus's crucifixion, from a leader of the mysterious Jewish sect of the Essenes in Jerusalem to another Essene leader who lived in Alexandria, Egypt. All elements of the supernatural are completely stripped away from the account's description of Jesus's life and death. Jesus is shown to have led a completely human life and to have died a completely human death. But not on the cross. Jesus survived his own crucifixion and lived for another six months.

The account was first published in German, in Leipzig, in 1849. English editions, all claiming to be authentic, were published in 1907, 1919, and 1975. There were also translations into French and Swedish.

The Latin letter was allegedly discovered on a parchment scroll in an old Greek monastery in Alexandria by a missionary who thought that its message was dangerous and so tried to destroy it. It was saved, however, by a learned Frenchman, who translated the account into German. The narrative was then brought to Germany by the Freemasons, understood to be modern-day descendants of the Essenes.

According to the account, Jesus himself was an Essene. When he was crucified, according to this "eyewitness," he did not expire. He was taken from the cross and restored to life by Joseph of Arimathea and Nicodemus, fellow Essenes, who knew the secret arts of healing preserved by the sect. When the women visiting the tomb thought they saw angels, these were Essene monks wearing their white robes. The women misunderstood that Jesus had been raised, when in fact he had never died. He did die, however, six months later, from the wounds he had sustained.

It has not been difficult for scholars to expose this Gospel as another fraud. The "eyewitness," allegedly an Essene, has no understanding of what the Essenes were really like. Today we know a good deal about this Jewish group, thanks to the Dead Sea Scrolls, which were unavailable to the forger, since they were discovered nearly a century after he produced his account. Nothing in the story corresponds to the historical realities of the group. For one thing, there is no way an Essene in Jerusalem would write his account in Latin, of all things.

There are other considerable problems. The account indicates that it was written seven years after the crucifixion, yet it explicitly mentions, by name, the Gospels of Matthew, Mark, Luke, and John, which were not written until forty to sixty years after Jesus's death. Moreover, these books were not known as a *group* of writings ("the four Gospels") until the end of the second century. Finally the exclusion of everything supernatural in the account is a thoroughly modern, post-Enlightenment concern, not an ancient one.

And, in fact, a modern scholar has shown where this concern, and indeed the entire story, came from. In 1936, a famous German scholar of the New Testament, Martin Dibelius, demonstrated that *The Crucifixion of Jesus* was virtually lifted, wholesale, from a now rather obscure work of historical fiction written by the German rationalist K. H. Venturini, *The Natural History of the Great Prophet of Nazareth* (two volumes, 1800–1802). Here too Jesus was an Essene whose life had nothing supernatural about it and who did not actually die on the cross, but was revived by Joseph of Arimathea. The author of *The Crucifixion of Jesus* simply took Venturini's two-volume work, condensed it into a readable booklet, and tried to pass it off as a historical account, when in fact it was a modern fabrication.

THE DEATH SENTENCE OF JESUS CHRIST

One of the striking and, to many people, surprising facts about the first century is that we don't have any Roman records, of any kind, that attest to the existence of Jesus. We have no birth certificate, no references to his words or deeds, no accounts of his trial, no descriptions of his death—no reference to him whatsoever in any way, shape, or form. Jesus's name is not even mentioned in any Roman source of the first century.[4] This does not mean, as is now being claimed with alarming regularity, that Jesus never existed. He certainly existed, as virtually every competent scholar of antiquity, Christian or non-Christian, agrees, based on clear and certain evidence. But as with the vast majority of all persons who lived and died in the first century, he does not appear in the records of the Roman people.

That is why the alleged discovery of an official copy of Pilate's *Death Sentence* made such an enormous impact in Europe and the United States when it was announced in the mid-nineteenth century.[5] The discovery was first mentioned in the French paper *Le Droit* in the spring of 1839. It was soon exposed as a fraud, but it resurfaced again in Germany ten years later and repeatedly elsewhere, including the United States, for many decades afterward.

The *Death Sentence* was allegedly found on a copper plate discovered in the southern Italian city of Aquila, near Naples, all the way back in 1280. A group of workers was said to have been excavating for Roman antiquities, when they uncovered an ancient marble vase. Inside the vase was a copper plate inscribed in Hebrew. When the text was translated, it was found to contain an official copy of Jesus's death warrant issued by Pontius Pilate. On the reverse side were directions for the warrant to be sent to all the tribes of Israel.

The plate allegedly came to be lost, but it was rediscovered during the French occupation of the Kingdom of Naples in 1806–15. When it was published a couple of decades later, it was touted as "the most impressive legal document in existence." In it, "Pontius Pilate, the acting governor of lower Galilee" states that "Jesus of Nazareth shall suffer death on the cross." This is said to have happened in the seventeenth year of the reign of the emperor Tiberius (31 CE), on March 27, "in the most holy city of Jerusalem."

The reason for the death sentence was that Jesus had committed six crimes. He was a seducer; he was seditious; he was an enemy of the law; he falsely called himself the Son of God; he called himself the king of Israel; and he entered the Temple followed by a multitude carrying palm branches. The death warrant is signed by four witnesses: Daniel Robani, Joannus Robani, Raphael Robani, and "Capet, a citizen."[6]

A top-flight scholar such as Edgar Goodspeed had no difficulty exposing the entire document as a hoax. It made no sense for a Roman official to try to justify his conviction of a criminal to the Jewish people or to send the justification to the "tribes of Israel," which had not in fact existed for many centuries. Pilate, a Roman official, would not have written in Hebrew, a language he didn't know. Pilate was not the governor of lower Galilee, but of Judea. As a non-Jew, he never would have referred to Jerusalem as "the most holy city." March 27 is a modern form of dating unknown to the ancient world. The term "Robani," used for three of the witnesses, appears to be a mistaken form of "Rabban," which means "teacher"; the author probably made the mistake because in direct address, such as in John 20:16, the word is spelled "Rabbouni." Joannus is not an ancient name in any of the relevant languages. Capet is a French name. And there is no Hebrew word for "citizen."

There are more problems, but these are enough to illustrate the case. Whoever made this account up did a rather poor job of it, even though his hoax had wide success, in both Europe and the United States, for over a century.

THE LONG-LOST SECOND BOOK OF ACTS

In 1904, the Anglican priest and physician Kenneth Sylvan Guthrie published a book called the *Long-Lost Second Book of Acts*, which, among other things, describes the teachings of Mary, the mother of Jesus, about reincarnation.[7] It is called the "second book" of Acts, because it begins by describing what happened to the apostle Paul after the events narrated in the New Testament book of Acts.

After being released from his Roman imprisonment, mentioned in Acts 28, Paul allegedly planned to go to Spain and then to Britain. But he eventually decides, instead, to go to Palestine. When he arrives, he goes to Jerusalem, to the house of the disciple John, where he finds Mary, the mother of Jesus, along with seven of the disciples. An elderly woman now, Mary prays for her death, and the angel Gabriel appears to tell her that her prayer is to be answered.

From her deathbed, reflecting on her mortality, Mary then divulges the secret doctrine of reincarnation. She herself has gone through seven incarnations; among other things she has been the wife of Noah, the woman who loved Zarathustra, the one who loved Siddhartha, and later still the one who loved Socrates.

Just before her death a storm comes, and Mary leads the disciples off to the Mount of Olives. Jesus appears from heaven and takes her in his arms. He tells the disciples that he too has had several previous incarnations, as Abel, Noah, Zarathustra, and Socrates.

This book is so obviously a fiction that it is hard to imagine its author expecting anyone to take it seriously. But given the reading public, who knows? Goodspeed, at any rate, thought that it was "simply a modern effort to claim that the Virgin Mary and Jesus himself endorsed the doctrine of reincarnation," and that "Guthrie doubtless thought it so transparent a device that it would deceive nobody."[8]

OTHER HOAXES AND DECEPTIONS

There are of course many other modern apocrypha that try to report on what Jesus and those associated with him really did. A book called *The Confession of Pontius Pilate* tells the story of Pilate going into exile in Vienna, where he feels deep remorse for what he did to Jesus and eventually commits suicide. Among other things, this account refers to a story in which Mary Magdalene presents the Roman emperor Tiberius with an Easter egg dyed red.[9] In *The Gospel of the Holy Twelve* Jesus is said to espouse a strictly vegetarian view in opposition to those who kill and eat animals. In this inventive narrative Jesus is said not to have eaten lamb at the Passover and to have fed the multitudes not with five loaves and two fish, but with five melons.[10]

One could argue that hoaxes are created not only by obscure figures trying to sensationalize accounts of Jesus (Jesus studied with the Brahmins!) or to authenticate their particular worldviews (Jesus was a vegetarian!), but also by scholars who may have had obscure reasons of their own.

One of the wildly popular books about Jesus during the 1960s and 1970s was Hugh Schonfield's *The Passover Plot: A New Interpretation of the Life and Death of Jesus*.[11] Schonfield was a brilliant and widely acknowledged scholar of ancient Judaism, with a complete set of bona fide credentials. But his historical reconstruction of what really happened to Jesus reads more like a Hollywood production than serious scholarship.

The short story is that Jesus from an early age "knew" that he was the messiah and so manipulated events during his public ministry to make it appear that he was fulfilling prophecy. In particular, he plotted with his disciples to feign his own death for the sins of others. He arranged to be drugged on the cross (when he was given the gall and vinegar, it was medicinal), so that his vital signs would slow down and he would appear dead. He would then be revived and appear to have been raised from the dead. The plot failed, however. Jesus had not counted on a Roman soldier spearing him in the side on the cross. He revived only briefly and was removed from the tomb by prior arrangement with coconspirators (not the disciples). He died of his wounds soon thereafter and was reburied elsewhere. The disciples, however, discovered the empty tomb and mistakenly thought they saw Jesus alive afterwards. They then proclaimed that he had been raised from the dead. And thus started Christianity.

The Passover Plot is not a forgery, of course. The author of the account, who writes in his own name, is a serious historian and lets his readers know it. And it is not exactly a fabrication, in that he claims that he is basing his account on historical research. Moreover, he presents it as a historical study. But as creative as it is, the major premise of the account is completely made up; there is no historical truth to it.

As a final example I might mention, again, the case involving one of the twentieth century's truly eminent scholars of early Christianity, Columbia professor Morton Smith. Smith claimed to have discovered a lost, alternate version of the Gospel of Mark. The account of the discovery appeared in two books Smith published in 1973, one a detective-like narrative for popular audiences and the other an erudite, hard-hitting research monograph for scholars.[12] In them Smith stated that in 1958, while visiting a monastery near Jerusalem, he discovered a handwritten copy of a letter, in Greek, by a second-century church father, Clement of Alexandria, in which he claimed that the author of Mark had published a second edition of his Gospel. This "Secret Gospel," as it came to be known, included a couple of stories not found in Mark, stories that sound mysterious and strange, about Jesus and his relationship with a young man he had raised from the dead.

Smith argued that this relationship was homosexual and that it provided evidence that Jesus had engaged in sexual activities with the naked men that he baptized during his ministry. Needless to say, Smith's books caused quite a stir. His scholarly book provided serious evidence that this really was a letter from Clement of Alexandria and that Clement really did know of such a Gospel. But since Smith's death in 1991, a number of scholars have come forward to argue that the letter is not authentic, that it was forged by none other than Smith himself. Two books have been published on the matter in recent years, both coming to the same conclusion, but on different grounds.[13] Other scholars, including those who knew Smith well, do not think so, and the debate goes on.[14]

Christian Forgeries, Lies, and Deceptions

THIS ISSUE OF MODERN hoaxes brings me back to a question I have repeatedly asked in my study of forgeries: "Who would *do* such a thing?" I hope by now you will agree with my earlier answer: "Lots of people." And for lots of reasons. And not just modern people. We have instances of Christian forgeries not only today, but also in the Middle Ages, in late antiquity, and in the time of the New Testament. From the first century to the twenty-first century, people who have called themselves Christian have seen fit to fabricate, falsify, and forge documents, in most instances in order to authorize views they wanted others to accept.

My particular interest in this book, of course, is with the forgeries of the early Christian church. No one doubts that there were lots of them. Today we have only a fraction of the ones that were produced in antiquity, as the vast majority of them have been lost or destroyed. But what we have is more than enough to give us a sense of how prominent the practice of forgery was. We have numerous Gospels, letters, treatises, and apocalypses that claim to be written by people who did not write them. The authors who called themselves Peter, Paul, John, James, Philip, Thomas, or—pick your name!—knew full well they were not these people. They lied about it in order to deceive their readers into thinking they were authority figures.

Some of these writings made it into the Bible. There are New Testament letters claiming to be written by Peter and Paul, for example, and James and Jude. But these books were written by other, unknown authors living after the apostles themselves had died. When the real authors of these books claimed to be apostles, they were consciously involved in deception. This practice was widely talked about in the ancient world and was almost always condemned as lying, illegitimate, and just plain wrong. But authors did it anyway.

I'm not saying that the authors who engaged in this activity were necessarily violating the dictates of their own conscience. We have no way of knowing what they really thought about themselves or about what they were doing. All we know is that when ancient people talked about the practice, they did not say positive things about it. Books that were forged were called false and illegitimate.

But one can imagine that the authors themselves may not have seen it this way. Whenever we have a record of those being caught in the act, they try to justify what they did. The second-century author who fabricated the story of Paul and Thecla, mentioned earlier, claimed he did it out of "love for Paul." The fifth-century forger Salvian of Marseille claimed he thought no one would think he meant it when he called himself Timothy and that he didn't mean any harm by it. And after all, no one would take seriously a book written by Salvian, whereas a book by Timothy might be widely read (see Chapter 1).

It is possible that many of the authors whose works we have considered, both within and outside of the New Testament, felt completely justified in what they were doing. If so, they were accepting the ancient view, held by many people still today, that lying is the right thing to do in some instances (as mentioned in Chapter 1). In the ancient world, this view was based on the idea that there could be such a thing as a "noble lie," a lie that serves a noble cause. If a doctor needs to lie to a patient in order to get her to take the medicine she needs, then that can be a good form of deception. If a commander-in-chief needs to lie to his troops that reinforcements are about to arrive in order to inspire them to fight more courageously, then that can be a good thing. Some lies are noble.

Other Christian authors, most notably Augustine, took precisely the opposite line, arguing that lying in all its forms was bad. Very bad. Very, very bad. It was not to be engaged in, no matter what. For Augustine, even if a lie could guarantee that your young daughter would not spend eternity in the fires of hell, but would enjoy the eternal bliss of heaven, that was not enough to justify telling the lie. You should never lie, period.

Most early Christians probably disagreed with Augustine, which is why he had to argue his point so strenuously. And most people today probably disagree as well. Most of us see lying as a complicated matter. Ethicists, philosophers, and religious scholars all disagree, even today, on when lying is appropriate and when it is not.[15] At the end of the day, this is a question that each and every one of us needs to decide for ourselves, based on our own circumstances and the specific situations we find ourselves in. Maybe sometimes it is okay to lie.

Maybe it is okay for parents to lie to their children about their own religious beliefs, to tell them that God exists even though they don't actually think so. Maybe it is okay for a spouse to lie to her partner about her extramarital affair, if it will prevent him from going through great turmoil and pain. Maybe it is okay to lie to one's parent about the prognosis after surgery, if it will keep the beloved parent from worrying about dying before their time. Maybe it is okay for church leaders to lie to their congregations about their personal beliefs or their less than perfect past, if they have to be seen as respected and stalwart leaders of the community. Maybe it is okay for elected officials to lie about budgets or deficits, shortfalls or windfalls, possible outcomes of policies, foreign intelligence, or the known outcomes of war—if the ends are sufficiently important to require lies instead of the truth.

And if lying is justified in some instances, what better reason for lying than to get people to understand and believe the truth? What would make better sense than writing a book that embodies a lie about a relatively unimportant matter (who *really* wrote this) in order to accomplish what really does matter (the truth being proclaimed)?

On the other hand, maybe the authors who forged these texts were wrong. Maybe they should not have tried to deceive their readers. Maybe it is better always to tell the truth, to stand by the truth, to be willing to take the consequences of the truth, even if you would much prefer the consequences of telling the lie.

Maybe children have the right to know what parents honestly believe. Maybe it is better for a spouse to tell her partner about an extramarital affair, if the alternative is to live a life of deceit and distrust. Maybe a dying parent (or grandparent, sibling, or anyone else) has the right to know that death is imminent, so he or she can prepare for the inevitable. Maybe it is better for church leaders not to mislead their people, but to tell them what they honestly know to be true (e.g., about church finances or about their own sinful past) or what they honestly believe (e.g., about God or the Bible). Maybe it is better for our elected officials to come clean and tell us the truth, rather than mislead us so as to be authorized to do what they desperately want to do domestically or on foreign soil. Maybe, on the whole, truth is better than lying.

To be sure, most people, in most circumstances, present, past, and very distant past, realize that there are times when it might be right and good to lie, if, for example, it can save a life or keep someone from physical harm. But the reality is that most of our lies are not so weighty. Certainly the lies manufactured by the forgers of early Christian texts were not told in order to protect life and limb. They were told in order to deceive readers into thinking that the authors of these books were established authority figures. If these texts were produced by reliable authorities, then what they say about what to believe and how to live must be true. True teachings were based on lies.

At the same time, the authors of these lies were no doubt like nearly everyone else in the world, ancient and modern; they too probably did not want to be lied to and deceived. But for reasons of their own they felt compelled to lie to and deceive others. To this extent they did not live up to one of the fundamental principles of the Christian tradition, taught by Jesus himself, that you should "do unto others as you would have them do unto you." Possibly they felt that in their circumstances the Golden Rule did not apply. If so, it would certainly explain why so many of the writings of the New Testament claim to have been written by apostles, when in fact they were not.

NOTES

Introduction: Facing the Truth

1. I am outlining here just the "orthodox" views that ended up winning the early Christian battles over what to believe. There were lots of Christians who held other views, as we will see later in the book. For further reflections, see my book *Lost Christianities: The Battles for Scripture and the Faiths We Never Knew* (New York: Oxford University Press, 2003).

2. Thus, for example, Irenaeus *Against Heresies* 3.2–4; 4.26; see also Tertullian *Prescription Against Heresies*.

3. This is why there is such a close connection in Christian antiquity between the content of a writing and its claim to authorship, as we will see. It was widely thought that if a writing promoted "false teachings," then it certainly could not have been produced by an established authority. In other words, the decision about who authored a work (an apostle?) was often made on the basis of whether the teachings in the work were acceptable. See the discussion of the Gospel of Peter in Chapter 2.

Chapter 1: A World of Deceptions and Forgeries

1. The authoritative discussion of the Hitler diaries, told with flair and in precise detail, is found in Robert Harris, *Selling Hitler* (New York: Viking Penguin, 1986).

2. For a fascinating account by one of modern times' most adroit forgery experts, see Charles Hamilton, *Great Forgers and Famous Fakes: The Manuscript Forgers of America and How They Duped the Experts*, 2nd ed. (Lakewood, CO: Glenbridge, 1996).

3. The story is told by the Greek historian Diogenes Laertius in his *Lives of the Philosophers* (5.92–93).

4. For a collection of some of the most interesting, see Bart D. Ehrman, *Lost Scriptures: Books That Did Not Make It into the New Testament* (New York: Oxford University Press, 2003). For a more comprehensive collection, see J. K. Elliott, *The Apocryphal New Testament* (Oxford: Clarendon, 1993).

5. Tertullian *On Baptism* 17. See also the discussion of ancient fictions about Paul in Chapter 3.

6. This is my own count.

7. As we will see later in Chapter 3, some scholars have maintained that the allegedly forged writing the author of 2 Thessalonians is referring to is none other than 1 Thessalonians!

8. Eusebius *Church History* 7.25.

9. Jerome *The Lives of Famous Men* 4.

10. Didymus the Blind, *Comments on the Catholic Epistles* (never translated into English), in Migne's *Patrologia Graeca* 39, 1774.

11. Clement of Alexandria *Miscellanies* 2.52.6.

12. This has recently been argued in Clare Rothschild, *Hebrews as*

Pseudepigraphon: The History and Significance of the Pauline At-tribution of Hebrews (Tübingen: Mohr Siebeck, 2009).

13. There may be some question, however, about Xenophon. The Greek philosopher Plutarch maintained that Xenophon used the pen name precisely to lend more credibility to his account by having it written by an outside party rather than writing about himself in the first person. If so, this is a pen name "with an edge."

14. For reasons for thinking that the Gospel of Matthew was not really written by the disciple Matthew, see Chapter 7, and in greater depth, John Meier, "Matthew, Gospel of," *Anchor Bible Dictionary* (New York: Doubleday, 1992), 4:618–41.

15. Galen *Commentary on Hippocrates' On the Nature of Man* 1.42.

16. Smith wrote two books about the discovery and its importance for understanding early Christianity and the historical Jesus, one an intriguing detective-like story for popular audiences, *The Secret Gospel: The Discovery and Interpretation of the Secret Gospel of Mark* (New York: Harper & Row, 1973), and the other a hard-hitting analysis for scholars, *Clement of Alexandria and a Secret Gospel of Mark* (Cambridge, MA: Harvard University Press, 1973). Recent years, however, have seen a spate of publications by scholars arguing that Smith in fact forged the document. See especially Stephen Carlson, *The Gospel Hoax: Morton Smith's Invention of Secret Mark* (Waco, TX: Baylor University Press, 2005); and Peter Jeffries, *The Secret Gospel of Mark Unveiled: Imagined Rituals of Sex, Death, and Madness in a Biblical Forgery* (New Haven, CT: Yale University Press, 2007). See also my discussion in Chapter 8.

17. Josephus *Jewish Wars* 1.26.3; trans. William Whiston, *The Works of Josephus* (Grand Rapids, MI: Baker, 1979).

18. See Wolfgang Speyer, *Die literarische Fälschung im heidnischen und christlichen Altertum* (Munich: Beck, 1971), p. 145.

19. For an English translation, see R. J. J. Shutt, "Letter of Aristeas," in James Charlesworth, ed., *The Old Testament Pseudepigrapha*, 2 vols. (New York: Doubleday, 1985), 2:7–34.

20. Martial *Epigrams* 7.12; 7.72; 10.3; 10.33. I am not saying, of course, that in this or any of the other cases I mention we actually know the real motivations of the forger. What we do know is that Martial read his motivations in this way.

21. Diogenes Laertius *Lives of the Philosophers* 10.3.

22. Pausanius *Description of Greece* 6.18.5.

23. The New Testament book of Revelation, written by an unknown John, is a very rare exception.

24. One of the most interesting discussions is in the writings of the church father Tertullian, who asked how the book of *Enoch*, written by the famous figure Enoch—a man who never died, but was taken up to heaven while still living seven generations after Adam—could have survived down to his, Tertullian's, own day. If there was a worldwide flood after Enoch's time in the days of Noah, wouldn't the book have perished? Tertullian goes out of his way to explain how it could, in fact, have survived the flood. Why does Tertullian have to go to the trouble of explaining this? Because he genuinely believed that it was written by Enoch. Tertullian was no dummy—far from it. He was one of the real intellectuals of the Christian third century. It is anachronistic for modern-day scholars to think that ancients must have seen through the ruse of apocalyptic forgery and recognized that the books produced were simply following the requirements of the genre.

25. Porphyry *Isagoge* pr. I.

26. For the letter and a full discussion of it, see A. E. Haefner, "A Unique Source for the Study of Ancient Pseudonymity," *Anglican Theological Review* 16 (1934): 8–15.

27. It is almost always claimed by scholars dealing with Christian pseudepigrapha that the author of the so-called *Acts of Paul* (or *Acts of Paul and Thecla*) was caught and punished. That is true, but his crime was not committing forgery. As I point out in Chapter 3 in greater detail, the *Acts of Paul* is not a book that claims to be written *by* Paul; it claims to be a true account *about* Paul. The author was punished not for lying about his identity, but for fabricating a fictitious account and trying to pass it off as a historical record.

28. Anthony Grafton, *Forgers and Critics: Creativity and Duplicity in Western Scholarship* (Princeton, NJ: Princeton University Press, 1990).

29. See Raffaella Cribbiore, *Gymnastics of the Mind: Greek Education in Hellenistic and Roman Egypt* (Princeton, NJ: Princeton University Press, 2001).

30. In Chapter 4 I deal with other explanations that try to sanitize the practice as well, including the claim that apparent forgeries can be explained by authors having used secretaries who used a different writing style and altered the content of what the authors wanted to say.

31. In addition, some ancient authors described the penning of works in a name other than one's own with the Greek and Latin equivalents of our verb "to make" (as in "to create," "to forge") or "to make up" (i.e., to "fabricate").

32. The most thorough examination is now forty years old, but it has never been equaled, let alone surpassed. Most New Testament scholars, alas, have never read it—Speyer's *Die literarische Fälschung im heidnischen und christlichen Altertum.* Also valuable, though considerably less thorough, is Norbert Brox, *Falsche Verfasserangabe: Zur Erklärung der frühchristlichen Pseudepigraphie* (Stuttgart: KBW, 1975). Most work on forgery in early Christianity focuses on the question of whether

any pseudepigraphical writings made it into the New Testament. The most recent work along these lines is Armin Baum, *Pseudepigraphie und literarische Fälschung im frühen Christentum* (Tübingen: Mohr Siebeck, 2001). Together these authors give a comprehensive survey of all the ancient sources on forgery. And all of them agree that forgers intended to deceive their readers.

33. Herodotus *Histories* 7.6.

34. Plutarch *The Oracles at Delphi* 407B.

35. Athenaeus *The Banqueters* 13.611B.

36. Speyer, *Die literarische Fälschung*, p. 3; translation mine.

37. Aristotle *Nicomachean Ethics* 4.7.

38. Xenophon *Memorabilia* 4.2.14–18.

39. Plato *Republic* 382C; 389B; Heliodorus *Ethiopica* I.26.6.

40. The fullest and most compelling study of Augustine's view of lying is David J. Griffiths, *Lying: An Augustinian Theology of Duplicity* (Grand Rapids, MI: Brazos, 2004).

41. Origen in his lost book the *Miscellanies*, discussed by Jerome in *Against Rufinus* 1.18; Clement *Miscellanies* 7, 9, 53, 1–4.

Chapter 2: Forgeries in the Name of Peter

1. In the fuller account of the story, George's father is so proud of his son for speaking the truth in the face of possible adversity that he takes him into his arms and praises him to the heavens.

2. There are a number of interesting books on lying for a general audience. One of the most influential has been Sissela Bok, *Lying: Moral Choice in Public and Private Life*, 3rd ed. (New York: Vintage, 1999).

3. For lying in antiquity, see especially the collection of essays in Christopher Gill and T. P. Wiseman, eds., *Lies and Fiction in the Ancient World* (Austin: University of Texas Press, 1993).

4. Exceptions *may* be some kinds of fantasy and science fiction, but even there plausibility is an important feature; postmodern novels, to no one's surprise, are a different kettle of fish.

5. Polybius *Histories* 2.56.10–12; trans. W. R. Paton, Loeb Classical Library (New York: Putnam, 1922).

6. For English translations of these stories, collectively known as the *Acts of Peter*, see J. K. Elliott, *The Apocryphal New Testament* (Oxford: Clarendon, 1993), pp. 390–430; and Wilhelm Schneemelcher, *New Testament Apocrypha*, trans. R. McL. Wilson, from the sixth German edition, 2 vols. (Louisville, KY: Westminster John Knox, 1991–92), 2:271–321.

7. Eusebius *Church History* 6.12.

8. For an English translation, see Bart D. Ehrman and Zlatko Plese, *Apocryphal Gospels: Texts and Translations* (New York: Oxford University Press, 2010).

9. It is debated among scholars whether it is the "evildoer" who is punished by not having his legs broken or Jesus. I tend to think the former, since it doesn't make as much sense to think that the soldiers got angry at Jesus for something the other fellow said.

10. Some scholars have argued that these verses are not *actually* docetic. Here I'm not arguing that the author intended them to be read docetically. I'm simply saying that a hostile reader like Serapion may well have thought they were meant docetically, even if they were not.

11. Note again the relation of an "author" to "authority" and vice versa. In Serapion's view a false account such as the *Gospel of Peter* could not have been written by an authority such as

Peter. And so the book was pseudepigraphical, written "under a false name" by someone else.

12. For English translations, see Wilhelm Schneemelcher, *New Testament Apocrypha*, trans. R. McL. Wilson, from the sixth German edition, 2 vols. (Louisville, KY: Westminster John Knox, 1991–92), 2:493–94. I have taken my quotations from there.

13. Though not in Paul's own writings. See the discussion of Gal. 2:11–14 in the section on the noncanonical *Epistle of Peter* in Chapter 6.

14. I deal with the matter for a general audience in my book *Lost Christianities: The Battles for Scripture and the Faiths We Never Knew* (New York: Oxford University Press, 2003). For a more thorough and heavy-hitting study, see Harry Gamble, *The New Testament Canon: Its Making and Meaning* (Philadelphia: Fortress, 1985). For a fully authoritative account, see Bruce Metzger, *The Canon of the New Testament: Its Origin, Development, and Significance* (New York: Oxford University Press, 1987).

15. English translations can be found in Elliott, *Apocryphal New Testament*, pp. 593–612; and Schneemelcher, *New Testament Apocrypha*, 2:620–38.

16. Eusebius classifies the *Apocalypse of Peter* among the *notha*—the "bastard," forged writings—rather than among the books he accepts as canonical. But the fact that he has to mention the book at all in this context suggests that there were other Christians who maintained that it should be accepted as Scripture, as with most of the other books he classified as *notha*, such as the *Didache*, the *Epistle of Barnabas*, and the *Shepherd of Hermas*. The *Apocalypse of Peter* is also received as canonical (tentatively) in the late second-century Muratorian Canon, a document I discuss in Chapter 3.

17. For a discussion of the book, which includes evidence that it was

not written by Peter, see J. H. Elliott, "Peter, First Epistle of," *Anchor Bible Dictionary* (New York: Doubleday, 1992), 5:269–78.

18. Jesus of course would have been speaking Aramaic. The Aramaic word for "rock" is Kephas, and that is how Peter's name occurs when given in its Aramaic form. I am not saying that I think the account in Matthew is historically accurate in describing Peter as the "rock" of the church, but I do think it highly probably that Jesus renamed Simon "the Rock" during his public ministry.

19. It should not be objected that Peter did not actually see the crucifixion of Jesus and so was not a "witness" to his sufferings. Whoever wrote this book almost certainly did not have the Gospels to read; we can't know what he thought about Peter's involvement in Jesus's last hours.

20. For a discussion of the book, which includes evidence that it was not written by Peter, see J. H. Elliott, "Peter, Second Epistle of," *Anchor Bible Dictionary*, 5:282–87.

21. Simeon appears to be the Hebrew form of "Simon." Why the author mixes Hebrew (Simeon instead of Simon) with Greek (Peter instead of the Aramaic Kephas) is a puzzle.

22. Paul himself did not think that he was writing "Scripture." He was writing personal letters to his churches. They too treated these writings, when they received them, as personal correspondence. It was only later, after Paul's lifetime, that different churches and individuals collected these letters and started regarding them as Scripture. For insightful comments on the early collections of Paul's letters, see Harry Gamble, *Books and Readers in the Early Church* (New Haven, CT: Yale University Press, 1993), pp. 58–65.

23. There are other reasons for assuming Peter did not write this letter. In 3:2 the author slips and refers to "your apostles" as if

he is not one of them. Moreover, the author uses the book of Jude and so must have written later than that forged letter. And he knows 1 Peter (since he refers to this book as his "second" letter), which, as I will argue more fully now, could not have been by Peter either, but was written later, at least after the fall of Jerusalem in the year 70.

24. William Harris, *Ancient Literacy* (Cambridge, MA: Harvard University Press, 1989).

25. Among the many excellent studies of ancient education systems, see especially the study of Raffaella Cribbiore, *Gymnastics of the Mind: Greek Education in Hellenistic and Roman Egypt* (Princeton, NJ: Princeton University Press, 2001).

26. Catherine Hezser, *Literacy in Roman Palestine* (Tübingen: Mohr Siebeck, 2001).

27. Mark Chancey, *The Myth of a Gentile Galilee* (Cambridge: Cambridge University Press, 2002); see also his more recent study, *Greco-Roman Culture and the Galilee of Jesus* (Cambridge: Cambridge University Press, 2005).

28. Jonathan Reed, *Archaeology and the Galilean Jesus* (Harrisburg, PA: Trinity Press International, 2000), pp. 140–69.

29. The famous synagogue that tourists see on the site today was built centuries later.

Chapter 3: Forgeries in the Name of Paul

1. For an English translation, see J. K. Elliot, *The Apocryphal New Testament* (Oxford: Clarendon, 1993), pp. 350–89; and Wilhelm Schneemelcher, *New Testament Apocrypha*, trans. R. McL. Wilson, from the sixth German edition, 2 vols. (Louisville, KY: Westminster John Knox, 1991–92), 2:213–70.

2. For a full account of the Thecla traditions, see Stephen Davis,

The Cult of Saint Thecla: A Tradition of Women's Piety in Late Antiquity (New York: Oxford University Press, 2001).

3. Tertullian *On Baptism* 17.

4. The classic study of Marcion, which is still worth reading today, was published by the great German scholar Adolf von Harnack in 1924; it has been partially translated into English by John E. Steely and Lyle D. Bierma as *Marcion: The Gospel of the Alien God* (Durham, NC: Labyrinth, 1990). The most recent overview is Heikki Raïsänen, "Marcion," in Antti Marjanen and Petri Luomanen, eds., *A Companion to Second-Century Christian "Heretics"* (Leiden: Brill, 2008), pp. 100–124.

5. For an English translation, see Bruce M. Metzger, *The Canon of the New Testament* (New York: Oxford University Press, 1987), pp. 305–07. Some scholars date the Muratorian Canon to the fourth century, but this view has not proved convincing to most.

6. For an English translation, see Elliott, *Apocryphal New Testament*, pp. 380–82; and Schneemelcher, *New Testament Apocrypha*, 2:254–57.

7. Benjamin White, "Reclaiming Paul? Reconfiguration as Reclamation in 3 Corinthians," *Journal of Early Christian Studies* 17 (2009): 497–523.

8. For an English translation, see Elliott, *Apocryphal New Testament*, pp. 547–52; and Schneemelcher, *New Testament Apocrypha*, 2:46–52. My quotations here follow Schneemelcher's translation.

9. For a fuller description of Gnosticism, see Chapter 6.

10. The scholarly literature on the pastoral letters is so massive that it is difficult to know where to refer interested readers who want to see the basic arguments about their authenticity. Possibly it is best to start with Jerome D. Quinn, "Timothy and Titus, Epistles to," *Anchor Bible Dictionary*, ed. David Noel Friedman (New

York: Doubleday, 1992), 6:560–71. As is true of everything I talk about in this book—as is true, in fact, for virtually anything any biblical scholar talks about—there are differences of opinion even here. For a representative of the minority view that Paul actually was the author of the pastoral letters, see the lively discussion in the introduction in Luke Timothy Johnson, *The First and Second Letters to Timothy* (New York: Doubleday, 2001).

11. For example, Michael Prior, *Paul the Letter Writer in the Second Letter to Timothy* (Sheffield: Sheffield University Press, 1989).

12. Among other things, this means that if any one of these letters is forged, they're all forged.

13. A. N. Harrison, *The Problem of the Pastoral Epistles* (Oxford: Oxford University Press, 1921).

14. This is the case even with scholars who want to argue that Paul did write the letters. One of the most recent studies is Armin Baum, "Semantic Variation Within the *Corpus Paulinum:* Linguistic Considerations Concerning the Richer Vocabulary of the Pastoral Epistles," *Tyndale Bulletin* 59 (2008): 271–92. Baum points out that in the other letters of Paul, the fewer total number of words that can be found in a letter means that there are fewer *different* words used. But not with the pastoral letters, which have fewer words than many of Paul's letters, but more *different* words. Baum still wants to think that these books are written by Paul, however, and so comes up with an explanation that sounds perhaps like a case of special pleading. In his view, Paul took more consideration and time with these letters than his others, since he was composing them in writing rather than orally. That seems highly unlikely to me. Paul certainly put a lot of time and effort into composing letters like Romans and Galatians. Moreover, Baum doesn't cite any evidence to suggest that the Pastorals were composed in writing by Paul rather than dictated, by Paul or anyone else.

15. Unfortunately, the article is available only in German: Norbert Brox, "Zu den persönlichen Notizen der Pastoralbriefe," *Biblische Zeitschrift* 13 (1969): 76–94.

16. Dennis Ronald MacDonald, *The Legend and the Apostle: The Battle for Paul in Story and Canon* (Philadelphia: Westminster, 1983).

17. Once again, the scholarship on this question is voluminous. A good place to start is Edgar Krenz, "Thessalonians, First and Second Epistles to the," *Anchor Bible Dictionary* (New York: Doubleday, 1992), 6:515–23.

18. F. F. Bruce, *Paul: Apostle of the Heart Set Free* (Grand Rapids, MI: Eerdmans, 1977).

19. J. Christiaan Beker, *Paul the Apostle: The Triumph of God in Life and Thought* (Philadelphia: Fortress, 1980).

20. See J. Christiaan Beker, *Heirs of Paul: Paul's Legacy in the New Testament and in the Church Today* (Minneapolis: Fortress, 1991).

21. See Victor Paul Furnish, "Ephesians, Epistle to," *Anchor Bible Dictionary* (New York: Doubleday, 1992), 2:535–42.

22. See Victor Paul Furnish, "Colossians, Epistle to the," *Anchor Bible Dictionary*, 1:1090–96.

23. Unfortunately, the book has never been translated into English: Walter Bujard, *Stilanalytische Untersuchungen zum Kolosserbrief: Als Beitrag zur Methodik von Sprachvergleichen* (Göttingen: Vandenhoeck & Ruprecht, 1973).

Chapter 4: Alternatives to Lies and Deceptions

1. It didn't occur to me at the time that the author of 2 Timothy would have been speaking only about the Scriptures he knew, the "Old Testament," and that his doctrine of inspiration may not have coincided with my own view that the Bible was com-

pletely without error, a view that in fact came into existence only in modern times.

2. A partial exception may be the view of evangelical scholar Donald Guthrie, who tries to argue on historical, rather than dogmatic, grounds that there can be no forgeries in the New Testament; see his "The Development of the Idea of Canonical Pseudipigrapha in New Testament Criticism," *Vox Evangelica* 1 (1962): 43–59.

3. These views of Daniel and Ecclesiastes are almost universally held by critical scholars today. For an introductory discussion, see two of the leading textbooks on the Hebrew Bible in use throughout American universities today: John J. Collins, *Introduction to the Hebrew Bible* (Minneapolis: Fortress, 2004); and Michael Coogan, *The Old Testament: A Historical and Literary Introduction to the Hebrew Scriptures* (New York: Oxford University Press, 2006).

4. Another approach is to acknowledge that false authorial claims do indeed constitute forgery—lies with the intent to deceive—but to insist that the Bible *should* not have such books in it. This is the claim of one of the most recent scholars of forgery who has come out of Germany, Armin Baum, who thinks that if it can be shown that a book really is forged, it should be removed from the New Testament (implied in his book *Pseudepigraphie und literarische Fälschung im frühen Christentum* [Tübingen: Mohr Siebeck, 2001] and confirmed by private correspondence). As you might imagine, given such a view, Baum is reluctant to consider too many of the books of the New Testament forgeries. But he is willing to concede, for example, along with the vast majority of scholars, that 2 Peter is.

5. A. N. Harrison, *The Problem of the Pastoral Epistles* (Oxford: Oxford University Press, 1921), p. 12.

6. A. W. Argyle, "The Greek of Luke and Acts," *New Testament Studies* 20 (1974): 445.

7. M. J. J. Menken, *2 Thessalonians* (London: Routledge, 1994), p. 40.

8. Andrew Lincoln, *Ephesians* (Nashville: Thomas Nelson, 1990), p. lxx.

9. R. McL. Wilson, *Colossians and Philemon* (London: Clark, 2005), p. 31.

10. For an assessment of how certain books came to be considered part of the canon of Scripture, see my study *Lost Christianities: The Battles for Scripture and the Faiths We Never Knew* (New York: Oxford University Press, 2003). A fuller discussion can be found in Harry Gamble, *The New Testament Canon: Its Making and Meaning* (Philadelphia: Fortress, 1985).

11. Bruce M. Metzger, "Literary Forgeries and Canonical Pseudepigrapha," *Journal of Biblical Literature* 91 (1972): 15–16.

12. Norbert Brox, *Falsche Verfasserangabe: Zur Erklärung der frühchristlichen Pseudepigraphie* (Stuttgart: KBW, 1975), p. 81; translation mine.

13. Wolfgang Speyer, *Die literarische Fälschung im heidnischen und christlichen Altertum* (Munich: Beck, 1971), p. 3; translation mine.

14. Kurt Aland, "The Problem of Anonymity and Pseudonymity in Christian Literature of the First Two Centuries," *Journal of Biblical Literature* 12 (1961): 39–49.

15. James Dunn, "The Problem of Pseudonymity," in *The Living Word* (Philadelphia: Fortress, 1987), pp. 65–85.

16. David Meade, *Pseudonymity and Canon: An Investigation into the Relationship of Authorship and Authority in Jewish and Earliest Christian Tradition* (Tübingen: Mohr Siebeck, 1986).

17. Markus Barth and Helmut Blanke, *Colossians* (New York: Doubleday, 1994), p. 123.

18. Margaret Y. MacDonald, *Colossians and Ephesians* (Collegeville, MN: Liturgical, 2000), p. 8.

19. Two additional sources come from centuries later still and are of almost no historical worth, as I argue below.

20. The passage is discussed at some length, for example, in Baum, *Pseudepigraphie und literarische Fälschung*, pp. 53–55.

21. Ibn Abi Usaybi'a, *Kitab 'uyun al-anba 'fi tabaqat al-atibba'*, ed. 'Amir al-Najjar, 4 vols. (Cairo: al-Hay'a al-Misriyya al-'Amma lil-Kitab, 2001), 1:244–45.

22. Iamblichus *Life of Pythagoras* 31.

23. See Leonid Zhmud, *Wissenschaft, Philosophie und Religion im frühen Pythagoreismus* (Berlin: Akademie, 1997), p. 91.

24. See, for example, Holger Thesleff, *Introduction to the Pythagorean Writings of the Hellenistic Period* (Åbo: Åcademi, 1961).

25. Two later Neoplatonic philosophers, Olympiodorus and Elias, living some two and a half centuries after Iamblichus, make roughly similar comments (Olympiodorus *Prolegomenon* 13.4–14.4; Elias *In Porphyrii Isagogen et Aristotelis Categorias Commentaria* 128.1–22). But they are so long after the fact that they cannot help us know what was happening in the time of the New Testament, half a millennium earlier (any more than the editorial practices in vogue today can tell us what was happening in the 1500s). Moreover, the comments of Olympiodorus and Elias may ultimately derive from the tradition starting with Iamblichus, some two hundred fifty years earlier.

26. E. Randolph Richards, *The Secretary in the Letters of Paul* (Tübingen: Mohr Siebeck, 1991).

27. Richards, *Secretary*, p. 108.

28. Richards, *Secretary*, pp. 110–11.

Chapter 5: Forgeries in Conflicts with Jews and Pagans

1. See John J. Collins, *The Scepter and the Star: The Messiahs of the Dead Sea Scrolls and Other Ancient Literature* (New York: Doubleday, 1995).

2. For an English translation of the Gospel of Nicodemus, see Bart D. Ehrman and Zlatko Plese, *Apocryphal Gospels: Texts and Translations* (New York: Oxford University Press, 2010).

3. For an English translation, see Ehrman and Plese, *Apocryphal Gospels*.

4. For an English translation, see Ehrman and Plese, *Apocryphal Gospels*.

5. For an English translation, see Ehrman and Plese, *Apocryphal Gospels*.

6. Tertullian *Apology* 21.24; Eusebius *Church History* 2.2.

7. For an English translation, see Ehrman and Plese, *Apocryphal Gospels*.

8. Tertullian *Apology* 21.24.

9. For an English translation, see Ehrman and Plese, *Apocryphal Gospels*.

10. For a fuller discussion, see my *Misquoting Jesus: The Story Behind Who Changed the Bible and Why* (San Francisco: HarperSanFrancisco, 2005), pp. 63–65.

11. In the history of the interpretation of the passage the question has always been, "What was he writing?" Some have thought that he must have been writing out the sins of the woman's accusers. Or a particularly apt quotation of scripture. Or a declaration of condemnation of unjust judges. Or something else!

12. Chris Keith, *The Pericope Adulterae, the Gospel of John, and the Literacy of Jesus* (Leiden: Brill, 2009).

13. Augustine *On the Harmony of the Gospels* 1.10.

14. Other writings allegedly written by Jesus are referred to in several church fathers, such as Augustine (*Against Faustus* 28.4) and Leo the Great (*Sermon* 34.4).

15. My reasoning in this case is that it is not a letter that existed outside of its fictional context, a piece of correspondence that circulated independently as a writing of Jesus.

16. For English translations of both letters, see Ehrman and Plese, *Apocryphal Gospels*.

17. An English translation of excerpts of Egeria's diary is provided by Andrew Jacobs in Bart Ehrman and Andrew Jacobs, *Christianity in Late Antiquity, 300–450 CE: A Reader* (New York: Oxford University Press, 2003), pp. 333–46.

18. Tertullian *Apology* 40; trans. S. Thelwell, in Alexander Roberts and James Donaldson, eds., *The Ante-Nicene Fathers* (reprint, Grand Rapids, MI: Eerdmans, 1995).

19. Minucius Felix *Octavius* 9.6–7; in G. W. Clarke, ed., *The Octavius of Minucius Felix* (Mahway, NJ: Paulist, 1974).

20. Minucius Felix *Octavius* 9.5.

21. For English translations of a range of accounts, see Herbert Musurillo, *Acts of the Christian Martyrs* (Oxford: Clarendon, 1972).

22. Eusebius *Church History* 9.5.

23. Ovid *Metamorphoses* 14.136–46.

24. For an excellent study of the Sibyl and her oracles, see H. W. Parke, *Sibyls and Sibylline Prophecy in Classical Antiquity*, ed. B. C. McGin (London: Routledge, 1988).

25. For a full analysis and translation of the surviving oracles, see John J. Collins, *Sibylline Oracles*, in James Charlesworth, ed.,

Old Testament Pseudepigrapha, 2 vols. (New York: Doubleday, 1983–85), 1:317–472.

26. All translations are by Collins, in Charlesworth, ed., *Old Testament Pseudepigrapha*.

27. Justin *First Apology* 20.

28. For example, the pagan critic Celsus around 177 CE, as quoted by the church father Origen in his book *Against Celsus* (5.61.615; 7.53.732; 7.56.734); also see a Latin oration attributed to the (Christian) emperor Constantine found in Eusebius's *Life of Constantine*, in which the emperor claims that the pagan charges of forgery are false.

Chapter 6: Forgeries in Conflicts with False Teachers

1. John J. Gunther, *St. Paul's Opponents and Their Background* (Leiden: Brill, 1973).

2. Thomas Sappington, *Revelation and Redemption at Colossae* (Sheffield: JSOT, 1991); Richard DeMaris, *Colossian Controversy: Wisdom in Dispute at Colossae* (Sheffield: Sheffield University Press, 1994); Clinton Arnold, *Colossian Syncretism: The Interface Between Christianity and Folk Belief at Colossae* (Tübingen: Mohr Siebeck, 1995); Troy Martin, *By Philosophy and Empty Deceit : Colossians as Response to a Cynic Critique* (Sheffield: Sheffield Academic Press, 1996).

3. I have taken all translations of the *Pseudo-Clementine Writings* from Thomas Smith, "The Pseudo-Clementine Literature," in Alexander Roberts and James Donaldson, eds., *The Ante-Nicene Fathers*, vol. 8 (reprint, Grand Rapids, MI: Eerdmans, 1995).

4. They are called this because they consist of twenty sermons allegedly given by Clement, in which he tells his tales of journeys and adventures with the apostle Peter.

5. There has been a spate of books on the historical James in recent years. For a competent treatment by a good scholar (with whom I disagree on a number of points), see John Painter, *Just James: The Brother of Jesus in History and Tradition* (Edinburgh: Clark, 1997).

6. See, for example, the discussion in my *Jesus, Interrupted: Revealing the Hidden Contradictions in the Bible (And Why We Don't Know About Them)* (San Francisco: HarperOne, 2009), pp. 53–58.

7. Scholars have come up with four major possible explanations for these "we passages." Three of the four explanations simply don't seem to work. The traditional explanation is that the author really was Paul's companion. That view is problematic though, since the author makes so many mistakes about Paul's life and teachings that he doesn't seem to be a close companion. Other scholars have maintained that the author, whoever he was, had access to a companion of Paul's travel itinerary and inserted it in a few places, creating the odd use of "we" on occasion (since that was how the itinerary was worded). This is an attractive option, but it does not explain why the writing style and vocabulary of the "we passages" is virtually the same as the rest of Acts. If the itinerary came from a different author, you would expect the style to be different. Other scholars have argued that the author is using an age-old technique of describing travel narratives—especially those involving sea journeys—in the first person. But still other scholars have pointed out that there are lots of sea-travel narratives not written in the first person, so this does not seem to explain these passages. The fourth explanation is the one that seems to me to have the fewest problems: the author has edited these sections of Acts to make his readers assume that he was actually with Paul for these parts of the story, even though he was not. This would explain why the "we" sections begin and end so abruptly: it was just a stylistic

device used by the author to insert himself into the story in a few places.

8. Irenaeus *Against Heresies* 3.14.1.

9. See note 6.

10. Scholars today are widely split on how to discuss Gnosticism or even whether to consider Gnosticism a single broad phenomenon. For three very different perspectives from leading scholars, see Karen King, *What Is Gnosticism?* (Cambridge, MA: Harvard University Press, 2005); Bentley Layton, *The Gnostic Scriptures: Ancient Wisdom for the New Age* (New York: Doubleday, 1987); and Birger Pearson, *Ancient Gnosticism: Traditions and Literature* (Minneapolis: Fortress, 2007).

11. For a fresh translation of the Nag Hammadi writings, see Marvin Meyer, ed., *The Nag Hammadi Scriptures* (San Francisco: HarperOne, 2007).

12. Epiphanius *The Medicine Chest* 26.

13. Whether Epiphanius actually knew and read these other books or instead was making them up is anyone's guess.

14. Both Didymus and Thomas mean "twin"; Jude was his name. He is talked about as the twin of Jesus in the ancient Syrian book the *Acts of Thomas*, which describes his missionary journey to India after Jesus's death.

15. For an English translation, see Meyer, *Nag Hammadi Scriptures*, pp. 487–97. I have taken my quotations from there.

16. For an English translation, see Meyer, *Nag Hammadi Scriptures*, pp. 235–45. I have taken my quotations from there.

17. For an English translation, see Wilhelm Schneemelcher, *New Testament Apocrypha*, trans. R. McL. Wilson, 2 vols. (Louisville, KY: Westminster John Knox, 1991–92), 1:249–84.

Chapter 7: False Attributions, Fabrications, and Falsifications:
Phenomena Related to Forgery

1. Thus Johannes Quasten, *Patrology* (Utrecht: Spectrum, 1950), 2:412–13.

2. It is included as part of the canon of the New Testament, for example, in a famous biblical manuscript of the fifth century, Codex Alexandrinus.

3. For the variety of expectations of what the future messiah would be like, see John J. Collins, *The Scepter and the Star* (New York: Doubleday, 1995) and my brief discussion in Chapter 5.

4. Irenaeus *Against Heresies* 3.7.11.

5. Papias indicates that he received this information from someone who had known the apostles; that is, it comes to us third-hand. See the next note.

6. For the full text of Papias's comments, see Bart D. Ehrman, *The Apostolic Fathers*, 2 vols., Loeb Classical Library (Cambridge, MA: Harvard University Press, 2003), 2:103.

7. Tertullian *Against Marcion* 4.5.

8. I argue this case in my book *Jesus, Interrupted: Revealing the Hidden Contradictions in the Bible (and Why We Don't Know About Them)* (San Francisco: HarperOne, 2009), pp. 102–12, and probably don't need to give all the arguments and information yet again here.

9. For an argument that the author intends to make his readers think he was Paul, see Clare Rothschild, *Hebrews as Pseudepigraphon* (Tübingen: Mohr Siebeck, 2009).

10. For an English translation, see Ehrman, *Apostolic Fathers*, 2:3–83.

11. For an English translation, see Bart D. Ehrman and Zlatko

Plese, *Apocryphal Gospels: Texts and Translations* (New York: Oxford University Press, 2010).

12. See David Dungan and J. K. Elliott, *Art and the Christian Apocrypha* (New York: Routledge, 2001).

13. For an English translation, see Ehrman and Plese, *Apocryphal Gospels.*

14. For an English translation, see Ehrman and Plese, *Apocryphal Gospels.*

15. The fullest, most recent study is Reidar Aasgaard, *The Childhood of Jesus: Decoding the Apocryphal Infancy Gospel of Thomas* (Eugene, OR: Cascade, 2009).

16. See my *Jesus, Interrupted.* As I stress there, this view that the Gospels contain nonhistorical accounts is not just my idiosyncratic idea; it is the consensus of modern critical scholarship and has been for a very long time.

17. This is the subject of my earlier book *Misquoting Jesus: The Story Behind Who Changed the Bible and Why* (San Francisco: HarperOne, 2005). Here I summarize just a few of the most important points.

18. See my *Misquoting Jesus,* pp. 65–68.

19. See the discussion in Gordon Fee, *The First Epistle to the Corinthians* (Grand Rapids, MI: Eerdmans, 1987) or, more briefly, *Misquoting Jesus,* pp. 183–86.

20. Robert Funk, Roy W. Hoover, and the Jesus Seminar, eds., *The Five Gospels: The Search for the Authentic Words of Jesus* (New York: Macmillan, 1993), p. 22.

21. *The Architecture of Marcus Vitruvius Pollio,* trans. Joseph Gwilt (London: Priestley and Weale, 1826).

22. Polybius *Histories* 9.2.12.

23. Martial *Epigrams* 1.66; trans. Walter C. A. Ker, Loeb Classical Library (Cambridge MA: Harvard University Press, 1979).

24. Diogenes Laertius *Lives* 2.60; 5.93; 8.54; trans. R. D. Hicks, Loeb Classical Library (Cambridge, MA: Harvard University Press, 1931).

Chapter 8: Forgeries, Lies, Deceptions, and the Writings of the New Testament

1. Edgar J. Goodspeed, *Modern Apocrypha* (Boston: Beacon, 1956); Per Beskow, *Strange Tales About Jesus: A Survey of Unfamiliar Gospels* (Philadelphia: Fortress, 1983).

2. Discussed in Goodspeed, *Modern Apocrypha*, pp. 3–14; and Beskow, *Strange Tales*, pp. 57–65.

3. See Goodspeed, *Modern Apocrypha*; Beskow, *Strange Tales*, pp. 20–28; 42–50.

4. By Roman source I mean any source written by a pagan author of the Roman Empire; Jesus is mentioned in Christian sources, of course, and twice in the writings of the Jewish historian Josephus, though by no other source of the first century.

5. See Goodspeed, *Modern Apocrypha*, pp. 92–96; Beskow, *Strange Tales*, pp. 16–24.

6. I have taken the translation from Goodspeed, *Modern Apocrypha*, pp. 92–93.

7. See Goodspeed, *Modern Apocrypha*, pp. 97–101.

8. Goodspeed, *Modern Apocrypha*, p. 101.

9. Goodspeed, *Modern Apocrypha*, pp. 45–49. This tale is based on old traditions, especially popular in the Byzantine Christianity, about Mary and a red egg, which arguably provide the origin for the custom of coloring Easter eggs.

10. According to Beskow, this account was written by the Anglican clergyman Gieon Ouseley (1835–1906), a committed vegetarian who wrote ten books on vegetarianism and the occult.

11. Hugh Schonfield, *The Passover Plot* (New York: Bantam, 1965).

12. See Chapter 1, n. 16.

13. See Chapter 1, n. 16.

14. One of Morton Smith's most avid supporters, who argues vehemently that the letter of Clement is authentic, is Scott Brown; his fullest study is *Mark's Other Gospel: Rethinking Morton Smith's Controversial Discovery* (Waterloo, ON: Laurier University Press, 2005).

15. For a popular treatment, see Sissela Bok, *Lying: Moral Choice in Public and Private Life*, 3rd ed. (New York: Vintage, 1999).

INDEX

Abgar, King, 162–163

Abraham, 30, 42, 194–196

abstinence teachings. *See* sexual abstinence teachings

Acts of Paul (and Thecla), 18, 81–83, 88, 103–104, 128–129, 233, 262, 270n27

Acts of Peter, 18, 50–52, 233

Acts of Peter and Paul, 155

Acts of Pilate, 172–173

Acts of the Apostles, 202–209; authorship of, 23, 206–209, 220–221, 286n7; differing from Paul's writings, 204–206, 208; as a forgery, 208–209; inaccurately aligning Paul with apostles, 63, 202–206; noting Peter's illiteracy, 75; Paul's conversion account, 191; summary of, 202–204

Adam, 30, 94

Aeschines, 247

afterlife, 6, 8, 64–65, 89, 106, 213. *See also* second coming beliefs

Against All Heresies, 221–222

Against Heresies (Irenaeus), 225

Aland, Kurt, 124

Alexander (son of Herod), 27, 40

Alexander the False Prophet (Lucian), 28

Anaximenes, 29

Ancient Literacy (Harris), 70–71

ancient world: copying texts, 240–241; historical writing, 47–49; libraries, 26–27; literacy and education, 70–73; notions of fiction, 45–48; plagiarism, 246–247; religion, 5–7; use of secretaries, 134; view of "noble lie," 41, 42, 263. *See also* forgery in the ancient world; Roman Empire

angels, 89, 112, 185

anonymous writing: to boost authority, 223–225; as equivalent to forgery, 119–120; included in New Testament, 10, 23, 220; wrongly attributed, 24, 140, 221–222, 249–250

anti-Semitism, 55–56, 59, 151–152

Antitheses (Marcion), 85–86

Apocalypse of John (Revelation), 21, 30, 64, 105

Apocalypse of Paul, 213

Apocalypse of Peter, 18, 30, 63–65, 274n16

apocalyptic forgeries, 18, 29–31
apocalyptic teachings, evangelical,
105–106
apologetics/apologists, 4, 169–170
apostles: apostolic succession,
7–8; forgeries associated with,
20, 217; Gospels formerly
"memoirs of the," 225; as illiterate, 8; Paul's relationship to
the, 61, 89, 199, 202–203, 205,
206; spirit-inspired writing
from the, 123–125
Apostolic Constitutions, 20, 22, 35,
37, 160, 248–249
Apostolic Tradition, 249
Aramaic, 72, 74, 75, 76, 198
Aristotle, 26, 27, 31
asceticism, 32, 49, 94, 96, 185
Athenagoras, 169
Augustine, 41–42, 160–161, 263
Aurelian, Emperor, 27–28
authority, attribution and, 222–
224

Babylon, 68
baptism, 82, 83, 111
Barnabas, 149, 229–232
Beker, J. Christiaan, 109
Beskow, Per, 252, 254
Bible. *See* New Testament; Old
Testament
biblical "conduct codes," 2, 94
biblical infallibility, 3, 5, 115–117
biography, 46, 47
Birth of Mary, 213
Book of Thomas the Contender,
215–216
Brox, Norbert, 102, 123
Bruce, F. F., 109
Brutus, 134, 137

Buddhism and Jesus hoax, 252–
254
Bujard, Walter, 113

Caldwell, Taylor, 79–81
canonical Gospels: as anonymous,
23, 24, 220–221; cast as continuous with Old Testament,
224–225; and the *Gospel of
Peter*, 55–59; lack of resurrection accounts, 17, 57–58;
misattributions of, 223–228;
possible plagiarism in, 248
Capernaum, 74
celibacy teachings. *See* sexual abstinence teachings
Cerinthus, 21, 217
childbearing, 94, 100, 103
Christ. *See* Jesus
Christian apologists, 4, 169–170
Christianity: evangelical, 2–4,
105–106, 115–117, 145–146;
legacy of lies and deceptions,
40–42, 261–265; messianic
claims, 145–149; second coming beliefs, 105–106; violence
and conflict in, 143–145, 176–
178. *See also* early Christianity;
modern forgeries and hoaxes
Church History (Eusebius), 52–53,
54, 156, 162
church leaders: authorship of *1
Clement*, 222; debates over
suspicious documents, 18–19,
21; development of hierarchy,
101–102; encouraging mar-
riage of, 99–100, 103; forged
documents to direct, 103;
on lying, 41–42; on role of
women, 82–83, 94, 103–105

Cicero, 134, 136, 137, 138

Claudius, Emperor, 155

Clement of Alexandria, 42, 261

Clement of Rome, 20, 62, 190, 222

Cleobius, 88, 89, 160

coauthoring theories, 77, 114, 136–137

Colossians, 112–114, 121, 128, 129, 185, 207

"conduct codes," 2, 94

Confession of Pontius Pilate, The, 259

Coptic Apocalypse of Peter, 213–214

Coptic church, 153

copying texts, 87, 240–242

Corinthian church, 101, 181, 222

creation, 88–89, 95–96

credibility motive, 8–9, 31–32

creeds, 6, 7

crucifixion of Jesus. See Jesus, crucifixion of

Crucifixion of Jesus, by an Eye-Witness, The, 254–256

Daniel, 30, 117, 131

Dante, 64

David (Aristotle commentator), 31

David, King, 146, 224

Dead Sea Scrolls, 255

debates, early Christian, 180–183, 218. See also false teachings

deceptions. See lies and deceptions

Decius, Emperor, 164

deicide, 149

deutero-Pauline letters, 92–93

Dibelius, Martin, 256

Didache, 248–249

Didascalia, 249

Didymus the Blind, 22

Diogenes Laertius, 29, 247

Dionysius (3rd-century scholar), 21

Dionysius the Renegade, 16–17, 27, 29

Diotimus, 29, 40

discovery narrative, 35

divine authority, 7–8

Divine Comedy (Dante), 64

divine knowledge/spark, 96, 210, 211, 214, 215

docetism, 53–54, 57, 59–60, 86, 89

Douglas, J. Archibald, 254

early Christian forgery: blaming Jews for crucifixion, 55–57, 148, 149–152, 171; church leader debates over, 18–19, 21, 22; emergence of, 8–11; evangelical views on, 115–117; false teachings put down by, 88–90, 94, 95, 103, 183–188, 216–218; falsehood to promote "truth," 144, 216, 217, 218, 250, 265; to fend off pagan attacks, 145, 170–173, 177–178; by Gnostics, 212–216; miracles in, 49–52; New Testament, 9–10, 65–70, 118, 262; noncanonical books, 17–19; overview on, 19–22, 139–141, 262; possible justifications for, 40–42, 262–265; in support of Paul, 87, 199–202; writings of Jesus, 159–163. See also pastoral letter forgeries; Pauline forgeries; Petrine

early Christian forgery (continued)
forgeries; scholarly justification of forgery

early Christian forgery list: Acts
of Peter, 50–52, 233; Apocalypse
of Peter, 18, 30, 63–65; Apostolic
Constitutions, 20, 22, 35, 37,
160; Book of Thomas the Contender, 215–216; Colossians,
112–114, 129–130, 185; Coptic
Apocalypse of Peter, 213–214;
Ephesians, 108–112, 129–130,
143–144; Epistle of Peter, 62–63;
Epistula Apostolorum, 217;
Gospel of Nicodemus, 150–152,
172–173; Hebrews, 22, 221,
229; James, 192–198; Jude,
186–188; Letters of Paul and
Seneca, 18, 90–92, 114, 171;
Pseudo-Clementine Writings,
62–63, 190–192; Second Treatise
of the Great Seth, 161; Sibylline
oracles, 174–176; 3 Corinthians, 88–90, 216; Timothy to the
Church, 32–33. See also Acts of
the Apostles; Gospel of Peter;
pastoral letter forgeries; Pilate
Gospels

early Christianity: based on conflict, 143–145; challenges of
apostolic succession, 7–8; faith
and works debate, 194–198;
falsifications in, 240–245; marriage beliefs, 18, 82–83, 94,
99–100, 103–104, 105; overview on debates in, 180–183,
218; pagan opposition to, 67,
145, 165–170, 177; question
of plagiarism, 247–249; and
the Roman Empire, 163–164;

rooted in truth claims, 5–7;
salvation through Jesus in, 61,
81, 85, 99, 100, 109–111, 200;
spiritual gifts and equality,
100–101; splits over sex, marriage, role of women, 82–83,
103–105. See also church leaders; early Christian forgery;
fabrications; false attribution;
false teachings; Gnosticism;
Jewish/Christian conflicts;
Jewish law and Christians;
second coming beliefs; sexual
abstinence teachings

Ecclesiastes, 117

Edessa, 162–163

Egeria, 163

Empedocles, 247

Enoch, 30

Ephesians, 108–113, 120, 128,
129, 136, 137, 138, 143–144,
197–198

Epicurus, 29, 40

Epiphanius, 212, 213

Epistle of Barnabas, 149, 229–232

Epistle of Peter, 62–63, 189–190,
204

Epistula Apostolorum, 217

equality, 101, 104

Eros, 27–28

Essenes, 255–256

ethical views, 40–42

Euripides, 26, 27

Eusebius, 21, 52–53, 54, 64, 156,
162, 173

evangelical Christians, 2–4, 105–
106, 115–117, 145–146

Eve, 94

evidence, 4

exclusivity, religious, 6, 7

fabrications, 232–240; about Peter, 49–52; *Acts of Paul*, 81–83; *Acts of Peter and Paul*, 155; *Gospel of Pseudo-Matthew*, 236–237; *Infancy Gospel of Thomas*, 237–239; in the New Testament, 239–240; overview on, 232–234; *Proto-Gospel of James*, 234–236

faith, and works, 194–198

false attribution, 220–232; *Epistle of Barnabas*, 229–232; to increase authority of writing, 222–223; misattribution of the Gospels, 223–228; mistaken, 221–222; New Testament, 220–221, 229; as pseudepigraphy, 24

false teachings, 180–218; attribution of the Gospels and, 225–226, 227; context and authorship, 267n3; and controversy surrounding Paul, 180–182, 188–189, 199–202; early Christian debates overview, 180–183, 218; forgeries to put down, 88–90, 94, 95, 103, 183–188, 216–218; forgery to promote, 8–9; of Marcion, 84–88; targeting Judaism / aligned with Paul, 229–232. *See also* Gnosticism; Paul, forgeries in opposition to

falsehood. *See* lies and deceptions

falsifications, 240–245

fiction, 45–48

1 Clement, 222

1 Corinthians, 93, 99, 100–101, 111, 193, 244–245

1 John, 23, 221, 223, 229

1 Kings, 224

1 Peter, 66–68, 75–76, 131, 134–139, 171–172, 199–200, 204

1 Samuel, 115, 224

1 Thessalonians, 93, 106–108, 113, 200

1 Timothy, 22, 94–100, 102–103, 138, 188, 208, 232, 244

Five Gospels, The (Jesus Seminar), 246

flesh, 88–90, 96, 211–212, 214–217

the flesh, 89–90, 96

forgery, literary: as deceptive, 9, 10, 25, 36, 37–38, 40; defining, 24–25; detection of, 33; Hitler diaries, 13–15; "honest," 121; intention of, 25–26, 38–39, 141, 249; as multifunctional, 170–171; techniques of forgers, 19–20, 33–35. *See also* early Christian forgery; modern forgeries and hoaxes; motivation for forgery; scholarly justification of forgery

forgery in the ancient world: as accepted practice, 119–120, 123–125; apocalyptic, 30–31; condemnation of, 9, 25, 36–37, 39, 140–141, 262; Dionysius's ruse, 16–17; intention to deceive, 38–39, 119–123, 126; methods of, 33–35; negative words to describe, 37–38, 140; prevalence of, 15, 36; punishment for, 39–40. *See also* early Christian forgery

fundamentalist Christians, 2–4, 105–106, 115–117, 145–146

Galatians, 61, 93, 99, 101, 110, 113, 134, 189, 191, 193, 195, 204–205
Galen, 26–27, 36–37, 39
Galilee, 73–74
Genesis, 195, 196
genre, literary, 46
Gentile Christians and the law. *See* Jewish law and Christians
George Washington illustration, 44–45
Gnosticism, 209–217; divine knowledge/spark in, 96, 210, 211, 214, 215; forgeries in opposition to, 216–217; forgeries to promote, 161, 212–216; overview on, 209–212; pastoral letter forgeries linked to, 95–96; salvation through transcendence of the flesh, 96, 211, 214; views on Jesus, 96, 182, 210, 211–212, 214
God: in apocalyptic writings, 30; Bible as inspired by, 115–116, 117; gift of the Spirit of, 100; in Gnosticism, 95–96, 210–211; Marcion's beliefs on, 85–89, 95, 231; messiah from, 146–149; objective knowledge of, 3; as truth, 41; use of deception by, 42
Golden Rule, 265
"good works" teachings, 99, 110, 194–198
Goodspeed, Edgar, 252, 254, 258
Gospel of Nicodemus, 150–152, 172–173
Gospel of Peter, 52–60; account of Jesus's death and resurrection, 17, 55–59; blaming Jews for

crucifixion, 55–57, 149–150; early source information on, 52–54; fabrication in, 233; as forgery, 54, 59–60, 233; as fragmentary, 55, 59; as heretical, 88; intention of author, 38; rediscovery of, 52, 54–55
Gospel of Philip, 17, 31, 212, 213
Gospel of Pseudo-Matthew, 236–237, 248
Gospel of the Holy Twelve, The, 259
Gospel of Thomas, 17, 31, 213
Gospels, New Testament. *See* canonical Gospels
Gospels, noncanonical, 17
Grafton, Anthony, 33
Great Lion of God (Caldwell), 79–81
Greek language proficiency, 71–76, 138–139, 198
Greek Septuagint, 67, 75, 76
Guthrie, Kenneth Sylvan, 258–259

Handing Over of Pilate, 157–159
Harris, William, 71
Harrison, A. N., 98
Hebrew Bible. *See* Old Testament
Hebrew language, 72–73, 75, 198
Hebrews, book of, 22, 23, 115, 221, 229
Heliodorus, 41
hell, 7, 18, 65
Hemis monastery, 252–253, 254
Heraclides of Pontus, 16–17, 27, 247
heresiologists, 221
heretical views. *See* false teachings
Herod, King, 27, 29, 40, 56, 149, 239

Herod Antipas, 153–154
Herodotus, 39
Hesiod, 247
Hezser, Catherine, 72–73
historical writing, 44–45, 47–49, 232–234
Hitler diaries, 13–15
Holy Spirit, gifts of the, 100–101
Holy Spirit-inspired forgery, 123–125
Homer, 247
Homilies, 190–192, 204
homonymous writing, 23
homosexual acts by Jesus, 261
hope, forgery to inspire, 29–31
Hosea, 145, 200
human body/flesh, 88–90, 96, 211–212, 214–217
humiliation of rival, 27
humility of disciple, writing to demonstrate, 129–133

Iamblichus, 131–133
India, accounts of Jesus in, 253–254
Infancy Gospel of Thomas, 237–239
influence, forgery increasing, 8–9, 31–32
intention to deceive, 25–26, 38–39, 122
Irenaeus, 207, 212, 213, 225–226
Isaiah, 30, 127–128, 145, 146, 162
Israel, king of, 146–147, 224
Issa stories, 252–254

James, book of, 192–198
James, brother of Jesus, 60, 61, 62, 187, 193, 197–199, 203, 205, 206, 209, 213, 234, 236
Jenkins, Jerry, 105

Jeremiah, 145
Jerome, 21
Jerusalem's destruction, 56–57, 59, 68, 149–150
Jesus: and the adulterous woman, 160, 242; birth of, 89, 235–236, 239; bringing the sword, 143; childhood miracle accounts, 236–239; divine revelation through, 7; docetists views of, 53–54, 57, 59–60, 86, 89; early church schisms and, 61–63, 182, 183; as engaging in homosexuality, 261; in forged apocalypse, 18; Gnostic views of, 96, 182, 210, 211–212, 214; Golden Rule, 265; in *Gospel of Nicodemus*, 150–152, 172–173; James's relationship to, 193–194; as Jewish messiah, 145–149, 224–225; "lost years" stories, 252–254; as misinterpreted, 87; in modern-day hoaxes, 252–254, 259–261; pagan views of, 166, 169; and Paul's conversion, 79–81, 191–192, 202; questioned about the afterlife, 64–65; salvation through, 61, 81, 85, 99, 100, 109–111, 200; in the Sibylline oracles, 175–176; teachings in Gnostic forgeries, 161, 212–215; transfiguration of, 68–69; as truth, 3; as vegetarian, 259; writings attributed to, 8, 18, 31, 159–163. *See also* second coming beliefs
Jesus, crucifixion of: blaming Jews for the, 55–57, 148, 149–152, 163, 171; *Crucifixion of Jesus, by*

Jesus, crucifixion of (continued)
an Eye-Witness, The, 254–256;
Gnostic account of, 213–214;
Pilate's Death Sentence hoax,
257–258; Roman Empire in
accounts of, 55–58, 151, 152,
156. See also Pilate Gospels

Jesus, resurrection of: account
in Gospel of Peter, 17, 57–59;
adding to the account in
Mark, 242–243; as of the flesh,
211–212, 217; in Gospel of Nicodemus, 152; modern forgery
discounting, 254–256

Jesus Seminar, 246

Jewish/Christian conflicts, 145–
159; alleged cover-up of Jesus's
resurrection, 58, 59; blaming
Jews for crucifixion, 55–57,
148–152, 163, 171; Christian
forgeries in answer to, 149–
152, 163, 177; Jewish reaction
to Christian claims, 145–149,
176–177; maligning Judaism
in Barnabas, 149, 229–231. See
also Pilate Gospels

Jewish law and Christians: Barnabas discrediting, 149, 230;
early church schism over,
60–63, 181, 218; forgeries
addressing, 109–110, 112,
189–190, 195–198, 203–205,
208; James's commitment to,
193; Marcion's views on, 85,
231–232; Paul on salvation
through Jesus over, 80–81, 85,
99, 191, 195–196, 231

Jews/Judaism: apocalyptic writing
in, 29–30; king of Israel, 146–
147, 224; linking Gospels with,

224–225; literacy and language
skills, 72–75; pagan views of,
165, 169; as united with Gentile Christians, 109; varied
messianic beliefs, 146–147;
writing forgeries to support,
28–29, 174–175

John, Apostle (son of Zebedee),
21, 23, 227, 229

John, author of Revelation, 21, 23

John, Gospel of, 9, 10, 23, 56,
150, 160, 162, 193, 223–229,
242, 244, 250

John the Baptist, 153, 154

Jonah, 42

Joseph, husband of Mary, 234–239

Joseph of Arimathea, 255

Josephus, 27, 40, 73

Joshua, 86, 224

Jude, 21, 69, 186–188, 247–248

Judges, 224

justification of forgery. See scholarly justification of forgery

Justin Martyr, 149, 169, 176,
225, 226

Justus of Tiberius, 73

knowledge of the divine, 96, 210,
211, 214, 215

Kujau, Konrad, 13, 14, 15, 26

LaHaye, Timothy, 105

last days. See second coming
beliefs

Late, Great Planet Earth, The
(Lindsey), 105

Left Behind series (Jenkins and
LaHaye), 105

Letter of Aristeas, 28–29, 67

Letter of Herod to Pilate, 153–155

Letter of Pilate to Claudius, 155–156
Letter of Pilate to Herod, 154–155
Letters of Paul and Seneca, 18,
    90–92, 114, 171
libraries, ancient, 26–27
lies and deceptions: ancient views
    on, 41–42; beyond literary
    forgery, 219–220, 249–250;
    Christianity's legacy of, 40–42,
    261–265; falsifications, 240–
    245; forgery as, 9, 10, 25, 36,
    37–38, 40; George Washington
    illustration, 44–45; "noble/
    medicinal lie," 41, 42, 263;
    nuances of falsehood, 45–46;
    plagiarism, 220, 245–249; to
    promote "truth," 144, 216,
    217, 218, 250, 265. *See also*
    early Christian forgery; fabri-
    cations; false attribution; mod-
    ern forgeries and hoaxes
Lindsey, Hal, 105
literary genre, 46
Long-Lost Second Book of Acts,
    258–259
Longinus, 154, 155
Lucian of Samosata, 28, 48
Luke, Gospel of, 23, 55, 86–87,
    206, 220–221, 223, 225–228,
    239, 248
Luke the physician, 206–209
Luther, Martin, 196
lying. *See* lies and deceptions

MacDonald, Dennis, 103, 104
Marcion, 84–89, 104, 182, 211,
    216, 231–232
Marcion's canon, 86–87
Marcus Aurelius, 134, 136,
    137, 167

Mark, Gospel of, 23, 55, 57, 70,
    223–228, 242–244, 248, 250,
    260–261
marriage, 18, 82–83, 94, 99–100,
    103–104, 105
Martial, 29, 37, 39, 247
Mary, mother of Jesus, 89, 234–
    239, 258–259
Mary Magdalene, 17, 259
Matthew ("Matthaias"), 215
Matthew, Gospel of, 9, 10, 23, 24,
    55–58, 63, 69, 143, 151–152,
    162, 193, 223–228, 239, 248
Maximin Daia, 173
Meade, David, 126–127, 129
"medicinal lie," 41, 42, 263
Melito, 149
messianic claims, 145–149, 224–225
Metzger, Bruce, 4, 123
Micah, 145
military forgeries, 27
Minucius Felix, 167–168
miracles: accounts of Jesus's child-
    hood, 236–239; in forgeries
    about Peter, 49–52, 62; of
    Jesus, 152, 156, 157, 158, 172
misattribution, 24, 140, 221–222,
    249–250
modern forgeries and hoaxes,
    252–261; *The Confession of Pon-
    tius Pilate,* 259; *The Crucifixion
    of Jesus, by an Eye-Witness,*
    254–256; *The Gospel of the Holy
    Twelve,* 259; *Long-Lost Second
    Book of Acts,* 258–259; *The Pass-
    over Plot,* 260; Pilate's *Death
    Sentence,* 256–258; Smith's
    "Secret Gospel" of Mark, 260–
    261; *The Unknown Life of Jesus
    Christ,* 252–254

Moody Bible Institute, 2, 3, 5
Moses, 229–230
motivation for forgery, 25–32;
    credibility and being heard,
    8–9, 31–32; defending religion,
    28–29; humiliation of rival, 27,
    29; inspiring hope by apoca-
    lypse, 29–31; and intention,
    25–26, 38–39, 122; political or
    military ends, 27–28; profit,
    15, 26–27; pulling a ruse,
    15–17, 27
Müller, Max, 254
Muratorian Canon, 87–88
mythology, 45, 233

Nag Hammadi library, 161, 212–
    213, 215
Narrative of Joseph of Arimathea,
    161
Natural History of the Great Proph-
    et of Nazareth (Venturini), 256
Nero, Emperor, 67, 68, 70, 91,
    92, 155
New Testament: anonymous
    works of the, 10, 23, 220,
    229; Apocalypse of Peter and,
    63–64; containing fabrica-
    tions, 239–240; discrepancies
    in, 5; falsifications in the,
    242–245; forged out of con-
    flict, 183; four literary genres,
    17; overview on forgeries in,
    9–10, 65–70, 118, 262. See also
    canonical Gospels
Nicodemus, 255
"noble lie," 41, 42, 263
noncanonical books, 17–19
nothos (illegitimate child), 37,
    38, 48

Notovitch, Nicolas, 252–254
Numbers, 115

objective truth, 3–4, 5
Old Testament: apocalypse in, 30;
    attempts to link Gospels with,
    224–225; Barnabas on broken
    Jewish covenant, 149, 229–231;
    deception by God in, 42; forg-
    eries in the, 117, 126–128, 131;
    Marcion rejecting the, 85–89,
    231–232; on the messiah,
    145–149; Septuagint, 67, 75,
    76; varied early church views
    on, 182
Onomacritus of Athens, 39
Origen, 42, 169, 234
orthonymous writing, 22–23

pagans, 163–176; beliefs of, 6,
    164–165; as bowing to Jesus,
    151, 237; Christian forgeries
    to fend off, 145, 170–173, 177–
    178; converting to Christianity,
    169–170, 202; opposition to
    Christians, 67, 145, 165–170,
    177; and the Sibylline oracles,
    173–176
Palestine, 72
Papias, 226–227
Parthenopaeus (play; Dionysius),
    16–17, 27
Passover Plot, The (Schonfield),
    260
pastoral letter forgeries, 93–105;
    absent from Marcion's canon,
    86–87; 1 and 2 Timothy copy-
    ist view, 97–98; first scholarly
    suspicions about, 95–96; Har-
    rison's statistics of word usage,

98; looking at historical context, 100–102; overview on, 93–97; possible reasons for, 103–105; and reactualizing the tradition, 128–129; verisimilitude in 1 and 2 Timothy, 102–103; word comparisons, 99–100, 278n14

Paul, Apostle: as aligned with Peter, 199–204, 209; ancient fabrications about, 81–83, 155; associating *Barnabas* with, 231–232; attribution of Luke and, 228; authentic letters by, 22–23, 93; beliefs on the flesh, 90; coauthoring by, 77, 114; controversy surrounding / opposition to, 60–63, 180–182, 188–189, 199–202; conversion of, 79–81, 191–192, 202; death of, 70, 92; on faith, 99, 195–198; falsification of writings of, 244–245; forgeries in support of, 87, 199–202; forgery of Jesus writing to, 161; linked to sexual abstinence teachings, 18, 82, 103–105, 233; modern fictions of, 79–81, 258; Peter and authority of, 190–192, 206; philosophers linked with, 18, 91–92; salvation through Jesus over Jewish law, 80–81, 85, 99, 191, 195–196, 231; second coming beliefs of, 90, 99–102, 106–108, 110–111. *See also* Acts of the Apostles

Paul, forgeries in opposition to, 188–198; book of James, 192–198; noncanonical *Epistle of Peter*, 189–190; overview, 188–189; the *Pseudo-Clementine Writings*, 190–192

Pauline forgeries, 84–93; *Apocalypse of Paul*, 213; Colossians, 112–114, 129–130, 185; deutero-Pauline letters, 92–93; as disciples writing in name of Paul, 129–133; Ephesians, 108–112, 129–130, 143–144; Hebrews, 22, 221; *Letters of Paul and Seneca*, 18, 90–92, 114, 171; overview on New Testament, 92–93, 188; perpetrated by Marcion, 84–88; scholars' reluctance to label forgeries, 118, 119; 2 Thessalonians, 19–21, 105–108, 120; secretary hypothesis and, 108, 114, 134–135; 3 Corinthians, 88–90, 216. *See also* pastoral letter forgeries

Pausanias, 29

pen names, 23–24

persecution, 66–67

Peter, Apostle: in *Acts of Peter and Paul*, 155; *Acts of Peter* fabrication, 18, 50–52, 233; ancient literacy and education, 70–73; attribution of Mark and, 223, 226, 227, 228; authority and Paul, 190–192, 206; death under Nero, 68, 70; forgeries aligning Paul with, 199–204, 209; forgery of Jesus writing to, 161; Gentile Christians and Jewish law, 60–63, 189–190, 203, 204; as illiterate, 75, 138; miracles allegedly performed by, 49–52, 62; possibility of Greek proficiency, 73–75,

Peter, Apostle (*continued*)
138–139; stories about, 49–52;
supposedly appointing Clement, 222

Petrine forgeries, 52–70; *Apoca-*
lypse of Peter, 18, 30, 63–65;
Coptic Apocalypse of Peter, 213–
214; as disciples writing in
name of Peter, 131–133; early
church schism and, 60–63;
Epistle of Peter, 62–63; 1 and 2
Peter, 65–70, 75–77, 199–202;
and the secretary hypothesis,
118, 134–139. *See also Gospel of*
Peter

Philemon, 93, 200, 207

Philippians, 80, 81, 93, 110, 113

philosophers: associating Paul
with, 18, 91–92; converting to
Christianity, 169–170; forgeries of works by, 26–27, 37; on
lying, 41; plagiarism by, 247;
story of Dionysius, 16; theory
of disciples writing in name of,
129–133

Pilate Gospels, 152–159; *Handing*
Over of Pilate, 157–159; *Let-*
ter of Herod to Pilate, 153–155;
Letter of Pilate to Claudius,
155–156; *Letter of Pilate to*
Herod, 154–155; overview on,
152–153; purpose of, 159,
171; *Report of Pontius Pilate*,
156–157, 158

plagiarism, 220, 245–249

Plato, 26, 27, 31, 37, 39, 41,
42, 71

Plutarch, 34, 39, 269n13

poetry, epic tragic, 45–46, 48

political forgeries, 27–28

Polybius, 48, 246

polytheistic religions, 6

Pontius Pilate, 3, 55–56, 58, 150–
153, 169, 172–173, 257–258,
259. *See also* Pilate Gospels

Porphyry, 130, 131

Procla, 154–155

profit motive, 15, 26–27

Proto-Gospel of James, 234–236,
248

Psalms, 145, 146, 236

pseudepigraphal writing, 24–25.
See also forgery, literary

Pseudo-Clementine Writings, 62–
63, 190–192

pseudonymous writing, 23–24,
140

pseudos (falsehood), 37–38

Pythagoras, 130–133, 247

Rahab, 42

rapture beliefs, 105–106

reactualizing tradition, 125–129

Reed, Jonathan, 74

reincarnation, 258–259

religion, ancient, 5–7

religious conflict, 143–145,
176–178

religious forgery, 28–29

Report of Pontius Pilate, 156–157,
158

resurrection of Jesus. *See* Jesus,
resurrection of

resurrection of the faithful. *See*
second coming beliefs

Revelation, 21, 30, 64, 105

Rhossus congregation, 53–54

Richards, E. Randolph, 134–138

Roman Empire: Christianity
unique in, 6–7; consulting

Sibylline oracles, 173–174; destruction of Jerusalem, 56–57, 68, 149–150; and Jesus's trial and crucifixion, 55–58, 151, 152, 156; lack of records on Jesus, 256–257; literacy in, 72–73; Paul unknown in, 91; treatment of Christians in, 67, 163–164; use of secretaries, 134–138

romances, 45–46

Romans, book of, 86, 93, 99, 134, 138, 200

Rome, 68, 92

Salome, 235

salvation: Gnostic transcendence of the flesh, 96, 211, 214; through Jesus, 61, 81, 85, 99, 100, 109–111, 200

Salvian, 31–33, 262

Sarah, 42

Schleiermacher, Friedrich, 95–96

scholarly justification of forgery, 119–140; coauthoring theories, 77, 114, 136–137; disciples writing as act of humility, 129–133; nondeceptive intent view, 119–123, 126; overview on, 118, 139–140; pseudepigraphy in the Spirit, 123–125; reactualizing the tradition, 125–129. See also secretary hypothesis

Schonfield, Hugh, 260

scribes, 87, 240–244, 250

scribes, forgeries by. See secretary hypothesis

second coming beliefs: docetist, 89; Gnostic, 211–212; messianic predictions and, 148;

mocked by scoffers, 69–70; modern rapture beliefs, 105–106; Paul's views, 90, 99–102, 106–108, 110–111; as spiritual / already occurring, 111, 112, 113

2 Corinthians, 93

2 John, 23, 221, 223, 229

2 Kings, 86, 224

2 Peter, 21–22, 68–70, 75, 76, 127, 128, 131, 134, 135, 138, 201–202, 204, 247–248, 275n23

2 Samuel, 224

2 Thessalonians, 19–21, 22, 35, 37, 105–108, 120

2 Timothy, 22, 86, 93–98, 102–103, 115, 188

Second Treatise of the Great Seth, 161

Secret Book of John, 213

Secret Gospel of Mark, 27, 260–261

secretary hypothesis, 133–139; arguments against, 138–139; four uses of secretaries theory, 135–138; overview of, 133–134; and Pauline/Petrine forgeries, 108, 114, 134–139

self-knowledge, 96, 210, 211, 215

Seneca, 18, 91–92, 114, 171

Septuagint, 67, 75, 76

Serapion, 53, 54, 57, 59–60, 233

sexual abstinence teachings: apologists supporting, 170; divided views on, 82–83, 103–105; in forgeries about Peter, 49–50; forgers linking to Paul, 18, 82, 103–105, 233; of the Gnostics, 96

Sibylline oracles, 173–176

Silvanus, 76, 200
Simon Peter. *See* Peter, Apostle
Simon the Magician, 50–52, 62, 88, 89, 155, 160, 190, 191, 217, 233
Smith, Morton, 27, 260–261, 269n16
Socrates, 41, 71, 247
Solomon, 117
Sophocles, 16, 26
Speyer, Wolfgang, 40, 123
Spirit-inspired forgery, 123–125
Spirit of God, 100–101
spiritual battle, 144
Stern (magazine), 13, 14
Stoics, 16
stories, true. *See* true stories
subjectivity, 3
submissiveness in women, 83, 94, 103–104, 172, 244
suffering, 53–54, 57, 59–60, 66–67

techniques of forgers, 19–20, 33–35
Tertius, 134
Tertullian, 18, 83, 84, 156, 165–166, 169, 212, 213, 221–222, 233, 270n24
Thecla, 81, 82–83, 103, 104, 105, 262
Theopompus, 29
3 Corinthians, 88–90, 216
3 John, 23, 221, 223, 229
Thomas, Judas Didymus, 213, 215
Thucydides, 47, 48
Tiberius, Emperor, 155, 156, 158, 259
Tibetan Issa stories, 252–254

Timothy to the Church (Salvian), 32–33, 262
Tiro, 137
Titus, 49–50, 86, 93, 95, 96, 99, 101, 102, 103, 115, 188, 197
tradition, reactualizing, 125–129
tragic poetry, 45–46, 48
transfiguration scene, 68–69
Trevor-Roper, Hugh, 13, 14
true stories, 43–49; ancient historical writing, 47–49; ancient notions of fiction, 45–48; and falsehood, 45; George Washington illustration, 44–45; nature of, 43–44
truth: apostolic truth, 7–8; Christianity's truth claims, 5–7; as complex, 43; evangelical Christians' commitment to, 3–5; objective truth, 3–4; reconciling Christianity with, 4–5; use of falsehoods to promote, 144, 216, 217, 218, 250, 265
truth claims, 5–7, 44–45

Unknown Life of Jesus Christ, The, 252–254

vegetarianism, 259
Venturini, K. H., 256
verisimilitude, 34–35, 102–103
virgin birth story, 235–236
Vitruvius, 246

Washington, George, 44–45
Weems, Mason Locke, 44
women in the church, 82–83, 94, 100, 103–105, 172, 244–245
works, 99, 110, 194–198

writing: ancient literacy and, 70–73; biography, 46, 47; epic poetry, 45–46, 48; fabrication, 232; falsifications, 240–242; historical writing, 44–45, 47–49, 232–234; homonymous writing, 23; literary genre, 46; notions of fiction, 45–48; orthonymous writing, 22–23; plagiarism, 220, 245–249; pseudepigraphal writing, 24–25; pseudonymous writing, 23–24. *See also* anonymous writing; forgery, literary; scholarly justification of forgery; secretary hypothesis; true stories

Xenophon, 41

Zechariah, 145